BEITRÄGE ZUR
GESCHICHTE DER BIBLISCHEN EXEGESE

Herausgegeben von

OSCAR CULLMANN, BASEL/PARIS · ERNST KÄSEMANN, TÜBINGEN
HANS-JOACHIM KRAUS, HAMBURG-VOLKSDORF·
HARALD RIESENFELD, UPSALA
KARL HERMANN SCHELKLE, TÜBINGEN · PAUL SCHUBERT, NEW HAVEN
ERNST WOLF, GÖTTINGEN

10

The New Testament Logia on Divorce

A Study of their Interpretation

from

Erasmus to Milton

by

V. NORSKOV OLSEN

WIPF & STOCK · Eugene, Oregon

Wipf and Stock Publishers
199 W 8th Ave, Suite 3
Eugene, OR 97401

The New Testament Logia on Divorce
A Study of their Interpretation from Erasmus to Milton
By Olsen, V. Norskov
Copyright©1971 Mohr Siebeck
ISBN 13: 978-1-5326-4267-8
Publication date 10/30/2017
Previously published by Mohr Siebeck, 1971

Every effort has been made to trace the current copyright
owner of this publication but without success. This licensed
edition published by special permission of Mohr Siebeck GmbH & Co. KG

FOREWORD

The New Testament teaching on marriage and divorce has exercised a deep influence upon Western civilisation. This is especially the case with the logia on divorce which are recorded in the Gospels of Matthew v. 32, xix. 3—12, Mark x. 2—12 and Luke xvi. 18. The Apostle Paul deals with the subject in 1 Corinthians vii. 1—15. Within the Christian churches the statements in these texts are considered authoritative concerning the questions of whether or not marriage is indissoluble, and whether divorce and remarriage are allowed for one or several reasons.

The purpose of this study is to examine the interpretation of the New Testament divorce texts during the Reformation period. The significance of the exegetical results achieved by the reformers can be appreciated only in the light of the medieval sacramental concept of marriage and the work of the Christian humanists; accordingly, the investigation begins with an examination of these two subjects, as well as the reaction of Roman Catholic exegetes to the interpretation of Erasmus. The interpretations of Luther and his associates and those of the prominent Reformed theologians follow. The works of representative English theologians have been studied, beginning with William Tyndale and Thomas Cranmer and ending with John Milton, whose works on divorce from an exegetical point of view terminate a period during which the meaning of the divorce texts was explored.

The investigation has been confined to primary sources, in which marriage and divorce have been considered in the light of the texts under discussion. An attempt has been made to seek the answer as to what motivated the expositors in their interpretations and to compare the exegetical results of the various writers. Such are the objectives and the scope of this study.

The original manuscript was presented to the Faculty of Theology of the University of Basel as a partial fulfillment of the requirements for the Dotcor of Theology degree.

The writer is greatly indebted to his adviser Professor Dr. Bo Reicke for his invaluable help and unfailing encouragement during the years devoted to the preparation of this book. Heartfelt thanks are owed to Dr. Heinrich Baltensweiler, who read the entire manuscript and suggested desirable amendments. Since he is author of the book, *Die Ehe im Neuen Testament*, his insight holds a special value. Professor Dr. Oscar Cullmann's personal interest is greatly appreciated. The writer is most thankful for his recommendation to have this study published in the series, „Beiträge zur Geschichte der biblischen Exegese".

Thanks are also due to the University of Basel and the Loma Linda University, California, which made generous grants available for the publication. The extensive correspondence across the Atlantic with Dr. jur. h. c. Hans Georg Siebeck of the J. C. B. Mohr's (Paul Siebeck) publishing house in Tübingen during the preparation for the publication of this book has been most cordial. The publishers deserve sincere gratitude.

CONTENTS

Foreword
The New Testament Divorce Texts 1

I. THE INTERPRETATION OF ERASMUS AND ROMAN CATHOLIC REACTION

Marriage as a Sacrament 2
    The Development of the Sacramental Idea of Marriage 2
    The Sacramentum or Mysterion of Ephesians v. 32 6
The Christian Humanists 10
    Lorenzo Valla 11
    Jacques Lefèvre D'Étaples 12
    John Colet 13
    Thomas More 14
Desiderius Erasmus 15
    Divorce and the Roman Catholic Impediments of Marriage 18
    Erasmus' Interpretation of the Divorce Texts 20
Edward Lee versus Erasmus 27
    Edward Lee's Criticism 27
    Erasmus' Reply 29
Natalis Bedda and Sorbonne versus Erasmus 30
    Natalis Bedda's Criticism 31
    Erasmus' Reply 32
Cardinal Cajetan 33
The Augsburg Interim Declaration of Religion 36
The Council of Trent 38
    The Canons of the Council 38
    The Catechism of the Council 39
The Rheims-Douai Bible 40

II. MARTIN LUTHER AND ASSOCIATES

Martin Luther 43
Philip Melanchthon 57
John Brenz 61

III. THE REFORMED THEOLOGIANS

Huldreich Zwingli	64
Heinrich Bullinger	70
Martin Bucer	76
Bucer's Commentary on the Gospels	76
De Regno Christi	80
Pietro Martire Vermigli	88
John Calvin	94
Theodore Beza	104
Commentary on the New Testament	104
Tractatio De Repudiis Et Divortiis	106

IV. ENGLISH EXPOSITORS

Early English Reformers	110
William Tyndale	110
Thomas Cranmer	112
John Hooper	115
The Influence of the Continental Reformers	117
Continental Writers	117
The Reformatio Legum Ecclesiasticarum	118
Anglican and Puritan Exposition	120
John Milton	128
Summary and Conclusion	143
Bibliography	150
Index of Names	158
Index of Bible References	160

The New Testament Divorce Texts

Matthew v. 32

> But I say unto you, That whosoever shall put away his wife, saving for the cause of fornication, causeth her to commit adultery: and whosoever shall marry her that is divorced committeth adultery.

Matthew xix. 9

> And I say unto you, Whosoever shall put away his wife, except it be for fornication, and shall marry another, committeth adultery: and whoso marrieth her which is put away doth commit adultery.

Mark x. 11–12

> And he saith unto them, Whosoever shall put away his wife, and marry another, committeth adultery against her. And if a woman shall put away her husband, and be married to another, she committeth adultery.

Luke xvi. 18

> Whosoever putteth away his wife, and marrieth another, committeth adultery: and whosoever marrieth her that is put away from her husband committeth adultery.

1 Corinthians vii. 15

> But if the unbelieving depart, let him depart. A brother or a sister is not under bondage in such cases: but God hath called us to peace.

The Authorized King James Version is used in our Biblical quotations, unless otherwise indicated. This version, not being influenced by any party spirit, was the final product of the sixteenth century Biblical scholarship which is being examined in this study. Further, it was the recognized Bible of the English speaking world for more than three centuries.

I. The Interpretation of Erasmus and Roman Catholic Reaction

Marriage as a Sacrament

For the late medieval Church the doctrine of marriage as being one of the seven sacraments was the pivot around which all aspects of marriage theologically and exegetically moved, making divorce unlawful in the true sense of the word, and claiming that jurisdiction over marriage matters belonged to the Church only. Without going into any discussion of the whole development of the Roman Catholic sacramental idea and the conflict between the *realists* and *nominalists* on the meaning of the *universals* within the scholastic theology, it will be necessary to mention briefly the high points of this development regarding marriage as a sacrament.

The Development of the Sacramental Idea of Marriage

Augustine exercised upon Christian theology, including the concept of marriage, a profound influence, which continued through the time of the Reformation. The Catholic theologians and the Protestant reformers of the sixteenth century alike quoted him. The former sought to find in him a supporter for placing marriage among the sacraments by the fact that he compares marriage to baptism and holy orders. Luther is indebted to him for his concept of marriage as a most sacred thing, only short of being a sacrament in a *technical* sense. Examining the Augustinian concept of marriage it is found that its whole structure rests on three cornerstones: procreation, faithfulness, and sacrament[1].

---

[1] Augustine, *Contra Julianum*, V. xii (46), Migne, *Patrologia Latina*, XLIV. 810. For an English translation see: *Saint Augustine Against Julian*, in *The Fathers of the Church*, ed. Roy Joseph Defarrari, XXXV, New York, 1957; Augustine, *De Genesi Ad Litteram*, IX. vii (12), *Patrologia Latina*, XXXIV. 397; Augustine, *De Nuptiis Et Concupiscenta*, I. x (11), xvii (19), *Patrologia Latina*, XLIV. 420, 424. For an English translation see: *On Marriage and Concupiscence*, in *A Select Library of the Nicene and Post-Nicene Fathers of the Christian Church*, ed. Philip Schaff, V., Grand Rapids, Mich., 1956; Augustine, *De Gratia Christi Et De Peccato Originali*, II. xxxiv (39), xxxvii (42), *Patrologia Latina*,

Procreation: according to the Genesis record the purpose of marriage was to produce children who would "be lovingly welcomed, kindheartedly reared and religiously educated". This purpose persists, and carnal relationships beyond this responsibility are, while not a crime since not adulterous, still a sin, though a venial one[2].

Faithfulness: chastity between the spouses and the power which, according to the Apostle Paul (1 Corinthians VII. 4), a married couple have over the body of one another, is by Augustine termed faithfulness. The law of fidelity is transgressed when one of the partners commits adultery. The latter is the only cause for separation, but adultery does not permit the innocent party to remarry[3]. In his exegetical work on the New Testament divorce texts he upholds this view[4], and the same is the case in his other discussions of the marriage institution[5].

Contrary to the views of Augustine, a contemporary of his, Pollentius, had presented the argument that one who had committed adultery should be considered as dead, since the law of Moses prescribed that such a person should be stoned. The Apostle Paul had written: "The wife is bound by the law as long as her husband liveth; but if her husband be dead, she is at liberty to be married to whom she will; only in the Lord" (1 Corinthians VII. 39). Consequently, the innocent party was allowed to remarry. Luther and Calvin as well as other reformers of the sixteenth century advanced the same view as a basic reason for remarrying. Pollentius had further anticipated the view, which was held by some of the Protestant reformers, that an incurable disease, which hindered sexual relationship, was a sufficient reason for divorce and remarriage. Augustine denied the validity of such a proposition[6].

XLIV. 404, 406. For an English translation see: *A Treatise on the Grace of Christ, and on Original Sin*, in *Nicene and Post-Nicene Fathers*, V.

[2] Augustine, *De Genesi Ad Litteram*, IX. VII (12), *Patrologia Latina*, XXXIV. 397; Augustine, *De Bono Conjugali*, I. VI (6), *Patrologia Latina*, XL. 377. For English translations see: *The Good of Marriage*, in *The Fathers of the Church*, XXVII; *On the Good of Marriage*, in *Nicene and Post-Nicene Fathers*, III.

[3] Augustine, *De Bono Conjugali*, I. IV (4), *Patrologia Latina*, XL. 376.

[4] Augustine, *De Conjugiis Adulterinis Ad Pollentium*, Migne, *Patrologia Latina*, XL. For an English translation see: *Adulterous Marriages*, in *The Fathers of the Church*, XXVII.

[5] See p. 2, n. 1 above.

[6] Augustine, *De Conjugiis Adulterinis Ad Pollentium*, II. II (2), III (3), XV (15), X (9), *Patrologia Latina*, XL. 471, 472, 481, 476. For the opinion of capital punishment for adultery by Luther, Brenz, Bullinger, Peter Martyr, Calvin, Beza and Tyndale see: pp. 52, 62, 74, 75, 93, 98, 105, 111 below. Luther, Melanchthon, Brenz and Calvin did not allow divorce for any incurable disease but Zwingli and Bucer did. See: pp. 51, 59, 61, 68, 83, 91 below.

Sacrament: Augustine's concept of the absolute indissolubility of the marriage tie, which denies remarriage even in the case of adultery, led him to the third fundamental principle of marriage, namely that expressed by his usage of the Latin word: *sacramentum*. *Sacramentum* is not used in the theological sense of Thomas Aquinas as a *causa gratiae*, but to express the sanctity and indissolubility of the marriage union, thus also conveying the meaning of a sign or a pledge[7]. It is with the same concept in mind that Augustine compares marriage to baptism. Just as one who has apostatized from the faith cannot lose "the sacrament of faith" (sacramentum fidei), which he received in baptism, likewise something pertaining to marriage remains as long as husband and wife are alive[8]. The same sacredness of the marriage tie is illustrated by comparing marriage to the sacrament of orders, which continues to be valid even if one ordained to the priesthood should be removed from office because of some fault[9].

Marriage is a sacrament or mystery in the sense that it is a symbol or an analogy of Christ's unity with the church, as expressed by the Apostle Paul: "For this cause shall a man leave his father and mother, and shall be joined unto his wife, and they two shall be one flesh. This is a great mystery: but I speak of Christ and the Church" (Ephesians v. 31—32)[10]. In the patriarchal age when "the mystery of salvation was still veiled in prophetic signs" (propheticis sacramentis), the patriarchs were allowed to have several wives, because they were motivated not by lust, but by piety and the duty of procreation. The City of God or the New Testament church is made up of many souls; yet, they are one in soul and heart toward God, and on account of this perfect unity the sacrament or symbol of marriage has now been limited to one man and one woman. Further, the sacrament of marriage as applied to the patriarchs was a prophetic sign or symbol of the multitude that should be subject under God as the several wives were under one husband. In New Testament times the sacrament of marriage with one wife illustrates the unity of the believer with Christ and His church[11]. Turning to the theologians of scholasticism it is found that

---

[7] Augustine, *De Bono Conjugali*, I. VII (6), XIII (15), XV (17), XVIII (21), *Patrologia Latina*, XL. 378, 384, 385, 387.

[8] Augustine, *De Nuptiis Et Concupiscenta*, I. x (11), *Patrologia Latina*, XLIV. 420. For a similar example see: Augustine, *De Conjugiis Adulterinis Ad Pollentium*, II. v (4), *Patrologia Latina*, XL. 473.

[9] Augustine, *De Bono Conjugali*, I. XXIV (32), *Patrologia Latina*, XL. 394.

[10] Augustine, *De Nuptiis Et Concupiscenta*, I. x (11), *Patrologia Latina*, XLIV. 420.

[11] Augustine, *De Bono Conjugali*, I. XIII (15), XVIII (21), XX (24), XXV (33), XXVI (34). *Patrologia Latina*, XL. 383, 387, 389, 395.

a gradual change took place in the Augustinian concept of *sacramentum nuptiarum*.

Stimulated by the contact with the Graeco-Arabian civilization through the Crusades, the eleventh century saw the awakening of a new intellectual life which gave birth to early Scholasticism. The theology of Peter Abelard, 1080—1143, Hugo of St. Victor, 1097—1141, and Peter Lombard, ?—1160, marks a new step in Catholic teaching of the sacraments. They distinguish the sacraments of the Church from her other ceremonies, and, defining the sacraments as a cause of grace, they assert Christ's real presence in the Eucharist[12]. Abelard includes marriage among the five sacraments, which he lists as Baptism, Confirmation, Eucharist, Extreme Unction, and Marriage. However, he makes a distinction between the first four sacraments and marriage. The last does not confer the gift of grace, but is a means against fornication for those who cannot live the life of celibacy[13]. Nevertheless, placing marriage alongside four sacraments which cause grace, he brings it closer to the final Roman Catholic sacramental concept.

Hugo of St. Victor, in his *Dogmatica*, has two sections on *De Sacramento Conjugii*[14], but in neither does he speak about marriage as a sacrament in the later Roman Catholic sense. He refers to Augustine when he states that the sacramental concept of marriage consists of it being a sign of the indissoluble relationship between Christ and the Church[15]. Marriage is also expressed as a twofold symbol of the unity between God and the soul of man and the unity between Christ and the Church, but he does not state that the sacrament of marriage conveys grace[16].

Peter Lombard, the most influential theologian before Aquinas, lists the seven sacraments as they have since been reckoned by the Roman Catholic Church[17]. For him too, the sacrament is given as a sign of God's grace and not only as a symbol of the invisible grace,

---

[12] C. W. Dugmore, *The Mass and the English Reformers*, London, 1958, pp. 39—58.

[13] Peter Abelard, *Epitome Christianae Theologiae*, xxxi, Patrologia Latina, CLXXVIII. 1745.

[14] Hugo of St. Victor, Dogmatica, Patrologia Latina, CLXXVI. 153—74, 479—520.

[15] Hugo of St. Victor, *Summa Sententiarum Tractatus Septimus*, iv, Patrologia Latina, CLXXVI. 157.

[16] Hugo of St. Victor, *De Sacramentis Christianae Fidei*, II. (xi). iii, Patrologia Latina, CLXXVI. 482.

[17] Peter Lombard, Sententiarum, IV. (ii). 1, Patrologia Latina, CXCII. 841—842.

but also as a cause of what it symbolizes[18]. When dealing with the sacrament of marriage he denies this sacramental grace. The grace consists only in the fact that marriage as an institution is remedial. Listing the sacraments he differentiates between those that supply grace, such as baptism, and others which are only remedial, such as marriage[19].

The scholastic doctrine of the sacrament of marriage achieved its greatest synthesis in Thomas Aquinas, 1225—1274. In his treatment of marriage as a sacrament the Angelic Doctor of the Latin Church defines it as equal to the other six. Having referred to Ephesians v. 32, of the Vulgate: "This sacrament is great", he states that it "transmits grace" (per hoc sacramentum gratia conferatur)[20]. In his *Commentary on the Sentences* he also deals with marriage as a sacrament. Discussing whether or not it causes grace, he states that as a sacrament, it is a "causa gratiae"[21]. What Aquinas thus taught became the perfect exposition of the doctrine of marriage within the Roman Catholic Church, and four centuries later the Council of Trent confirmed it to be an absolute truth of faith.

The Sacramentum or Mysterion of Ephesians v. 32

In Jerome's version the Greek *mysterion* of Ephesians v. 32 is translated by the Latin *sacramentum;* but it has been noticed that by the ancient Church it was understood to mean a mystery, symbol, sign, or most sacred thing.

When marriage had become one of the seven sacraments, and when, in the hands of the scholastic theologians, the Bible was used as an arsenal of texts to prove a certain given doctrine (the meaning of a text was often detached from its context and its historical events), Ephesians v. 32 became the textual foundation for the scholastic sacramental idea of marriage with its indissolubility even in the case of adultery. To a very large degree the sacramental concept stood or fell with the word *sacramentum*. For example, Luther and Calvin said that the whole misunderstanding of this doctrine could have been avoided if only the theologians had read the Greek New Testament[22]. The usage of the two words in either upholding or denying the sacra-

---

[18] Peter Lombard, *Sententiarum*, IV. (i). 2, *Patrologia Latina*, CXCII. 839.

[19] Peter Lombard, *Sententiarum*, IV. (ii). 1, *Patrologia Latina*, CXCII. 842.

[20] Thomas Aquinas, *Summa Contra Gentiles*, IV. LXXVIII, *Opera*, Paris, 1874, XII. 590.

[21] Thomas Aquinas, *Commentum in Lib IV. Sententiarum*, XXVI. II. III. 4, *Opera*, XI. 73.

[22] See pp. 45, 95 below.

mental concept, is clearly reflected in Latin and vernacular versions of the New Testament during the sixteenth century.

In his first edition of the Greek New Testament, 1516, Erasmus gives a Latin translation parallel with the Greek text. In this edition and in the subsequent ones the Latin text reads: "Mysterium hoc magnum est." In his annotations to the 1516 edition he makes this remark:

> I do not want those to be unaware who from this text make matrimony one of the sacraments, not that it should be doubted, but that here it is not greatly implied. Indeed this special little clause, 'But I' [verse 32], is sufficient to indicate, that this great mystery pertains to Christ and the church, not to husband and wife. It is in fact not a great sacrament if a man is joined to his wife, for the heathens have the same custom[23].

In the annotations to the 1519 edition Erasmus enlarges his statement somewhat. He begins by saying: "I would not want you to be unaware that some from this text make matrimony one of the seven sacraments. Not that there should be any doubt about this, since, probably this tradition comes from the apostles, or without doubt it has been further developed for us by the holy fathers." Erasmus asserts that Augustine and Jerome do not call it a sacrament as it was later understood. He then remarks: "Not that I say this, as if calling in doubt whether matrimony is a sacrament, but because from these words of the Apostle it does not easily appear on the surface." He then repeats the statement from the first edition and closes by saying that the Greek "does not actually signify a sacrament of the kind of which the church has seven, but means hidden and secret, which word is frequently used by Paul and about other things, which are far different from the nature of a sacrament"[24].

In his paraphrases on Ephesians v. Erasmus describes the great mystery as the unity between Christ and the Father and between Christ and the Church. This unity was to become an example for husband and wife to love one another. No reference is made to the sacramental problem[25]. In the annotations Erasmus presents two points of view, and he seems to play one against the other. On the one hand he does not wish to appear contrary to the teaching of the Church, but

---

[23] Erasmus, *Novvm Instrumentum omne ... cum Annotationibus*, Basel, 1516, p. 533.

[24] Erasmus, *Novvm Testamentvm omne ... cum Annotationibus*, Basel, 1519, p. 428.

[25] Erasmus, *The Paraphrase of Erasmus vpon the Newe Testamente*. London, 1548—49, II.

on the other he brings forth evidences which undermine the official teaching of the Church.

Luther used Erasmus' text as soon as it came out, as may be noticed from his lectures on the Apostle Paul's Epistle to the Romans. In a letter dated February 14, 1519, the well-known printer and publisher of Basel, John Froben, informs Luther about the second edition of Erasmus' New Testament[26]. In his German translation of the New Testament, 1522, Luther translates the Vulgate *sacramentum* and the Greek *mysterion* with *Geheimnis*. In a marginal note he speaks about the relationship between Christ and the Church, and likewise between husband and wife, *as Geheimnis*[27].

The first complete German Bible printed during the Reformation period was the Zürich Bible, 1529. It was published five years before Luther's complete Bible of 1534. However, it was a reprint of those books of the Bible which Luther at that time had translated. As would be expected the text reads: "Die geheimnuss ist gross." It has the same marginal note as found in Luther's translation.

In France the modern history of vernacular versions of the Bible begins with the humanist Jacques Lefèvre. His New Testament appeared in 1523 and the Old Testament five years later. Together they were published as the Antwerp Bible in 1530, and a revised edition was printed in 1534. Lefèvre follows the Vulgate but makes corrections from the Greek. He does not retain the Latin rendering of Ephesians v. 32 but corrects it in the light of the Greek text. Accordingly, his translation reads: "Le mystère est grand." In his commentary on the Epistle to the Ephesians he does not enter into any discussion concerning the usage of *mysterion* and *sacramentum*. This is so much more strange since at the end of each chapter he makes special comments on some of the key words. A possible answer will be given in another discussion of Lefèvre. At the end of chapter five he makes remarks on some words in verse thirty-one, passes by verse thirty-two, and goes on to verse thirty-three. The commentary has his own Latin translation parallel with the Vulgate. The *sacramentum* of the latter is rendered by *mysterium* in the former. In his interpretation of verse thirty-two in the major section of his commentary he confines himself to explaining the "great mystery" as one not seen with carnal eyes but with spiritual eyes, as it pertains to Christ's sacrifice for the relationship to the Church as His bride. The practical application for husband and wife is that "so ought a husband be earnestly desirous for

---

[26] "Joh. Froben an Luther, Basel, 14. Februar, 1519." This letter appears as No. 146 in *Briefwechsel*, I. 331–33, *D. Martin Luthers Werke*. Kritische Gesamtausgabe, Weimar edition (hereafter referred to as *W. E.*).

[27] Martin Luther, *Die Deutsche Bibel*, *W. E.*, VII. 207.

the salvation of his wife, which is his body, and of which he is the head"[28].

When the Waldenses held their synod in 1532, it was decided that they should contribute to the Protestant cause by sponsoring a Protestant French version of the Bible. Pierre Robert Olivetan, a cousin of Calvin, produced this translation, which was published in 1535. In harmony with the Greek text he translates the sentence under discussion with the words: "Le secret est grand."

Olivetan's version became the basis for the Geneva Bible, which in turn influenced the many English translations. The various English versions translated by Protestants, from Tyndale's Bible, 1525, to the Authorized Version, 1611, made use of the *mystery* or *secret*.

The Roman Catholics could not let the success of the Protestant vernacular Bibles remain unchallenged. In Germany Hieronymus Emser produced an anti-Lutheran New Testament which was published in 1527. He used Luther's New Testament as a basis for his translation but corrected it to accord with the Vulgate. His rendering of Ephesians v. 32 is a compromise, reading: "Das ist eyn gros Sacrament vnd heymlickeit."

The Emser translation became in turn the basis for the one of Johann Dietenberger, 1534. From a Catholic doctrinal point of view he improves the reading, for he renders it: "Das ist ein gross Sacrament." An annotation leaves no doubt as to the meaning of this statement, referring to the translation as a Hussite text, which by the use of *Geheimnis* offers a detrimental or prejudicial interpretation against the holy sacrament of marriage[29].

John Eck, Luther's old opponent, produced another German version, 1537. He renders the text as did Dietenberger, and a marginal note stating that marriage is a sacrament.

The faculty of theology at the University of Louvain authorized a new French version. The first edition was published in 1550, but it was revised in 1572 and again in 1578. It is known as the Louvain Bible. It was printed in order to counteract the influence of Protestant translations. Accordingly, Ephesians v. 32 reads: "Ce sacrement est grand."

---

[28] Jacques Lefèvre, *Epistolae Divi Pauli Apostoli* [Paris], 1515.

[29] An annotation on Ephesians v reads: In disem Capittel da die Elymasiter aber auss jrem Hussischen text dolmetschen, Saufft euch nit vol weins, darauss ein vnordenlich wesen volget: saget weder der Griechisch noch vnser text, darauss ein vnordenlich wesen volget: sonder, darinn vnkeuscheit ist. In dem letzten vnderscheid, volgen sie aber im Hussischen text, da er von dem ehelichen wesen sagt, Das geheimniss ist gross: dann wie vnser text laut, so soll es heissen, Diss

René Benoist, professor of theology at the University of Paris, produced a French version, 1566. In the preface he recommends the reading of the Bible in the vernacular in order to fight off Protestant heresy. Since the Benoist translation was essentially a reproduction of the Olivetan version only with some emendations, it was condemned by the theological faculty of the University for its Protestant flavour. However, his translation, "Ce sacrement est grand", follows the Latin versions and is accompanied by a marginal note stating that "this place shows, what is the holy thing of which the sacrament of marriage is a sign"[30].

The English Catholic Version of the New Testament (the Rheims Version), 1582, will be considered later. Here it suffices to say that it has the translation: "This is a great sacrament", and an annotation explaining matrimony as a sacrament in harmony with the canons and decrees of the Council of Trent. Having referred to the Protestants, who say that there are only two sacraments, the annotation states that they "do not likevvise folovv the Catholike Church in calling matrimonie by the same name, vvhich is here so called of the Apostle, specially vvhereas the signification in it, is a great as in any other of the Sacraments, and rather greater".

The usage of the Greek *mysterion* and the Latin *sacramentum* by Protestant and Catholic translators respectively as well as the explanations and marginal notes, confirms the exegetical significance of the two words in the discussion of marriage and divorce as mentioned in the beginning of this section[31].

The Christian Humanists

Since the early part of the fourteenth century the Italian humanists had been at work in recovering the culture of Ancient Greece and Rome. The awakening of an interest in the classical literature gave birth to new intellectual inquiries and a revised interest in the study of the Hebrew and Greek languages. These historical and philological studies broke away from medieval scholasticism. The Christian humanist sought to go back beyond the Thomist-Aristotelian Christianity by replacing the scholastic theology with a biblical theology. In their historical and philological approach their quest was to ascertain

Sacrament ist gross, vnd nit allein, dise geheimniss, wie dise dem heiligen Sacrament der Ehe zu nachtheil verdolmetschet haben.

[30] The marginal note to Ephesians v. 32 reads: Ce lieu monstre qui est la chose saincte de laquelle le sacrement du mariage est signe.

[31] For a study of the history, significance and characteristics of the various Bible translations see: *The Cambridge History of the Bible. The West from the Reformation to the Present Day*, Cambridge, 1963.

what a given text actually meant in the contest of Christ's teaching and primitive Christianity.

The results of the philological approach have been illustrated in the *mysterion* of Ephesians v. 32, and it remains now to consider the exegetical results of the historical approach as related to Erasmus' interpretation of the divorce texts. But first an examination should be made of the interpretation and approach of a few of the Christian humanists whose lives and works are of significance for Erasmus and for Christian humanism generally because of the role they played in the formative phase of the Protestant Reformation and particularly in the interpretation of the New Testament logia on divorce.

Lorenzo Valla

In his *Annotations* on the New Testament, 1444, Lorenzo Valla laid the foundation for modern New Testament textual criticism. In comparing three Greek manuscripts with three Latin translations he found many instances in which the Latin departed from the meaning of the Greek. Unfortunately the Vulgate had incorrect renderings which affected matters of doctrine. Valla's historical and textual criticism disproved the belief that the Apostles' Creed was composed by the Apostles and also exposed the falsity of the Donation of Constantine.

In 1504 Erasmus found a copy of Valla's *Annotations* in the Abbey of Parc just outside of Louvain. He took it with him to Paris and edited it; the next year it was printed and prefaced by a letter which he had written to Christopher Fisher, an Englishman who served as the Papal Protonotary and with whom Erasmus lodged in Paris. The letter is a general plea for the work of the humanists who are often condemned or envied by vested interests. Erasmus recommends Valla's book because it upholds the standards of the humanists by going back to the original sources. He also thinks that tribute should be given to Valla's good judgment and findings in place of the biased criticism so often expressed against him[32]. The question will now be asked: Does Valla make any remarks about the divorce texts? Since he confines himself to a few grammatical observations, which have no bearing upon the exegetical results, and makes no reference to the Greek *mysterion* in his comments on Ephesians v. 32, but retains the rendering of the Vulgate, it would be correct to say that he did not

---

[32] Lorenzo Valla, *Lavrentii Valae, viri tam Graecae quam Latinae linguae doctissimi, in Nouum Testamentum Annotationes, appri me utiles. Cum Erasmi Praefatione, & euisdem in hasce Annotationes castigationibus ad calcem adpositis*, Basel, 1541.

influence Erasmus' interpretation of the divorce texts in a direct way. However, Erasmus' publication of the *Annotations*, in the face of Valla's unpopularity in theological and ecclesiastical circles, clearly revealed the impression made on him by Valla's humanistic approach and indicated the scope and direction of his own future studies.

Jacques Lefèvre

In France the chief representative of Christian humanism was Jacques Lefèvre D'Étaples, also called Faber Stapulensis, 1455—1536. He aimed at a reform within the Church which was based upon the Bible. Accordingly, his greatest contribution is in the field of biblical studies. He wrote a Latin commentary on the Pauline Epistles, 1512, and one on the Gospels, 1521, both of which were printed in several editions. Reference has already been made to his French New Testament. Guillaume Farel, Calvin's forerunner in Geneva, was greatly influenced by Lefèvre.

It has already been noticed that Lefèvre, in his French translation of the New Testament, renders Ephesians v. 32 by "Le mystère est grand". This could have suggested that he would deviate from the common Catholic interpretation of the divorce texts, but it will be observed that this is not the case. In fact, apparently hoping to avoid an issue, he omits any discussion of the passage in his annotations. By this omission he may have hoped to avoid the issue which could arise from his use of the Greek rendering instead of the Vulgate.

The main point of emphasis in his comments on the divorce texts in the Gospels is that according to the teaching of Christ, it is not lawful to remarry even in the case of adultery[33]. Roman VII. 2—3 is brought into bearing upon the divorce question, confirming that a wife who marries another while her husband is alive shall be considered an adulteress[34]. In his interpretation of 1 Corinthians VII the statement of verses ten and eleven: "Let not the wife depart from her husband: But and if she depart, let her remain unmarried, or be reconciled to her husband: and let not the husband put away his wife", is brought into relationship with the divorce texts of the Gospels, supporting the interpretation that in case of adultery both parties should seek reconciliation but, failing this, should remain unmarried. The Apostle's counsel in verse fifteen, that the believing party dismissed by the unbelieving one "is not under bondage", is not discussed. Without seeking support from Ephesians v. 32, Lefèvre asserts the indissolubility of the marriage tie.

---

[33] Jacques Lefèvre, *Comentarii Initiatorii in Qvatvor Evangelia* [Paris], 1526.
[34] Lefèvre, *Epistolae Pauli*, sig. 80r.

John Colet

Having finished his education at Oxford, Colet went to Italy "like a merchant seeking goodly wares", as Erasmus puts it in his biography of Colet[35]. After imbibing the spirit of the new learning, he returned to England, 1496—97, and began to give his famous lectures, first on Romans, and then on 1 Corinthians. His objective was to bring out the practical meaning which Paul had sought to convey to his readers. He rejected the allegorical and anagogical exegesis of the scholastic theologians.

In 1498 Erasmus arrived at Oxford and attended Colet's lectures, and a friendship was created which lasted until Colet's death in 1519. When Erasmus published his Greek New Testament, 1516, Colet rejoiced and wrote him a letter of encouragement and appreciation. Realizing that many approved and admired Erasmus' work, he also knew that others disapproved and found fault with it. For his own part he writes:

> I am so devoted to your studies and so charmed with your new edition, that it produces in me a variety of emotions. At one moment I am full of sorrow that I have not learned Greek, without which we are nothing; at another I rejoice in that light which is emitted by the rays of your genius. Indeed, Erasmus, I am surprised at the fertility of your mind, which conceives so many projects, and brings such important works to birth day after day in such perfection, especially when you have no fixed abode, and are not assisted by any great or certain emoluments[36].

There is no indication as to what Colet thought of Erasmus' interpretation of the divorce texts. He himself does not deal with the question of divorce in his interpretation of 1 Corinthians VII, but from his comments it is obvious that he places less value upon marriage than does Erasmus. Colet's disparagement of the marriage estate and his praise of celibacy reflect the thinking of Augustine as expressed in the latter's treatises on marriage and virginity. Marriage is only allowed to those who have not the gift of continence. "But, if there be non reason of this kind, then rest assured that not even a first marriage is allowed. For marriage has nothing good in itself, save in so far as it is a remedy for necessary evil." In the beginning it was useful for procreation. "But now that the Bridegroom has come, and the truth of spiritual marriage is fulfilled, there is no longer any necessity for the

---

[35] Erasmus, *The Lives of Jehan Vitrier and John Colet*, trans. J. H. Lupton, London, 1883, p. 21.

[36] Francis Morgan Nichols, *The Epistles of Erasmus*, London, 1904, II. 286—88. Epistle 411, "John Colet to Erasmus" (June 20, 1516).

married state to exist as a figure of that which was to come. Nor indeed is conjugal union required in Christendom for the increase of offspring; since our way of increase is not by generation, but by regeneration in God." If all Christians were called to remain single "there would always be a surplus from heathendom", but if the question should be asked: "What would have been the result, supposing that the whole multitude of heathens had been converted to the worship of Christ", then they would be considered as an answer to the Lord's prayer about the coming of His kingdom. The same thought was expressed by Augustine[37]. In his comment on Romans VII. 2—3 no reference is made to marriage or divorce as found in Lefèvre's commentary[38].

Thomas More

Before the turn of the sixteenth century Thomas More and Erasmus had been student friends at Oxford. Both men were disciples of Colet, and in the same year as the first edition of Erasmus' New Testament appeared Thomas More published his *Utopia*[39]. More describes how marriage and divorce are considered in his ideal state. While he does not enter into any exegesis of the divorce texts, it is of interest to notice his viewpoints for the sake of comparison with the exegetical conclusions of the expositors. More lived and died as a Catholic; yet he expressed concepts contrary to the idea of marriage and divorce as held by the Church.

After having fallen from the grace of Henry VIII, 1504, More entered the ascetic life of a monk in a Carthusian Charterhouse intending to take the vow of a monk or priest. However, the following year he married. His own experience no doubt influenced him to make a re-evaluation of the virtues of married life and those of celibacy. Contrary to Colet, the Utopians hold that those who marry are wiser than those who remain celibate and that they discharge "a debt which they owe to human nature and to their country". Furthermore, "they would indeed laugh at any man, who from the principles of reason would prefer an unmarried state to a married . . . but they reverence and admire such as do it from the motives of religion".

---

[37] John Colet, *An Exposition of St. Paul's First Epistle to the Corinthians*, trans. J. H. Lupton, London, 1874, pp. 90—92; Augustine, *De Bono Conjugali*, I. x. *Patrologia Latina*, XL. 381.

[38] John Colet, *An Exposition of St. Paul's Epistle to the Romans*, trans. J. H. Lupton, London, 1873, pp. 20—24, 149.

[39] Thomas More, *Utopia*, printed in *Ideal Commonwealths*, London, 1901. For More's discussion of marriage and divorce see pp. 69—71, 89.

Divorce is allowed "in the case of adultery or insufferable perverseness". The Senate is given the authority to dissolve the marriage tie, and at the same time it grants the innocent party "leave to marry again". These thoughts must have appeared heretical in a time when marriage was a church matter and adultery warranted only separation from board and bed with no right to remarry. The adulterer was punished with slavery, but if the innocent party wanted reconciliation his only recourse was to follow the lost party into slavery, except that the Prince could void the sentence. "But those that relapse after they are once pardoned are punished with death." Aside from such breaches of the vow, divorce was only by mutual consent, even in cases of calamity or sickness. More writes:

> But it frequently falls out that when a married couple do not well agree, they by mutual consent separate, and find out other persons with whom they hope they may live more happily. Yet this is not done without obtaining leave of the Senate, which never admits of a divorce but upon a strict inquiry made, both by the Senators and their wives, into the grounds upon which it is desired; and even when they are satisfied concerning the reasons of it, they go on but slowly, for they imagine that too great easiness in granting leave for new marriages would very much shake the kindness of married people[40].

It seems that More laid down reasons for divorce which in modern terminology would be called divorce by mutual consent and for mental incompatibility. Regarding this view he was far in advance of even the Protestant reformers, Martin Bucer probably being an exception. The thread was first taken up by John Milton more than one hundred and twenty-five years later. The challenge which More, as a lawyer, brought to the Catholic foundation and structure of marriage and divorce from a judicial point of view, Erasmus, as a theologian, brought to the same from an exegetical point of view.

Desiderius Erasmus

At the publication of the English translation of Erasmus' *Paraphrases* of the New Testament early in the reign of Edward VI, 1548, the Catholic Bishop Gardiner of Winchester expressed his evalution of Erasmus and his literary activities. Strype's record reads:

> As to Erasmus' Paraphrase, the said Bishop pretended, 'He found divers things in it to condemn the Work: and that he agreed with them that said, Erasmus laid the Eggs, and Luther hatched them: and that of all the monstrous Opinions that have risen, evil Men had a wondrous Occasion

---

[40] More, *Utopia*, p. 70.

ministred to them from that Book'. He also wrote to the Protector the particular Objections he made against it. He said, 'He might term it in one word Abomination, both for the Malice and Untruth of much Matter out of Erasmus's Pen: and also for the arrogant Ignorance of the Translators of it"[41].

Strype does not omit to mention another and more favourable acceptance of Erasmus' work. Seeking to vindicate Erasmus he quotes from the translator's *Epistle Dedicatory:*

'I cannot but judg, that whose are prompt and hasty Condemners of Erasmus, or eager Adversaries unto his Doctrine, do, under the Name and Colour of Erasmus, rather utter their Stomach and Hatred against God's Word, and the Grace of the Gospel, which Erasmus for his part most diligently and most simply laboureth to bring to light"[42].

In order to promote true religion Archbishop Cranmer had initiated the composition of the *Books of Homilies* expecting that these, together with *The Paraphrase of Erasmus*, should be made available to the people in each parish[43]. The words of Gardiner and the value placed upon Erasmus' work by Cranmer, illustrate to a very large degree the attitude toward the writings of Erasmus by the Catholic and Protestant theologians, respectively, during the sixteenth century.

What thus applies in general, is specifically true when it comes to Erasmus' exposition of the New Testament logia on divorce. The opposition manifested toward him on this point from the one side, and the indebtedness expressed by the other, are here most evident. In his interpretation of the New Testament logia on divorce Erasmus reveals himself as a Christian theologian who seeks to solve an ethical problem within Church and society by finding a solution based on Scripture and centered in Christ[44]. No ecclesiastical institution should

---

[41] John Strype, *Memorials of Thomas Cranmer*, London, 1694, II. III. 151. To the Duke of Somerset Gardiner wrote: "By the doctrin of the Paraphrasis, whosoever had done away his wife for advotrie might mary again. By the Paraphrasis al men may mary, Bushops and Priests . . . By the Paraphrasis the keeping of a Concubine is called but a light fault." Strype, *Memorials of Cranmer*, Appendix XXXVI, p. 80.

[42] Strype, *Memorials of Cranmer*, II. III. 153.

[43] Strype, *Memorials of Cranmer*, II. III. 148—53.

[44] In a recent and pertinent study of Erasmus it has been conclusively proved that Erasmus was above all else a Christian theologian, anchored on Scripture and centered in Christ. The present study upholds this thesis. See Ernst-Wilhelm Kohls, *Die Theologie des Erasmus*, I—II, Basel, 1966. Published under the auspices of *Theologische Zeitschrift*, the Theological Faculty of the University of Basel, ed. Bo Reicke.

stand between the needy and the Good Samaritan. Erasmus appears not as an academic theorist but as a Christian pragmatist who is devoted to his Master in service for his fellow men.

Erasmus' genuine interest in these matters is reflected in some works on matrimony and related subjects. In one section of *Enchiridion Militis Christiani*[45] he warns against fornication and pleads with those fallen into its trap. The virtues of marriage are presented in *Apologia Pro Declamatione Matrimonii*[46]. *Christiani Matrimonii Institvtio* is dedicated to Catherine of Aragon[47]. Its influence, through Bullinger, on English domestic conduct books has been asserted[48].

The sources for an examination of Erasmus' exegesis of the divorce texts are the *Annotations* of his New Testament, which were first printed in 1516 in collaboration with John Oecolampadius[49] and slightly enlarged in the 1519 edition[50], the *Paraphrases* of the Gospels, which were published in 1522—24, and those of the Epistle to the Corinthians, 1519[51]. The main source is however found in the *Annotations* on 1 Corinthians VII[52]. His exegesis of this chapter is theological and homiletical rather than grammatical. He makes the text a basis for a long doctrinal and ethical discussion of marriage and divorce. In this approach he is imitated by the Protestant reformers at large. Luther and Peter Martyr are notable examples of

---

[45] Erasmus, *Enchiridion Militis Christiani*, printed in *Des. Erasmi Rot. Opervm*, Basel, 1540, V. 3—55. This edition of Erasmus' collected works is hereafter referred to as *Opera*.

[46] Erasmus, *Apologia Pro Declamatione Matrimonii, Opera*, IX. 91—94.

[47] Erasmus, *Christiani Matrimonii Institvtio, Opera*, V. 513—602.

[48] Alfred Weber, *Heinrich Bullingers "Christlicher Ehestand", seine zeitgenössischen Quellen und die Anfänge des Familienbuches in England*, Leipzig, 1929.

[49] Erasmus, *Novvm Instrumentum omne*, 1516; Ernst Staehelin, *Das theologische Lebenswerk Johannes Oekolampads*, Leipzig, p. 61.

[50] Erasmus, *Novvm Testamentvm omne*, 1519.

[51] Erasmus, *Paraphrasin in Euangelium Matthaei nunc primum natam & aeditam per D. Erasmvm Roterodamum: Paraphrases in omneis epistolas apostolicas, hoc est Pauli, Iacobi, Ioannis, Petri, Iudae, per eundem*, Basel, 1522; *In Evangelivm Marci Paraphrasis*, Basel, 1524; *In Evangelivm Lvcae Paraphrasis*, Basel, 1524; *Paraphrases Des. Erasmi Roterodami in Epistolas Pauli apostoli ad Rhomanos Corinthios & Galatas, quae commentarii uice esse possunt*, Basel, 1520. The preface is dated 1519 and the British Museum Catalogue lists a separate edition of 1 Corinthians for that year.

[52] For the annotations on 1 Corinthians VII see Erasmus, *Opera*, VI. 460—81. For an early English translation see: *The Censure and Iudgement of the Famous Clark Erasmus of Roterodam: Whyther dyuorsement betwene man and wyfe stondeth with the lawe of God . . . in the Book of his Annotations, upon these wordes of Paule*, trans. Nicholas Lesse, London [1550?].

those who give a long discourse on marriage and divorce in connection with their exegesis of 1 Corinthians VII. Thus a pattern was set by Erasmus. The annotations to the divorce texts in the Gospels as well as in the paraphrases on the same and on 1 Corinthians VII, do not add anything vital to the annotations of 1 Corinthians VII. The points in the *Paraphrases* which deviated from official Catholic teaching were attacked by the Sorbonne and a prominent Catholic theologian. An English theologian did the same with the *Annotations*. Their criticisms and Erasmus' replies will be examined[53]. Before turning to his comments on 1 Corinthians VII, his discussion on Catholic practices of divorce and separation should be considered.

Divorce and the Roman Catholic Impediments to Marriage

In order fully to appreciate Erasmus' and the Protestant reformers' interpretation of the divorce texts and the discussions connected therewith, it should be pointed out that the insistence of the Roman Church upon the indissolubility of the marriage tie did not mean that divorce was not practised, but divorce was understood and approached in a different way as compared with the Protestant theologians. Catholic theologians differentiate between two types of divorce. The first is separation from board and bed (divortium a mensa et thoro), and the other is an absolute annulment of the marriage tie (divortium a vinculo matrimonii), by asserting that the marriage from the very beginning (ab initio) had been unlawfully contracted.

Erasmus lists and discusses eighteen impediments advocated by the Church as hindrances for contracting marriage. They are as follows: a general or special ecclesiastical interdict; marriage not to be contracted in an inauspicious time of the year, otherwise to be annulled; certain conditions of one party unknown to the other; mistaken identity; vow of chastity; holy order; relationship in which grades and lineage are differentiated, but going further than prohibited by the law of Leviticus XVIII; birth without adoption; spiritual relationship which was extended to persons taking part in the baptism of a child (Erasmus lists twenty cases of spiritual relationship which opposed matrimony taking place and obviated what already had been contracted); affinity; lack of public honesty; custom or established law; admitted crime; difference of religion; fear because of threat; preceding obligation as to a former marriage or promise of marriage; impotence and insanity[54]. Introducing his discussion of these eighteen impediments Erasmus makes this comment:

---

[53] See pp. 27—33 below.
[54] Erasmus, *Christiani Matrimonii Institvtio, Opera*, V. 528 ff.

Some are of this kind that they do not invalidate the contract, or they do not allow a separation from a wife, but they obstruct the making of a contract, and they make the slighter of this impediment guilty of a crime. Some divorce for a time, others obstruct the making of marriage, and annul it when made. Some break up a contracted marriage, but not when it is consummated. Some so invalidate it, however contracted, that not even the Roman Pontiff has relaxed the rigour of the law. Others although not legally contracted, nevertheless can be approved by him, if it is desired. Others again separate from board and bed, others restore male or female to their former state . . . Now concerning one or other of these impediments a thousand questions come up for examination and the innumerable battles of human opinions[55].

It is evident from Erasmus' discussion of the Catholic impediments that he considers them to be contrary to the spirit and letter of the New Testament logia on divorce. Furthermore, the state of abuse into which these impediments had led, he found deplorable. While divorce, as he saw it in the light of Christ's words, was denied, it was possible through canonical laws to find ways and means to annul a marriage by *proving* it to have been illegal *ab initio*. Accordingly, his interpretation of the divorce texts was not an academic exercise, but he hoped that through a practical application of a correct interpretation of Christ's words a higher moral standard might be achieved for the marriage estate. This point will also be noticed in Luther's treatment of the impediments and the divorce texts. Having considered the matter of divorce as related to the impediments, he suggests that since thousands of people within the Christian commonwealth are in danger of falling into matrimonial snares, the leaders, as "learned physicians", should modify some of the ecclesiastical laws[56].

Having referred to one group of people who repudiate the authority of papal decrees and another group who equate them to the gospel or put them above the gospel, he takes a moderate position between these two views. Concerning his proposed suggestions he writes: "Hence, whatever I say here, I would not wish it to be accepted otherwise than as in a council in which the subject matter is treated; anyone you please reports his opinion from the turmoil of those sitting in session, being remiss to the better, and even making it a matter of ridicule, if it is deserved."[57]

The reaction of the Council of Trent to the matters proposed by Erasmus and the Protestant reformers will later be considered in some detail. Here it suffices to mention that the Council sought to restrict

---

[55] Erasmus, *Christiani Matrimonii Institvtio, Opera*, V. 528.
[56] Erasmus, *Christiani Matrimonii Institvtio, Opera*, V. 536.
[57] Erasmus, *Christiani Matrimonii Institvtio, Opera*, V. 536.

some of the impediments, such as spiritual relationship and public honesty. However under the section the *Sacrament of Matrimony*, canons IV, IX, and XI, clearly endorsed the other points under attack. Anyone holding any of the following opinions should be anathema:

> . . . the Church could not constitute impediments dissolving marriage; or that she has erred in constituting them . . . that clerks constituted in sacred orders, or regulars, who have solemnly professed chastity, are able to contract marriage, and that being contracted, it is valid, the ecclesiastical law, or vow, notwithstanding . . . that the prohibition of the solemnization of marriages at certain times of the year, is a tyrannical superstition of the heathen[58].

The subject of the impediments will be taken up again in connection with the examination of Luther's exegesis, remembering that Erasmus' discussion of them, as just referred to, was written in 1526, six years after Luther had presented the problems, and at a time when Erasmus was not interested in being identified with Luther. The question of the impediments may therefore be considered as a serious problem within the Church and society at that time.

Erasmus' Interpretation of the Divorce Texts

The Pharisees had asked Christ: "It it lawful for a man to put his wife away for every cause?" In his answer Christ made them to understand that Moses permitted the letter of divorce, not because he favoured divorce but because of the hardness of their hearts. It was feared that the husband, in his hatred toward his wife, might do her great harm, probably even kill her. Thus of two evils Moses chose the lesser. In other words the law was given to restrain evil, but the Jews used it to obtain divorce for any trivial reason[59].

As the ideal for Christian matrimony Christ points to the primeval condition, when husband and wife were made one flesh. The grace of the gospel should be able to amend the ways of an unpleasant wife or give patience to bear what difficulties may arise. Christ is stricter than Moses by allowing only one reason for divorce, namely adultery. On the other hand Erasmus makes statements which seem to imply

---

[58] Theodore Alios Buckley, trans., *The Canons and Decrees of the Council of Trent*, London, 1851, pp. 178, 179.

[59] For the annotations on Matthew V and XIX see Erasmus, *Opera*, VI. 29, 77. For the paraphrases on the same two chapters see *Opera*, VII. 25, 79—80. The English translation of the same is found in *The Paraphrase of Erasmus vpon the Newe Testamente*, London, 1548, I. sig. XXIIIR, LXXVV—LXXVIV.

that there could be other reasons, as when he says that Christ told His disciples that among Christians there should not be divorce for any light displeasures[60]. According to Erasmus Chrysostom emphasizes adultery to be the only exception, but Origen regards other crimes as equal to adultery or even worse, while Augustine equalled idolatry to adultery. Erasmus himself thinks "that adultery is made the exception, because it diametrically fights against the very nature of marriage"[61]. He confesses that the divorce texts are full of difficulties and the doctors of the Church do not share the same opinion about them. However, in his comments on 1 Corinthians VII he makes his interpretation of the logia on divorce very clear[62].

Erasmus begins his discussion by stating most carefully that he does not wish to bring up any new opinion which may cause contention, but his purpose is to help those who represent the pure and sound judgement of the Church[63]. At the same time he asserts that it ought not to be considered contumely, neither should any be offended, if a person finds a meaning which differs from that of an authority, no matter how great a name he may bear. He is well aware of the common opinion that once marriage has been contracted it cannot be dissolved except by the death of one of the partners. He also realizes that this opinion is approved by the consensus of the theologians of scholasticism. However, it has always been in the hearts of good men to change their opinions so as to deal fairly with a good cause. In the laws of pharmacy, medicine is accommodated to the nature of the sickness, and it should be considered if it would not be profitable to apply the same principle in matrimonial matters. Erasmus' conviction that enlightenment would usher in a new era and bring a reform within the Church, is reflected in his approach[64].

Two basic propositions are laid down. It should be permissible to dissolve certain marriages, not fortuitously but for very serious reasons, by the ecclesiastical authorities or recognized judges, and to give the innocent party freedom to marry again. These two views would of course be considered revolutionary and heretical by the theologians. Since it is wrong to cast doubt on fundamental Christian beliefs, as the divinity of Christ, etc., then according to the opinion of Erasmus the question of divorce belongs to another category. Here injunctions can be changed as time and necessity will require, even though they have been upheld by the authority of the Church. Of utmost importance is the exemplification of apostolic piety to procure the salvation

---

[60] Erasmus, *Paraphrase*, I. sig. xxIIIv; *Opera*, VII. 25.
[61] Erasmus, *Opera*, VI. 77.   [62] See note 52 p. 17.
[63] Erasmus, *Annotations*, sig. AIIIIv–Avr; *Opera*, VI. 467.
[64] Erasmus, *Annotations*, sig. AvIr; *Opera*, VI. 467.

of all men as much as possible and to succour the weak and sick members of the Church. In other words charity should come before any institutionalism, having preference over any ecclesiastical injunctions[65].

Having thus expressed the concept of apostolic charity, Erasmus brings the reader face to face with the problems of the many thousands who are unhappily coupled together with the result that both parties thereby perish. They could be saved if they were divorced and able to marry someone else. If this were possible without doing injury to the word of God, then it ought to delight all godly men. Furthermore, charity sometimes does what it legally is not able to do, and it is justified in doing so[66]. Erasmus realizes that this proposition may be regarded as unheard of and absurd, as well as being unworthy of being called into discussion. However, the writings of the early Church Fathers supplied him with evidences that in this proposition and the two previously mentioned about divorce and remarriage, he is nearer the truth than may be expected. Thus Origen records that certain bishops known to him had permitted some wives, who had divorced themselves from their husbands, to marry again. Origen admits that this was against the precept of the Lord and Paul, but he could not entirely condemn it, because it must have happened for good reasons. Otherwise some worse crimes might possibly have been committed because of the hardness of their hearts. The principal point, which should be observed, is that Origen noticed in this example that the wives were allowed that which he considered Paul had prohibited[67].

According to Erasmus Origen asserts that Christ permitted divorce only on account of adultery, but he faces the perplexing question of whether or not a husband was allowed to divorce a wife for parricide, poisoning, or witchcraft. On the one hand it was against the precept of Christ, but on the other it seemed unjust that a husband should have to bear these evil traits in his wife. For Erasmus the evidence was clear: Origen made exceptions other than adultery. Furthermore, Origen allowed the divorced person to remarry, which is evident by his illustration of Christ's relationship to the synagogue and the Christian Church. By God Christ was married to the synagogue, but when she became an adulteress and sought the death of her husband, she was divorced, and the Christian Church became the new wife[68].

Tertullian allowed both divorce and remarriage. In this respect he

---

[65] Erasmus, *Annotations*, sig. Aviir–Aviiv; *Opera*, VI. 467.

[66] Erasmus, *Annotations*, sig. Aviiir; *Opera*, VI. 467.

[67] Erasmus, *Annotations*, sig. Aviiiv–Biv; *Opera*, VI. 468.

[68] Erasmus, *Annotations*, sig. Biv–Bvr; *Opera*, VI. 468.

was just as orthodox as Ambrose, who conceded the right to marry another wife when the former was put away because of adultery. A believing wife was also permitted to remarry if divorced from an unbelieving husband. Reference is also made to other ancient theologians to the same effect[69].

Some assert that marriage can be dissolved before there has been coitus but not after. Erasmus is of the opinion that when a marriage has been contracted legally and by mutual consent, then whether or not there has been coitus, there is no serious cause sufficient for discrimination between the two. Therefore, when divorce is allowed in the first case, it should also be allowed in the second[70].

In his further plea against a divorce which is only a separation from board and bed, Erasmus becomes very specific in his references to the Papacy. First of all Christ did not demand virginity, neither that man should go against nature, but the laws of the Church add affliction to affliction upon those who should have been assisted. A man who is separated from his wife because she was unfaithful, is excluded from entering the honours and privileges of the marriage estate by human laws, but not by the law of the gospel[71]. Since canon law does not permit remarriage, the result is that a man has to live with a secret wife in sin. While Erasmus realizes that according to the law of the Church a marriage cannot be annulled after it has been entered upon, he still feels that the rigour of this law can be mitigated, when such causes often exist as to make it seem cruel not to come to the rescue of the sufferers. In view of the fact that this law seems to war against the equity of nature, it should be looked into if there may not be other interpretations which are to be read in the Gospels and the Epistles[72].

Realizing that this suggestion would be considered revolutionary, he appeals to the reader not to call upon heaven and earth in rage and say that this man wants to break the decretals of the Church. This is not his purpose as he wishes to reason out the matter. Thus again he expresses his desire for reform, but within the Church. He continues his discourse by emphasizing that on many points of doctrine there has not always been unanimity within the Church from century to century[73].

Certain injunctions were instituted by the Church which had value only for that time, but the Church and the bishop of Rome had au-

---

[69] Erasmus, *Annotations*, sig. Bvr–Ciiiir; *Opera*, VI. 468–70.
[70] Erasmus, *Annotations*, sig. Ciiir–v; *Opera*, VI. 469.
[71] Erasmus, *Annotations*, sig. Diir; *Opera*, VI. 471.
[72] Erasmus, *Annotations*, sig. Divr–v; *Opera*, VI. 471.
[73] Erasmus, *Annotations*, sig. Divv; *Opera*, VI. 471.

thority to change these if it was necessary for the betterment of mankind. Christ sought the lost sheep, therefore the Church should seek the salvation of those who suffer. No human laws ought to be valued except they are conducive to the salvation of men. Some theologians say that the bishop of Rome has authority to change anything, even that which the Apostles and Peter have ordained. Other doctors question this and say that he cannot decree against the gospel. With both concepts Erasmus can win his argument, since the first permits the Church to change present practices, and the second obliges the bishop of Rome to issue his injunctions in harmony with Christ's teaching and the spirit of the gospel. In ancient times people were not declared heretics for not believing what later was considered essential. This raises a double doubt: whether all the acts in a certain council are important, and with what words and spirit they are defined. If it is true, as some assert, that the Roman pontiff cannot err in judicial matters, then there is no need for a general council. However, in the opinion of Erasmus, the papal directives cannot be relied upon by the very fact that the Catholic concept of divorce is a result of tradition. This concept was probably first expressed by one or two bishops, then gradually it spread and became powerful with no one knowing how a custom once established acquired power. Erasmus emphasizes that he has brought forward all these points lest anyone should hastily reject the disputation about changing divorce laws as being absurd[74].

Erasmus now turns to the divorce texts of the Gospel of Matthew. Even though Christ allowed one exception for divorce, the Church circumscribes it and interprets Christ's words more rigidly than Christ Himself did. Augustine and the ancient theologians and lawyers did not interpret divorce to mean only separation from board and bed. Christ spoke to the Jews and they knew no other divorce than that which gave legal right to marry again. The Church's rigid interpretation of the divorce texts is contradictory to the general interpretation given to the other words in the Sermon on the Mount. For example, Christ forbad swearing more severely than divorce. Yet it is interpreted to be understood that we are commanded not to swear unadvisedly without a cause. Likewise, we have just as much right to say that no one should divorce his wife unadvisedly for every trifle[75].

Erasmus clearly states that Christ made one exception for divorce, namely adultery. On the other hand he also seems to imply that there could be other reasons. This apparent contradiction should be seen in the light of his statements which, according to the theology of Luther, would characterize the difference between the kingdom of Christ and

[74] Erasmus, *Annotations*, sig. Dvr-Eviir; *Opera*, VI. 471–73.
[75] Erasmus, *Annotations*, sig. Fiv; *Opera*, VI. 474.

the kingdom of the world. The words of Matthew v. 32 were not spoken to the multitudes but to the disciples who were the purest part of His body belonging to the kingdom of heaven. They had no need of laws, divorce, oath-taking, etc. But within the Church is another group referred to as the imperfect ones who are found in large numbers. They constitute the kingdom of the world and in this sphere it is not wrong to go to court, to use force in opposing wrong, to take oath, etc. On account of hardness of heart the Jews were permitted to put away their wives for any cause they pleased, lest they should do greater evils. Greater perils can be found among Christians, for besides unchastity are found cruel murders, poisonings, and incantations. The question is therefore if the same cause would not advocate the same remedy? When the Pharisees asked Christ whether or not it is lawful for a man to put away his wife for any cause, Christ restricted divorce to one cause, not because there is no more scandalous cause than adultery, but because it is in every way directly contrary to the very nature of matrimony[76]. Erasmus suggests that Christ gave one cause for divorce, namely, adultery, but the Apostle Paul enlarged the precept of the Lord[77].

Having expressed his disagreement with the concept that marriage on account of being a sacrament is indissoluble, as already discussed, Erasmus turns to the argument of Romans VII. 2–3: "For the woman which hath an husband is bound by the law to her husband so long as he liveth; but if the husband be dead, she is loosed from the law of her husband. So then if, while her husband liveth, she be married to another man, she shall be called an adulteress: but if her husband be dead, she is free from the law; so that she is no adulteress, though she be married to another man." This statement by Paul was quoted by Catholic theologians to prove that a second marriage was prohibited while one of the partners was still alive. Erasmus asserts that Paul is not reasoning about divorce, but he makes known that the law of Moses in now superseded by the gospel. The Christian should no longer cling to the law, since he is married to a new spouse, namely, Christ. Paul makes use of a parable, and a parable does not necessarily fit on all points. If Paul really had meant what some wish him to say, then he would not have referred to the law, for those to whom Paul spoke would not have known any other law than the one which permitted the husband to put his wife away by giving her a letter of divorce[78]. Thus it is indirectly pointed out that a certain text should

---

[76] Erasmus, *Annotations*, sig. FIIIR–FVV; *Opera*, VI. 474.

[77] Erasmus, *Annotations*, sig. FVV–FVIV; *Opera*, VI. 474–75.

[78] Erasmus, *Annotations*, sig. HVIV–HVIIR; *Opera*, VI. 478.

not be taken out of its context and used as a proof text for an already fixed concept. The Protestant theologians followed Erasmus' interpretation in their commentaries.

A parallel example of Romans VII. 2—3 is found in 1 Corinthians VII. 39: "The wife is bound by the law as long as her husband liveth; but if her husband be dead, she is at liberty to be married to whom she will; only in the Lord." Here again Erasmus emphasizes that Paul is not treating the subject of divorce, but only giving advice to virgins and widows especially[79].

Erasmus finds two different types of departing in 1 Corinthians VII. The first may be styled separation, the other divorce. When Paul says: "Let not the wife depart from her husband: But and if she depart, let her remain unmarried, or be reconciled to her husband: and let not the husband put away his wife", then he has in mind equal marriages of Christians. The more serious offences are included in the statement of verse fifteen: "But if the unbeliever depart, let him depart. A brother or a sister is not under bondage in such cases: but God hath called us to peace." Within this category is the case of an unbelieving husband refusing to live with a wife who has become a Christian, the crime of adultery, and similar or even worse cases[80]. In the same classification belongs the case of a youth who may have been caught into a marriage through wine and drunkenness. In such instances there are often mutual quarrels, irremediable hatred, dread of poisoning and of murder, anticipating nothing but evil. Neither can live continently and if they cleave to each other they perish twice, but if the marriage is dissolved and they are allowed to marry again, it is hoped that they both should be outside peril[81].

Thinking of the more serious offences mentioned above, and having in mind the difference between separation from board and bed expressed in verses ten and eleven, and actual divorce and remarriage allowed in verse fifteen, Erasmus thinks that perhaps it was because of such circumstances that the Apostle relaxed somewhat his earlier vigorous counsel. He suggests that Paul should be more affably interpreted than he is[82]. In this connection reference is made to Jerome's record of the case of Fabiola, who had been abused by her husband and therefore left him and remarried. In spite of being the innocent party she was required by the bishop to do public penance because she had remarried. Erasmus thinks that if this woman had sought advice

---

[79] Erasmus, *Annotations*, sig. HvIIIv—IIIr; *Opera*, VI. 478.
[80] Erasmus, *Annotations*, sig. IIIIr; *Opera*, VI. 478.
[81] Erasmus, *Annotations*, sig. IIIIIr; *Opera*, VI. 479.
[82] Erasmus, *Annotations*, sig. IvR; *Opera*, VI. 479.

from Paul, she would have been more kindly treated than by the bishop.

Concluding his comments on the divorce text of 1 Corinthians VII, Erasmus makes a few final inferences. It should be understood that his suggestions had not been prescribed for the purpose of opening the window repeatedly to divorces, but were given in the hope that divorce might be a remedy for an unfortunate marriage, when in vain all ways and means had been tried to help the partners. There was no reason that proper divorce laws should break up marriages everywhere, for this did not happen even among the pagans. He also felt it as a duty and right to state with what reasons his interpretation and concept were adduced. Finally, he hoped that his thoughts might come into fruitage through the authority of the ecclesiastical powers[83].

Edward Lee versus Erasmus

As would have been expected, a number of voices were raised in criticism against the *Annotations* of Erasmus, and in these voices the reaction of Rome was heard. One of those who caused Erasmus considerable worry and annoyance was Edward Lee, from 1531 until his death in 1544, Archbishop of York. Lee himself was deeply interested in biblical studies and had written a commentary on the Old Testament[84]. The writers' quarrel is reflected in their correspondence[85], but Lee's official assault is his *Annotations* on those of Erasmus.

Edward Lee's Criticism

Lee's specific reaction and opposition to Erasmus' interpretation of the divorce texts are expressed in his comments on some of Erasmus' annotations on Matthew XIX and Ephesians v. 32[86]. In connection with his discussion of the Mosaic divorce law Erasmus had raised the question, if the same causes would not allow the same remedies. Lee answers negatively, because marriage is counted as a sacrament according to Ephesians v. 32. Christ will not repudiate His Church, likewise should neither husband nor wife separate from one another ex-

---

[83] Erasmus, *Annotations*, sig. IvIR–KvIIv; *Opera*, VI. 479–481.

[84] William Hunt, "Edward Lee", *The Dictionary of National Biography*, XXXII. 347–49.

[85] H. M. Allen, *Opvs Epistolarvm Des. Erasmi Roterodami*, Oxford, 1913, III. letter 765; Oxford, 1922, IV. letters 998, 1037, 1061.

[86] Edward Lee, *Annotationes Edovardi Leei in Annotationes Novi Testamenti Desiderii Erasmi* [Basel, 1520].

cept in the case of adultery. He does not touch the question of remarrying, but his emphasis on marriage being a sacrament would most likely not allow this. He asserts that the indissolubility of the marriage tie "is maintained in Christ and the church, that living together in eternity they should be separated by no divorce"[87].

In his interpretation of Ephesians v. 32 Erasmus had said "that there is not very much to be gathered from this passage as to matrimony being a sacrament", but Lee expresses the opposite opinion, saying: "Nay rather from this place it is plainly implied, that matrimony is a sacrament."[88] Lee's exegetical arguments follow next. First the text says: "Husbands, love your wives, even as Christ loved the church." As a result of this men ought to love their wives as their own bodies", and it then follows that "a man shall leave his father and mother, and shall be joined unto his wife, and they two shall be one flesh". Subsequently the Apostle says: "This is a great sacrament. But I speak of Christ and the church." Lee states his deduction in the form of a question and answer. "Now I ask you, what sacrament does he mean, when he says (this is a great sacrament)? I do not think you will say of Christ and the church, for that would change the meaning. This sacrament of Christ and the church, is great in Christ and the church. Therefore, when he says (this sacrament), you cannot from these words have it to refer to anything else than the indissoluble union of husband and wife."[89]

Lee refers to Erasmus' statement that "not every mystery is one of the seven sacraments, and certainly there are great mysteries, as when Eve was formed from the side of Adam, which was a mystery and is designated a secret"[90]. Lee thinks that there is no reason why this question should have been brought up, for no one has contended that marriage is one of the seven sacraments, and "it is evident no one will deny it, nor desire to fight against the catholic church"[91]. Erasmus had attacked what was held as "a common opinion, and not to be despised, nor can there be a better one, that matrimony was instituted in paradise, not only in its function, but as a sacrament"[92]. In support of the latter Lee refers to Augustine.

From this examination of Lee's remarks it is evident that the cardinal issue was Erasmus' suggestion that the sacramental concept of marriage could not be founded on Ephesians v. 32, and consequently doubts were given to the common concept of marriage being a sacrament. Denying this concept as being supported by Ephesians v. 32,

---

[87] Lee, *Annotationes*, p. 21.   [88] Lee, *Annotationes*, p. 111.
[89] Lee, *Annotationes*, p. 112. [90] Lee, *Annotationes*, p. 112.
[91] Lee, *Annotationes*, p. 113. [92] Lee, *Annotationes*, p. 114.

Erasmus' approach to the interpretation of the divorce texts was incorrect.

Erasmus' Reply

Erasmus, as would be expected, concentrates his reply on the sacramental aspect of marriage. Thus his answer to Lee's annotations on Matthew XIX is referred to in his comments on Ephesians v. 32. He does not correct any part of his interpretation, but he denies the implications drawn by Lee. What worries him most of all is Lee's insinuation that he fights against the Catholic Church. His main remark to Matthew XIX. 9 is a categorial denial of this. "I am not in favour of divorce, but of perpetual living together, nor do I oppose the custom and constitution of the catholic church."[93]

Commenting on Lee's remarks as related to Ephesians v. 32, Erasmus' objective appears to be twofold. He wishes to assert that he is loyal to, and in full accord with the Church, but at the same time maintaining that his exegesis and use of the Fathers are correct. It is of significance to notice how he harmonizes this anomaly, as it is on account of this anomaly that the Protestant reformers deviated from Erasmus and he himself was attacked by Catholic theologians.

In his reply Erasmus does not add anything new exegetically. He reaffirms that whatever is called a mystery is not a sacrament, since there are mysteries which are not of this kind. When it was disputed whether or not this text sufficiently proved that matrimony was one of the seven sacraments, then he indicated that from this text there was not enough evidence. However, his personal belief was that "matrimony is a sacrament, not because it is called a mystery, but because the church reckons it among the seven"[94]. The same confession is made when he writes:

I confess it is a sacrament, and such a sacrament as the church includes in the seven, and although with most odious words she assails me, as though I was working my hardest to cast out Matrimony from that number. Although I am a little more favourable to matrimony than some theologians, even more modern ones, who deny that it is said to be a sacrament, unless the significance of that word be modified, so it becomes a sign of something sacred[95].

In spite of this confession Erasmus points out that none of the Ancient Fathers taught that marriage was counted among the seven

---

[93] Erasmus, *Respondet Annotationibus Eduardi Lei, Opera*, IX. 118.
[94] Erasmus, *Annotationibus Lei, Opera*, IX. 190.
[95] Erasmus, *Annotationibus Lei, Opera*, IX. 191.

sacraments. When it is asserted that marriage as a sacrament constitutes a cause of grace, then it should be remembered that Peter Lombard did not assign to marriage this primary distinction of a sacrament. "Therefore if anyone is of the same opinion, he is not going against the decretals of the catholic church or the practice and the mind of the Roman church, since it does not reprobate the opinion of these people."[96] When contemporary theologians want matrimony to be a sacrament by which spiritual grace is conferred, then anyone who rejects this opinion should not be branded as a heretic, since in the past the opposite view had been brought forth by celebrated theologians. In this connection Erasmus again confirms his loyalty to the Church, saying: "I myself embrace more the opinion of the more recent theologians, who think grace is conferred by the sacrament of matrimony, which is one of the number properly said to be a sacrament."[97]

Lee closed his remarks on the text under discussion by affirming that it proved marriage to be a sacrament. Erasmus brings his comments to an end by denying the same, but he does not hesitate to underline his belief in the teaching of the Church. He writes: "If anyone asks me, why do you believe it [marriage] to be one of the seven, if from this place or any other it cannot be sufficiently gathered? This is what I would reply impromptu: The authority and consensus of the church move me, but not in this matter only, but even in very many others also."[98]

While Erasmus in his own mind sought to harmonize his loyalty to the Church with the results of his exegetical, doctrinal, philological and historical studies, the Protestant reformers broke with the Church partly on account of these results, and the Catholic theologians opposed him for the same reasons. This illustrates how that process began which gradually isolated him from both groups.

Natalis Bedda and Sorbonne versus Erasmus

Noel or Natalis Bedda, principal of the College of Montaigu and one of the professors of theology at the Sorbonne, was a zealous champion of the Church. When Erasmus' German bookseller sought to have the *Paraphrases* printed in France, then that of Luke was submitted to Bedda for an examination and possible recommendation.

---

[96] Erasmus, *Annotationibus Lei, Opera,* IX. 192.
[97] Erasmus, *Annotationibus Lei, Opera,* IX. 192.
[98] Erasmus, *Annotationibus Lei, Opera,* IX. 192.

Bedda pointed out fifty propositions which were erroneous or suspicious. The matters were referred to the Faculty of the Sorbonne and both Bedda and the Faculty expressed their condemnation and published their criticisms, 1526, which included an attack on Erasmus' interpretation of the divorce texts. Bedda's *Annotations* also attacked the writings of Lefèvre[99].

Natalis Bedda's Criticism

In his annotations on Erasmus' interpretation of Matthew v. 32 Bedda presents two propositions relative to divorce: "A woman who goes away with another man ceases to be his wife... We want no other cause for divorce except that of fornication, for that wars against nature itself." His criticism of Erasmus is based on the understanding that Erasmus in these propositions teaches "that if one partner in the union commits adultery, then the marriage is broken and does not exist any longer for the innocent one, but this is simply heresy, being contrary to the divine Scriptures, spoken through the Apostle by the Holy Spirit"[100]. Bedda substantiates his criticism with reference to four Bible texts. According to Romans VII. 1—2, a wife is first free to marry another after the first husband is dead. Mark x. 11—12 confirms that the first spouse is still a husband, even if he is an adulterer. When Christ was tempted by the Pharisees about "this sacrament", He replied according to Matthew XIX. 6, that marriage was as an unbreakable link: "What therefore God hath joined together, let not man put asunder." This statement of verse six clearly indicates that verse nine does not give liberty to divorce or remarry. It is further made evident from the Apostle Paul's words in 1 Corinthians VII. 10. Quoting this text Bedda harmonizes it with Matthew XIX. 9 in the following way: "I command, yet not I but the Lord: If the wife depart from her husband because of fornication (for he allows no other cause) let her remain unmarried or reconciled to her husband."[101] Bedda makes no reference to 1 Corinthians VII. 15, and in his short note on the chapter as a whole he repeats the just mentioned statement as well as that on Romans VII. 1—3[102].

In his comments on Erasmus' paraphrases of Matthew XIX reference

---

[99] Natalis Bedda, *Annotationum Natalis Bedae Doctoris Theologi Parisien. in Iacobum Fabrum Stapulensem libri duo: Et in Desiderium Erasmum Roterodamum liber vnus, qui ordine tertius est . . . in Paraphrases Erasmi super eadem quatuor Euangelia, & omnes Apostolicas Epistolas*, Paris, 1526.

[100] Bedda, *Annotationes*, sig. 188R.   [101] Bedda, *Annotationes*, sig. 188v.

[102] Bedda, *Annotationes*, sig. 219v.

is made to the various points already mentioned, and his criticism is confined to Erasmus' assertion that only few are fitted for celibacy. Bedda considers this to be incorrect, for by faith it is possible. Finally, he accuses Erasmus of being "in the fullest sense a heretic"[103].

Erasmus' Reply

In his answer to Bedda, as in the case of Lee, Erasmus is most anxious to underline that he does not wish to teach anything contrary to the beliefs of the Church. Having referred to his annotations on 1 Corinthians VII, he writes:

There the reader will perceive, that I hope for a more exact discussion of this passage, if possible; neither have I ever sought to teach anything about divorce different from that which the church now follows, but simply to submit my intellect in obedience to the Roman seat. Nor do I propose anything else except that anyone who has discussed the matter more thoroughly shall be able to solve for me and others like me the question of scruples[104].

He also states that by the paraphrases he does not intend to exclude either the interpretations of others or what the Church condemns[105]. However, in his reply to Bedda he still contends that while the Lord did not allow divorce for mediocre offences, he did make an exception in the case of adultery[106]. Regarding the question of celibacy, Erasmus confirms his conviction that its life is only for a few, and whether or not a person can enter into it is determined by a certain ability of nature[107]. Bedda's and Erasmus' different attitudes toward celibacy could have an indirect influence on their concept of divorce, since Erasmus would reason that it is against nature that the innocent party in a divorce case should not be allowed to remarry, while Bedda would expect that God's grace should give a person strength to live a life of chastity.

The theological faculty of the University of Paris expressed similar criticisms to those made by Bedda, and to these Erasmus replied[108]. Erasmus verges on a recantation of his former interpretation. He

---

[103] Bedda, *Annotationes*, sig. 212v.

[104] Erasmus, *Divinationes Erasmi Rot. Adnotata Per Beddam, Opera*, IX. 471–72.

[105] Erasmus, *Adnotata Per Beddam, Opera*, IX. 384.

[106] Erasmus, *Adnotata Per Beddam, Opera*, IX. 472.

[107] Erasmus, *Adnotata Per Beddam, Opera*, IX. 384.

[108] Erasmus, *Declarationes ad Censvras Lvtetiae Vvlgatas Svb Nomine Facultatis Theologiae Parisiensis, Opera*, IX. 654 ff.

states that it appears to him that a man who commits adultery is no longer a husband; likewise, a woman no longer a wife. Also, in view of the understanding of Christ's hearer, that a divorce implied the privilege of remarriage, he admits difficulty in reading the meaning of separation only into the statements in Matthew v, xix. He then concludes by writing: "I qualify my remarks, that what I say about dissolving marriage and becoming divorced can be understood as separation from bed, not insinuating another word whereby I would make a law of marrying again."[109] This recantation was no doubt to a large degree only apparent, but may be accounted for by the fact that he was most sensitive to any criticism regarding his loyalty to the Church and to any suspicion that he might be in association with the Protestants. While he answered the Sorbonne as he did, he made most furious attacks on Bedda, who actually represented the Sorbonne in this controversy, and obtained the support of King Francis I by whose authority Bedda and the Faculty were silenced[110].

Not all Catholic expositors were in harmony with the official interpretation as reflected in Lee's and Bedda's attacks on Erasmus. A notable example is Cardinal Cajetan.

Cardinal Cajetan

Thomas De Vio or Cardinal Cajetan played, as papal legate, a prominent role in Luther's struggle with the Church. Between 1518 and 1520 he had several interviews with Luther and was one of those who drafted the bull *Exsurge Domine*, 1520[111]. His personal contact with the Protestants convinced him of the need of meeting them on their grounds. As a result he occupied himself with biblical studies and published a commentary on the Gospels, 1530, and one on the Epistles two years later. He died in 1534[112].

In his commentaries on the New Testament Cajetan deals with all the divorce texts, but of those in the synoptic Gospels he confines him-

---

[109] Erasmus, *Declarationes ad Censvras Lvtetiae Vvlgates Svb Nomine Facultatis Theologiae Parisiensis, Opera*, IX. 679.

[110] For a discussion of the controversy between Bedda and Erasmus see: John Joseph Mangan, *Life, Character and Influence of Desiderius Erasmus of Rotterdam*, New York, 1927, II. 256—68.

[111] Roland H. Bainton, *Here I Stand, A Life of Martin Luther*, New York, 1950, pp. 91—98, 101—5, 136, 139, 144—45.

[112] Thomas De Vio, Cardinal Cajetan, *Evangelia cvm Commen. Caietani*, n. p., 1530; *Epistolae Pavli et Aliorvm Apostolorum*, n. p., 1532.

self mainly to Matthew XIX. 9. From his exegesis of Matthew v. 32 it should however be noticed that while the divorce law of Deuteronomy XXIV. 1 left a wide margin of causes for putting away a wife, Jesus restricted divorce to fornication which is the only cause of breaking the marriage tie[113].

Christ's reference to the primeval marriage institution in Matthew XIX is considered at some length in order to emphasize that the Lord Jesus proves the indissolubility of marriage founded as a divine institution and by a special reason as an ecclesiastical sacrament[114]. The principle of divorce seems to contradict the ordinance: "What therefore God hath joined together, let not man put asunder", and brings up the question: "How can legal divorce break up marriage?" Cajetan's answer is that "that dissolving of marriage which the law of divorce permits, was not given by human but by divine authority, as the words of the prophet Malachi [II. 14] and the context of Deuteronomy [XXIV. 1] testify. The Lord shows that marriage came from the divine institution, and that divorce came only by some secondary way and was added to the old divine law"[115]. Cajetan therefore understands Christ's words to mean "that it is lawful for a Christian to send away his wife because of carnal fornication of his own wife, and that he may take another", but adds "if ever an explanation of the church is made valid"[116]. The latter has not been the case up to the present time, as the papal decretals on matrimonial matters cannot be regarded as definitions of faith. In his comments on 1 Corinthians VII he expresses himself to the effect that he does not only marvel but is amazed "that though Christ clearly made an exception of adultery, a great number of doctors do not allow that liberty to married people"[117].

Two points should be noticed in connection with Cajetan's interpretation of Mark x. 11—12. It is not necessary to hold that Mark's omission of the exception of adultery requires an interpretation of Matthew in the light of Mark, but rather that Mark's account is incomplete, for "no one should be perplexed by this, for what one Evangelist says another omits, and what one is silent about another supplies"[118]. The second point relates to an inequality between men and women in the matter of divorce. He quotes Mark x. 12 alone: "And if a woman shall put away her husband, and be married to another, she committeth adultery", asserting that Christ here makes no exception in the case of the woman, but considers man and woman

---

[113] Cajetan, *Evangelia*, sig. 15R.
[114] Cajetan, *Evangelia*, sig. 44R.
[115] Cajetan, *Evangelia*, sig. 44R.
[116] Cajetan, *Evangelia*, sig. 44v.
[117] Cajetan, *Epistolae*, sig. 62R.
[118] Cajetan, *Epistolae*, sig. 77R.

unequal as to the cause of putting away[119]. Cajetan is contradictory in these arguments in that he finds support for the inequality in the fact that Mark makes no exception whatsoever, but above he stated that Mark did not record all that Christ said. In his comments on 1 Corinthians VII this inequality is modified: "It is said that the Lord allowed this legal freedom, not to both partners, but to the husband only, as the text plainly shows. But Paul granted the law of freedom to both husband and wife, without doubt by divine authority, by which alone can be separated what God has joined, as in the word of the Lord about marriage, instituted at the beginning, not of Christendom, but of the world: What God has joined, let not man separate."[120]

While Cajetan emphasizes the divine origin of marriage in his interpretation of Christ's words, he also points out that in the light of Paul's words in 1 Corinthians VII, marriage is something of an impediment to the spiritual life[121]. In regard to the statement of verses ten and eleven Cajetan, in common with other Catholic expositors, brings it into relationship with Christ's words on divorce by stating that these universal precepts are contained under the command of the Lord in Matthew XIX. 9[122], but in harmony with his interpretation of the divorce texts in Mark and Luke his deduction is different. Since the exception clause in Matthew is not mentioned by Paul in 1 Corinthians VII. 10, Protestant writers make this verse apply to a separation from board and bed, which can be applied for less severe reasons than adultery. Catholic exponents bring the same text into relationship with the divorce texts of Mark and Luke, which do not mention the exception of adultery, and conclude that the exception mentioned by Matthew should be understood in the light of these texts. Protestant theologians bring 1 Corinthians VII. 15 into relationship with the divorce texts of Matthew, asserting that the record of Mark and Luke should be understood likewise. Catholic theologians consider the Pauline exception of verse fifteen as something specific with no relationship to the words of Christ, which is the way Protestants interpret verses ten and eleven. Cajetan brings verses ten and eleven into relationship with the divorce texts of Matthew, as he did with Mark and Luke, and thus he differs from both the common Catholic and Protestant exegeses of 1 Corinthians VII. 10—11.

In Cajetan's interpretation of the words: "A brother or a sister is not under bondage in such cases: but God hath called us to peace", the key words are "not under bondage" and "called us to peace". In

---

[119] Cajetan, *Epistolae*, sig. 77R.
[120] Cajetan, *Epistolae*, sig. 62R.
[121] Cajetan, *Epistolae*, sig. 61R.
[122] Cajetan, *Epistolae*, sig. 61v.

the filial and parental relationship a Christian should not be in bondage to the unbeliever, and the same applies in the relationship between husband and wife, but this does not mean "that the marriage tie may be broken, as the filial or parental tie cannot be broken". Since God has called us to peace, then the Christian should not go to court against the unbeliever who seeks separation, "but if he depart let him depart, for God has called us not to litigation but to peace"[123].

Contrary to common Catholic exposition Cajetan finds no support for the sacramental concept of marriage in Ephesians v. 32. He writes:

> This is a great sacrament or rather mystery. You do not, as a prudent reader, have it from Paul in this place that marriage is a sacrament. He does not say it is a sacrament, but it is a great mystery. And truly the mystery of these words is great. They declare indeed the indivisibility of marriage, as the Lord explained in Matthew. They contain the law of nature, that marriage means leaving father and mother. They imply the duty which a man owes to his wife more than to his parents. They imply the way in which Paul declared the wife to be the flesh of the husband. Hence this mystery is great. But I speak concerning Christ and the church, or, in Christ and the church. Paul implies great mystery according to the literal sense, and great according to the spiritual meaning, referring these things to Christ and the church[124].

Cajetan's interpretation is close to that of Erasmus. His readiness to submit his conclusions to any official injunctions by the Church, if such should come, made his exposition of a short duration since the Council of Trent took quite a different attitude.

Before turning to this council, a statement of faith, issued by Emperor Charles V, will be considered.

The Augsburg Interim Declaration of Religion

After his decisive victory over the German electors, 1547, Emperor Charles V attempted to establish religious unity by the promulgation of the *Declaration of Religion*, 1548[125]. It re-established most of the

---

[123] Cajetan, *Epistolae*, sig. 62R.
[124] Cajetan, *Epistolae*, 140R.
[125] B. J. Kidd, *Documents Illustrative of the Continental Reformation*, Oxford, 1911, pp. 358—59. Bullinger had encouraged Calvin to write a refutation. Calvin published *The Augsburg Interim Declaration of Religion* with the title: *The Adultero-German Interim*. He also wrote a refutation: *The True Method of*

Roman beliefs and practices, but appealed to the Protestants by asserting the doctrine of justification by faith in a modified form, the use of the cup by the laity in the Lord's Supper, and the marriage of the priests with some reservation, as well as some modifications of the sacrificial character of the Mass. In its description of the marriage institution and the concept of divorce it is thoroughly Roman Catholic.

Marriage was instituted to become a perpetual and undivided companionship for life, but during Old Testament times it degenerated in two ways; namely, through polygamy and by the letter of divorce. An analogy is expressed between polygamy, which was permitted by a dispensation, and Christ, who "would collect a Church to himself from the multitude of the Gentiles as well as from the Synagogue, that he would adopt her as his Spouse, and that, by the fecundity of several wives, they would sever Christ the Saviour". The divorce text of the Gospel should be understood in the light of 1 Corinthians VII. 10—11, stating that the wife should not depart from her husband, but if she does, then she should remain unmarried. Accordingly, "the bond of Marriage, once formed between two, is no more dissolved by any divorce, but only by the death of either. For in regard to the intimation by Christ, that the wife may be put away for fornication, this makes the spouses cease to live together at bed and board, but does not dissolve the bond of marriage". The sacramental concept of marriage is expressed in the following words:

Since Christ then made Marriage both by this own grace, and bound it, as it were, with a faster chain, as Christ is the one spouse of one Church, and that by an indissoluble tie, so a man is the one husband of one wife, and that by perpetual union, in like manner as Christ is perpetually joined with his spouse the Church. Wherefore, Marriage is not only the union of male and female, but is also a Sacrament, because of the grace of Christ, which is never wanting to it, in order that a man may be able to love his wife just as Christ loved the Church, to cultivate an undivided connection with her, and be contented with her for ever[126].

The *Declaration of Religion* may have satisfied the Catholics on the question of marriage and divorce but not the Protestants. It expresses

---

Giving Peace to Christendom and of Reforming the Church. Both were dedicated to Emperor Charles V and published in 1549. For Calvin's discussion about *sacramento matrimonii* see Calvin, *Corp. Reform.*, VII, 571—74. For an English translation see: John Calvin, *Tracts and Treatises in Defense of the Reformed Faith*, III, Grand Rapids, Mich., 1958, 217—20.

[126] Calvin, *Corp. Reform.*, VII. 573; *Tracts and Treatises*, III. 219.

the Catholic reaction to the exegesis of the divorce texts by the first generation of Protestant theologians; in this reaction there was no room for a compromise. This fact is made evident in the decisions made at the Council of Trent.

The Council of Trent

The twenty-fourth session of the Council of Trent, November 11, 1563, was the second to the last, and dealt with the *Doctrina de Sacramento Matrimonii*. Its canons[127] and Catechism set forth the official Roman Catholic concept of marriage and divorce.

The Canons of the Council

The indissolubility of the marriage tie was expressed by the father of the human race under the inspiration of the Holy Ghost in the words of Genesis II. 23, 24, and confirmed by the Lord in Matthew XIX. "But, the grace which might perfect that natural love, and confirm that indissoluble union, and sanctify the wedded, Christ Himself, the institutor and perfecter of the venerable sacraments, merited for us by His passion", in accordance with Ephesians v. 25, 32. It is asserted that "with reason have our holy Fathers, the Councils, and the tradition of the universal Church, always taught, that it is to be numbered amongst the sacraments of the new law". A violent reaction to the Protestant exegesis is made most evident. Having referred to marriage as numbered among the sacraments, it states:

... against which impious men of this age raving, have not only entertained false opinions touching this venerable sacrament, but, introducing according to their wont, under the pretext of the Gospel, a liberty of the flesh, they have by writing the word asserted, not without great injury to the faithful of Christ, many things alien from the sentiment of the Catholic Church, and from the usage approved of since the times of the apostles; whose rashness the holy and universal synod wishing to meet has thought proper, lest their pernicious contagion should draw more after it, that the more conspicuous heresies and errors of the schismatics aforesaid be exterminated, decreeing against the said heretics and their errors the following anathemas[128].

Twelve canons were formulated regarding the sacrament of marriage, each beginning with the words: "If any one shall say ..." and

---

[127] Theodore Alois Buckley, trans., *The Canons and Decrees of the Council of Trent*, pp. 176–79.

[128] Buckley, *The Canons and Decrees of the Council of Trent*, p. 177.

closing with the statement: " ... let him be anathema." Canons seven and eight express a clear condemnation of the Protestant exposition. They read:

If any one shall say, that the Church doth err in that she hath taught, and doth teach, according to the evangelical and apostolic doctrine, that the bond of matrimony cannot be dissolved on account of the adultery of one of the married parties; and that both, or even the innocent party, who gave not occasion to the adultery, cannot contract another marriage during the lifetime of the other married person; and, that he is guilty of adultery, who, having put away the adulteress, shall marry another wife, as also she, who, having put away the adulterer, shall wed another husband; let him be anathema.

If any one shall say, that the Church errs, in that she decrees that, for many causes, a separation may take place between husband and wife, in regard of bed or cohabitation, for a determinate or for an indeterminate period; let him be anathema[129].

An anathema is also expressed over those who say that marriage is not one of the seven sacraments; that the church cannot add or dispense with the degrees of consanguinity and affinity in Leviticus XVIII; that the Church had no right to constitute impediments whereby the marriage could be dissolved; that irksome cohabitation and desertion dissolve the marriage tie; that matrimony is to be preferred to the state of celibacy and marriage matters do not belong to the ecclesiastical judges. The decision by the Council, that the Vulgate should remain the authorized version of the Bible for the Roman Catholic Church and be the model of any other translation, ensured the preservation of the word *sacramentum* in Ephesians v. 32.

The Catechism of the Council

During the Council it was proposed that a catechism be written for religious instruction, and during the last session, December 24, 1563, Pope Pius IV was entrusted with the task. It was completed and printed in 1566 and soon translated into the various languages of Europe. Chapter seven deals with the subject of matrimony[130]. The indissolubility of the marriage tie is expressed in the language and with the arguments found in the canons of Trent. The basis for its indissolu-

---

[129] Buckley, *The Canons and Decrees of the Council of Trent*, p. 178.

[130] Theodore Alois Buckley, trans., *The Catechism of the Council of Trent*, London, 1852, pp. 336–43.

bility "arises chiefly from its nature as a sacrament". The scriptural foundation for the sacramental concept is Ephesians v. 28—32: "This is a great sacrament, no one should doubt that he referred to marriage; as if he had said: The conjugal union of man and wife, of which God is the author, is a sacrament, that is, a sacred sign, of the most holy union by which Christ the Lord is united with his Church." Since marriage as a sacrament signifies this union, it too is indissoluble. Christ's words confirm the same, and in this way they were understood by Paul according to 1 Corinthians VII. 10, 11. Verse thirty-nine of the same chapter asserts that only after the death of one of the partners is the other at liberty to remarry.

The *Tridentine Catechism* was published half a century after Erasmus' New Testament with annotations. Luther had been dead for twenty years and most of the second generation of Protestant reformers were in their graves. The Protestant interpretation of the divorce texts, which will be examined, had been crystallised. Trent thus expressed a clear denial of those exegetical results which had come from the pen of Erasmus fifty years earlier and were developed by the reformers into a part of Protestant belief and practice. Prior to Trent a Cajetan could say, as Erasmus did, that no council had made a decision which would make their interpretations heretical. Cajetan felt therefore free to interpret the divorce texts as he did, but with the reservation that he would submit his opinions to the decision of any future council. Trent made its decrees on marriage and divorce very definite, and the history of Catholic interpretation of the New Testament logia on divorce may therefore be considered to end here. While Catholic vernacular versions of the Bible were printed, it was assured by accompanied notes and annotations that the divorce texts were interpreted in harmony with Tridentine teaching.

The Rheims-Douai Bible

In view of the influence of the English Catholic version of the Bible and the opposition to it by Anglican and Puritan theologians, this version will now be examined. Its annotations can be considered as a typical example of the post-Tridentine interpretation of the texts under discussion.

After the accession of Queen Elizabeth I, a Catholic exile, William Allen, founded an English theological seminary in Douai, France, as a training center for priests for England. It was in this seminary, then moved to Rheims, that an English Catholic version of the New Testament was produced in 1582[131]. Later the seminary moved back to Douai, and here the Old Testament was published in 1609[132].

In the Rheims' Version the marginal note to Matthew v. 32 reads: "Marriage a Sacrament, and is not dissolued by diuorce", and in the parallel passages of Matthew xix, Mark x and Luke xvi it is stated: "Marriage after diuorce vnlawful." The annotations confirm this assertion: "The knot of Mariage is a thing of so great a Sacrament, that not by separation it self of the parties it can be loosed, being not lawful neither for the one part nor the other, to marie agayne vpon diuorce." This comment on Matthew v. 32 is referred to in the annotations on Matthew xix. 9, where it is said: "For aduoutrie one may dismisse an other. But neither party can marry againe for any cause during life." Attention is brought to Romans vii. 2—3 and to the case of Fabiola who made penance for remarrying, even though she was the innocent party in a divorce case. In this connection the marginal note to Romans vii. 2—3 should be noticed: "Nothing but death dissolueth the band betvvixt man and vvife: though for fornication one may depart from an others companie, therefore to mary againe is aduoutrie, during the life of the partie separated."

In the comment on Mark x. 11 it is pointed out that Christ's words on divorce, as expressed in the Gospel of Matthew, should be understood in the light of the divorce texts in Mark and Luke. "That which S. Matthew vttered more obscurely, and is mistaken of some, as though he meant that for fornication a man might put away his wife and marry an other, is here by this Euangelist (as also by S. Luke) put out of doubt, generally auouching, that whosoeuer putteth away his wife and marrieth an other, committeth aduoutrie."

The annotation to Luke xvi. 18 makes reference to the parallel passage in Mark and says: "The good Mariage through out al nations and men, is in issue and fidelitie of chastitie, but among the people of God it consisteth also in holines of Sacrament: Whereby it commeth to passe that it is a heinous crime to marry againe, though there be a diuorce made, so long as the parties liue." In the notes on 1 Corinthians vii no comments are made on verse fifteen, but verses ten and eleven are brought into relationship with Christ's saying on divorce, thus emphasizing the belief that though a married couple "be separated for fornication, yet neither may marry againe". The remarks on the Mosaic divorce law of Deuteronomy xxiv. 1 should

---

[131] *The Nevv Testament of Iesvs Christ, Translated Faithfvlly into English ... in the English College of Rhemes*, Rheims, 1582.

[132] *The Holie Bible Faithfvlly Translated into English . . . by the English College of Doway*, Douai, 1609.

also be noticed. Reference is made to all the New Testament divorce texts and the opinion is expressed, that while God allowed the letter of divorce in order to avoid a greater evil, "Christ either by correcting a fault, or by recalling a former dispensation, restored the insolubilitie of mariage to the first institution".

The annotations of the Rheims-Douai Version were one by one commented upon by the Anglican theologian William Fulke[133]. His work will be considered among the English expositors.

---

[133] See p. 122 below.

II. Martin Luther and Associates

Martin Luther

The beginning of the Protestant Reformation is generally dated from the memorable October 31, 1517, when Luther, according to the tradition, nailed the Ninety-five Theses on the door of the castle church in Wittenberg. However, Luther's final break with the Church of Rome came during the year 1520. His three treatises: *To the Christian Nobility of the German Nation, The Babylonian Captivity of the Church and A Treatise on Christian Liberty*, all written in that year, as well as the Bull of excommunication from Rome, made the break irreparable. It is in *The Babylonian Captivity of the Church* that Luther makes his first comments on the New Testament logia on divorce.

In the three treatises written during this stormy period Luther laid down the main principles of the Reformation. What is further written and accomplished in succeeding years is only a clarification and development of the tenets of that year. What is thus true of the Reformation in general applies equally well to Luther's interpretation of the divorce texts. Furthermore, the main principles of these three writings: the God-given responsibility of the secular power, the abuses of the sacramental system, and Christian liberty as understood in the light of the gospel, are basic concepts for Luther in his exegesis of the texts under discussion.

In order to evaluate Luther's exegetical results and comments on divorce as correctly as possible, it is necessary to observe the different motives, principles and biblical concepts, which he expresses in his discussion of marriage. While each of these will be examined later in more detail, it is of value to consider them in the setting in which his first explanations on divorce are made.

Dealing with the seven sacraments of the Church of Rome in *The Babylonian Captivity of the Church*, Luther also discusses the sacrament of marriage[1]. According to Luther marriage is not a sacrament

---

[1] Martin Luther, *De captivitate Babylonica ecclesiae praeludium. 1520*, 550—60.

as advocated by Rome, and he gives several reasons for his assertion. For example, marriage has been from the beginning of mankind and is also found among unbelievers, thus it cannot be a possession only of the Church or a sacrament of the New Testament[2]. Luther's main argument is an exegetical one, based on the Greek text. Thus in Luther's denial of marriage as a sacrament, which in turn is of basic importance to his concept of divorce, the Greek New Testament of Erasmus was a determining factor, as has been noticed previously.

Using the Greek New Testament Luther points out that where the Vulgate reads *sacramentum*, the Greek word is *mysterion*. Therefore, when the Vulgate reads: "They shall be two in one flesh. This is a great sacrament"[3], and "Let a man so account of us as the ministers of Christ, and dispensers of the mysteries of God"[4], then the first text could just as well read *mystery* and the second *sacrament*. "Nowhere in all of the Holy Scriptures is this word *sacramentum* employed in the sense in which we use the term; it has an entirely different meaning. For wherever it occurs it denotes not the sign of a sacred thing, but the sacred, secret, hidden thing itself."[5] Considering the Apostle Paul's statement: "And without controversy great is the mystery of godliness: God was manifest in the flesh, justified in the Spirit, seen of angels, preached unto the Gentiles, believed on the world, received up into glory", as written in the Vulgate[6] and in the Greek text[7], Luther asserts that *sacrament* or *mystery* signifies that wisdom of the Spirit, hidden in a mystery, which is Christ. Further, when the Catholics quote the Apostle Paul, stating that marriage is a sacrament, they twist the meaning of the text. When the Apostle wrote about *sacramentum*, he wrote about Christ and the Church. Luther therefore points out that Christ and the Church, as a great and secret thing, is a mystery and is to be represented by marriage, without therefore calling marriage a sacrament. If the Latin *sacramentum* and the Greek *mysterion* should be interpreted as done by the Catholics, then such an exegesis would create a thousand sacraments. This false exe-

---

Translation according to Martin Luther, "The Babylonian Captivity of the Church, 1520", printed in *Luther's Works* (hereafter referred to as *L. W.*), XXXVI, Philadelphia, 1959.

[2] Luther, *Bab. Capt.*, *L. W.*, XXXVI. 92—93.

[3] *Vulgate*, Ephesians v. 31—32. et erunt duo in carne una. Sacramentum hoc magnum est.

[4] *Vulgate*, 1 Corinthians IV. 1. Sic nos existimet homo ut ministros Christi, et dispensatores mysteriorum Dei.

[5] Luther, *Bab. Capt. L. W.*, XXXVI. 93.

[6] *Vulgate*, 1 Timothy III. 16. Et magnifeste magnum est pietatis sacramentum.

[7] *Greek New Testament*, 1 Timothy III. 16. mysterion.

gesis could have been avoided if the Catholics had read the Greek text[8].

Another factor, which must be taken into consideration when evaluating Luther's concept of marriage and divorce, is the concept of naturalism which was prevalent in his thinking during the early period of his life. Naturalism is clearly revealed in his treatment of marriage in the treatise under discussion. Luther realized that laws are necessary for the state; however, a wise magistrate will govern more successfully by natural inclination than by laws. In civil affairs it is much better to place good and wise men in position than to make laws, for these men are in themselves "the very best of laws". When knowledge of "divine law" is combined with "natural wisdom", then written laws are unnecessary, but above all love or charity needs no laws[9].

Having stated that love needs no laws, Luther refers to Christian liberty which is above the laws of men. This is specifically the case with laws given by the Pope. Marriage, as a divine institution, is superior to any such laws[10]. Luther, as Erasmus later did, deals with several of these papal laws. In explaining these he indicates several motives which also must be taken into consideration when his exegesis of the divorce texts is evaluated.

Luther disagrees with the principle that marriage should be hindered by spiritual and legal relationships or by disparity of religion which forbids marriage with any unbaptized person. St. Augustine's mother was married to a heathen; therefore he asserts that the same is permissible today. The "impediment of crime" would make a marriage unlawful if certain crimes had been committed, one of which could be that someone had married the person with whom he had lived in adultery. Luther would of course condemn the act, but when David could obtain forgiveness after having committed the double crime of adultery and murder in his relationship to Bathsheba and Uriah, then the law called "the impediment of crime" should not stand between God and His grace toward the sinner. In his discussion of the "impediment of a tie" Luther emphasizes the sanctity of the tie between a man and woman who are betrothed. Contrary to canon law he contends that the tie is not broken even if the man has carnal knowledge of a second woman after his betrothal. The second woman he has deceived and actually committed adultery with her[11]. Here the question could be raised as to whether or not Luther contradicts

---

[8] Luther, *Bab. Capt.*, *L. W.*, XXXVI. 93–96.

[9] Luther, *Bab. Capt.*, *L. W.*, XXXVI. 98.

[10] Luther, *Bab. Capt.*, *L. W.*, XXXVI. 98–100.

[11] Luther, *Bab. Capt.*, *L. W.*, XXXVI. 100–01.

himself, for he also teaches that divorce is legitimate when adultery has been committed. In answering this question it should be pointed out, even though it will be discussed later in greater detail, that Luther had a high concept of the marriage vow and thus could say: "For my part I so greatly detest divorce, that I should prefer bigamy to it."[12] Furthermore, he taught that everything should be done to preserve the marriage tie even if one of the partners had been unfaithful. In the defence of the sacredness of a promise of betrothal Luther met the Catholics with their own arguments which assert that a monastic vow makes a man no longer his own. Thus the same should apply to the given and received promise of betrothal. In this connection Luther makes a significant reference to Galatians v. 22: "But the fruit of the Spirit is love, joy, peace, longsuffering, gentleness, goodness, faith." Luther speaks about a promise of betrothal given and received, as faith given or received ("fides data et accepta"), and considers the promise or faith to be one of the fruits of the Spirit[13]. His arguments against the "impediment of a tie" are rooted in his high concept of the marriage in which the "fides data et accepta" is brought into relation with the meaning of faith (fides) as found in the Epistle to the Galatians. In other words matrimonial matters should be judged within the framework of the theology of that epistle. It is not possible to separate Luther's discussion of marriage and divorce from his basic concept of faith, law, and grace, or the Christian freedom and obligation as expressed in *A Treatise on Christian Liberty*.

Turning to the "impediment of ordination" Luther detests the fact that even a contracted marriage is made null by ordination. This is contrary to divine law which makes marriage a true and inseparable union[14]. The last of the many papal regulations, which makes either for unlawful divorce or for a hindrance to rightful divorce and marriage, is the "impediment of public decency". This regulation stated that no relatives of the deceased husband may marry the widow. Luther opposed this regulation by referring to the fact that the law of Moses not only allowed but compelled the next of kin to marry the widow. In this connection he points out that the people of Israel were supplied with the best laws; namely, the laws of God[15]. Luther believed that the laws of Moses had been abolished by the gospel; yet, their

---

[12] Luther, *Bab. Capt.*, *L. W.*, XXXVI. 105.

[13] Martin Luther, *De captivitate Babylonica ecclesiae praeludium. 1520, W. E.,* VI. 556—57. Si enim votum religionis facit alienum, cur non etiam fides data et accepta, cum haec sit praecepti et fructus spiritus Gal. v., illud autem arbitrii humani? Luther, *Bab. Capt., L. W.*, XXXVI. 101.

[14] Luther, *Bab. Capt., L. W.*, XXXVI. 101—02.

[15] Luther, *Bab. Capt., L. W.*, XXXVI. 102.

moral and judicial injunctions could be of practical value, not as a law but as guiding principles. Next, Luther lays down another basic principle when he asks if the people of Christian liberty should be subjected to more severe laws than those of legal bondage[16]. For example, under "the stress of youthful passion"[17] a young person may have a "fall", and since the Pope can grant dispensation under certain circumstances, then in the name of Christian liberty Luther also claims the right to grant dispensation. For Luther it is not a legal matter and should not be decided on the grounds of law, but the objective is to bring about the person's salvation. This is more important than any law. Luther therefore also begs for his right of Christian liberty: "For with what right am I deprived of my liberty by somebody else's superstition and ignorance? If the pope grants a dispensation for money, why should not I, for my soul's salvation, grant a dispensation to myself or to my brother? Does the pope set up laws? Let him set them up for himself, and keep hands off my liberty, or I will take it by stealth!"[18] If a woman is married to an impotent man, her situation should be decided by the judgement of charity[19].

In *The Babylonian Captivity of the Church* Luther suggests three reasons, in addition to the act of adultery, which justify the annulment of a marriage, namely, impotence, ignorance of a former contracted marriage, and desertion. Two years later Luther mentions the three reasons for divorce as being impotence, adultery, and a wife's objection to render the conjugal duty[20].

Having discussed the various papal laws relating to marriage and divorce and given his own counsel, Luther then turns to the divorce text of Matthew v. 32. From his comment on this text it is obvious that what he has said formerly is the exception to the rule. He first states that it is a question of whether or not divorce is allowed, and then adds that he himself detests it and would prefer bigamy but hastens to say that he would not make a decision[21]. However, in the case of Philip of Hesse he sanctioned bigamy but this whole affair cannot be taken as any norm, for time and circumstance may rather serve as an excuse. Commenting on Christ's words on divorce Luther states very categorically that Christ allowed divorce only in the case of adultery. "The pope must, therefore, be in error whenever he grants a

---

[16] Luther, *Bab. Capt., L. W.*, XXXVI. 102.
[17] Luther, *Bab. Capt., L. W.*, XXXVI. 103.
[18] Luther, *Bab. Capt., L. W.*, XXXVI. 103.
[19] Luther, *Bab. Capt., L. W.*, XXXVI. 104.
[20] Luther, *Vom ehelichen Leben. 1522, W. E.*, X (II). 287–90. See also *Tischreden, W. E.*, IV. 4499, 4792.
[21] Luther, *Bab. Capt., L. W.*, XXXVI. 105.

divorce for any other cause; and no one should feel safe who has obtained a dispensation by this temerity (not authority) of the pope."[22] Thus Luther's opposition to the Catholic impediments is rooted in this understanding that Christ allowed only one cause for divorce.

In his exegesis of the divorce texts in Matthew Luther generally brings his interpretation into relationship with the Pauline divorce text. When the Apostle Paul permits an unbelieving husband to depart from a wife who has become a Christian, then Luther asserts that according to 1 Corinthians VII the wife may marry again as long as the future husband is a Christian. From this Luther concludes that the innocent party in any divorce case should be allowed to marry again, as in the case of a wife whose husband deserts her or returns after ten years. It is significant to notice that Luther brings to an end his whole discussion of marriage and divorce by laying down the principle that whatever decision or interpretation is made, it should be done "in the name of Christ" and "in the spirit of Christ"[23].

It follows now to examine Luther's other writings to see how far he follows, modifies, or changes the views already expressed. When evaluating Luther's interpretation of the New Testament divorce texts, which is generally confined to the Gospel of Matthew and 1 Corinthians VII, it is of importance to notice that in the majority of cases the setting is found in his general dicussion of marriage in which the high dignity and honour of the marriage estate is emphasized. Whatever allowances Luther makes for divorce, he wishes first and foremost to make sure that this dignity is preserved.

In his sermon *Vom ehelichen Leben. 1522*, Luther emphasizes the honourable estate of marriage when he writes that God Himself has ordained it and has given it his very interest[24]. It should be mentioned that of the three parts into which this sermon is divided, the second deals with the question of divorce. The following year Luther wrote a letter to the German nobility concerning chastity. Commenting on 1 Corinthians VII Luther writes that God has honoured the marriage estate in the fifth commandment. Furthermore, nothing secular or ecclesiastical, and nothing in heaven or on earth is more highly honoured than marriage[25].

During the year 1523 Luther wrote an exposition on 1 Corinthians VII. In it he characterizes marriage as the most religious or spiritual

---

[22] Luther, *Bab. Capt., L. W.*, XXXVI. 106.
[23] Luther, *Bab. Capt., L. W.*, XXVI. 106.
[24] Luther, *Vom ehelichen Leben. 1522, W. E.*, X (II). 294.
[25] Luther, *An die Herren deutschs Ordens, dass sie falsche Keuschheit meiden und zur rechten ehelichen Keuschheit greifen, Ermahnung. 1523, W. E.*, XII. 241.

estate[26]. The significance of this exposition is revealed by the fact that in 1529 it was translated into English. Two German criticisms of it with common Catholic arguments were printed not long after its publication[27].

Luther's interest in the subject under discussion is further illustrated in two other sermons on the subject of marriage. In the first, preached in 1525, Luther refers to marriage as a holy estate[28], and in the second, delivered in 1530, it is emphasized that marriage is not only equal with, but above emperor and bishop, and is the most noble estate not only in the whole of Christendom but in the whole world[29]. In one of his Table-talks Luther speaks about marriage as the most beautiful arrangement made by God[30].

In another and very early sermon on marriage, 1519, Luther approves of the Fathers who refer to marriage as a sacrament, a holy sign, and a spiritual, holy, mystical and eternal thing, and compares it with baptism[31]. Reference has already been made to Luther's attack on the Catholic sacramental system and his denial of marriage as being a sacrament. As late as 1539 he expressed himself to the same effect[32]. However, Luther maintained a concept which may be styled as a *res sacra*. Marriage is not a sacrament in a *technical* sense; yet, it is a most holy thing and a mystery; this is emphasized in various connections where reference is made to Ephesians v. 31—32. Accordingly, Luther could speak about the unity of husband and wife as a sign and figure of a great sacrament or mystery[33]. Speaking about the marriage of Abraham, Luther refers to marriage as a sacrament and a spiritual interpretation of Christ and the Church[34]. In his sermon on marriage, 1519, when he speaks about marriage as a sacrament, reference is again made to the Apostle Paul's comparison between mar-

---

[26] Luther, *Das siebend Kapitel aus der Epistel S. Pauli zu den Chorinthern.* 1523, W. E., XII. 105.

[27] Luther, *An Exposition in to the seventh chaptre of the first pistle to the Corinthians*, n. p., 1529; H. Dungersheym, *Erzeigung der falscheit des unchristlichen Lutherischen comments über das sibende Capitel d'ersten Epistel zu den Chorinthern, so weyt es bedrifft die geistlichen*, n. p. [1525?]; C. Koellin, *Eversio Lutherani Epithalamii*, n. p., 1527.

[28] Luther, Eine predigt vom Ehestand. *1525*, W. E., XVII (1). 12.

[29] Luther, *Deudsch Catechismus (Der Grosse Katechismus). 1529*, W. E., XXX (I). 162.

[30] Luther, *Tischreden*, W. E., VI. 6907.

[31] Luther, *Ein Sermon von dem ehelichen Stand. 1519*, W. E., II. 168.

[32] Luther, *Von den Konziliis und Kirchen. 1539*, W. E., L. 636—39.

[33] Luther, *Resolutio disputationis de fide infusa et acquisita. 1520*, W. E., VI. 96—97; Luther, *Von den Konziliis und Kirchen. 1539*, W. E., L. 636—39.

[34] Luther, *Über das 1 Buch Mose. Predigten. 1527*, W. E., XXIV. 422.

riage and Christ and His Church[35]. Even though Luther seems to agree with the Fathers who compare marriage with baptism, it does not necessarily follow, as some have asserted, that, after speaking about a sacramental concept of marriage as taught by Thomas Aquinas, he then changed his opinion between 1519 and 1520[36]. Rather it is a case of clarification of his opinion, which is re-enforced by his discussion of Abraham and marriage as a sacrament in 1527. Here Luther not only refers to Ephesians v. 32 but also to the words in Ephesians v. 25—26, where another reference is made to baptism: "Husbands, love your wives, even as Christ also loved the church, and gave himself for it; That he might sanctify and cleanse it with the washing of water by the word."[37] There are good reasons to think that in both statements about the sacraments, 1519 and 1527, Luther had in mind the marriage estate, not as a sacrament in the Thomistic sense, but as a *res sacra* like the relationship between Christ and the Church. Furthermore, in the light of the whole development of the sacramental concept of marriage it is evident that Luther's interpretation is Augustinian. Luther's references to marriage as a sacrament and its comparison with baptism obviously have Augustine as their source and are pre-Thomistic in their meaning. In its article on marriage the *Württembergisches Glaubensbekenntniss* reflects Luther's teaching. It also seems to confirm the above interpretation of Luther's statements of marriage as being a sacrament. It asserts that according to the Apostle Paul marriage is called a mystery or a great sacrament of Christ and His Church as commonly interpreted[38]. It seems that Luther's exegesis of the Latin *sacramentum* and the Greek *mysterion* as

[35] See footnote 31.

[36] Discussing Luther's concept of marriage Emil Friedberg refers to Luther's sermon of 1519 in the following way: "Luther in seinem Sermon vom ehelichen Stande, der in das Jahr 1519. fällt, erkennt vollkommen die Sacramentalität der Ehe an, die er in dieser Beziehung der Taufe als ganz gleichberechtigt an die Seite stellt. Seine Beweisführung ist die der katholischen Dogmatik des Mittelalters und speciell die des Thomas von Aquino, der auch das Wesen des Ehesacraments gleichsam in der Legalisirung der sinnlichen Triebe suchte." Emil Friedberg, *Das Recht der Eheschliessung in seiner Geschichtlichen Entwicklung*, Leipzig 1865, p. 157. In his discussion of the same, George Elliot Howard, referring to Friedberg, makes a similar statement: "As late as 1519 he [Luther] declares that 'the marriage state is a sacrament', an outward 'symbol of the greatest, holiest, noblest, most worthy thing that has ever existed or can exist: the union of the divine and human natures in Christ';and this symbol he explains entirely in harmony with the 'dogmatism of the Middle Ages, notably that of St. Thomas Aquinas, who sought the motive of the marriage sacrament in legalization of the sensual impulse.'" George Elliot Howard, *A History of Matrimonial Institutions*, London, 1904, I. 386.

[37] Luther, *Über das 1 Buch Mose. Predigten. 1527, W. E.*, XXIV. 422.

[38] *Württembergisches Glaubensbekenntniss*, Stuttgart, 1848, art. 21. Wir beken-

expressed in *The Babylonian Captivity of the Church* was basic in all his discussions of marriage as a sacrament.

In view of Luther's *res sacra* concept of marriage it is not surprising that he detested divorce and also stated that adultery is the greatest robbery on earth[39]. In a sermon preached on Genesis XVI Luther refers to Matthew XIX. 8, 9 and 1 Corinthians VII. 9—11 and makes the statement that if a person is a Christian, he must not divorce[40]. On a number of occasions Luther expressed himself to the effect that there should be no act of divorce, because in the New Covenant the institution of marriage is the same as was established by God as recorded in Genesis. Only because of hardness of heart had Moses allowed the people to give a letter of divorce, but in the New Covenant this is not permissible. Commenting on Christ's words in Matthew v. 32 Luther affirms that those who wish to be Christians should not divorce for what "God hath joined together, let not man put asunder"[41].

During the years from 1537 to 1540 Luther preached a series of expository sermons over Matthew XVIII to XXIV[42]. Dealing with the divorce text of Matthew XIX Luther states that married people are not permitted to divorce one another because they are angry or disagree with one another. Furthermore, marriage, as a godly institution, should not be severed except by death[43]. In the sermons on marriage preached in 1522 and 1525, Luther categorically stated that sickness is not a reason for divorce, neither if one of the partners, because of sickness, is not able to render the conjugal duty[44]. In 1530 when Luther preached about marriage and divorce, he states that marriage is dissolved only by death. In the same sermon he strongly emphasized that if a person who had committed adultery asked for forgiveness, the innocent party ought to forgive[45].

---

nen, dass der eheliche Stand sey von Gott eingesetzt und bestättiget, und sey ein Geheimnus, das ist (wie man es gemeiniglich ausgelegt) ein gross Sacrament in Christo und seiner Kirchen, wie Paulus sagt.

[39] Luther, *Sas siebend Kapitel aus der Epistel S. Pauli zu den Chorinthern. 1523, W. E.*, XII. 101. der ehebruch der grössist raub und diebstal ist auff erden.

[40] Luther, *Über das 1 Buch Mose. Predigten. 1527, W. E.*, XXIV. 305.

[41] Luther, *Wochenpredigten über Matth. 5—7. 1530—32, W. E.*, XXXII. 378. Luther, *Matth. 18—24 in Predigten ausgelegt. 1537—40, W. E.*, XLVII. 320; Luther, *Über das 1 Buch Mose. Predigten. 1527, W. E.*, XXIV. 304—5; Luther, *Antwort auf den Dialogum Hulrichi Nebulonis. 1542, W. E.*, LIII. 196—97; Luther, *Von Ehesachen. 1530, W. E.*, XXX (III). 214—15.

[42] Luther, *Matth. 18—24 in Predigten ausgelegt. 1537—40, W. E.*, XLVII. 232 to 627.

[43] Luther, *Matth. 18—24 in Predigten ausgelegt. 1537—40, W. E.*, XLVII. 319.

[44] Luther, *Vom ehelichen Leben. 1522, W. E.*, X (II). 291.

[45] Luther, *Von Ehesachen. 1530, W. E.*, XXX (III). 241.

During his whole life Luther advocated the dignity of the marriage estate and was also consistent with his statement of the year 1520, when he wrote that he detested divorce. He is likewise consistent in his exegesis of the logia on divorce in the Gospel of Matthew. Reference has already been made to his explanation in *The Babylonian Captivity of the Church*. In his various sermons on marriage and in his expository sermons on Matthew v and xix and 1 Corinthians vii, covering a period of twenty years, Luther states that Christ allowed divorce only on the grounds of adultery[46].

The question could be asked: When Luther states that Christ permits divorce only on account of adultery and yet justifies divorce for other reasons, does Luther not contradict himself? In the attempt to answer this question it is hoped that the apparent anomaly may disappear, or at least that Luther's justifications and exegetical reasons may clearly be seen[47].

Luther permitted the innocent party, who was divorced because of adultery, to remarry. Luther's starting point is that only death can separate the marriage tie and make the partner free to marry again. However, the act of adultery makes the offender as dead, in his relationship both to the spouse and to God. Referring to the fact that the laws of Moses demanded that the adulterer be put to death, Luther expressed the opinion that the secular powers ought to do the same in the Christian dispensation. Even though this is not done, the adulterer is still considered as dead in the eyes of God[48]. Now it becomes clear why he allowed remarriage, and we are ready to follow his argument for other causes.

Interpreting the Pauline text in which the Apostle deals with the relationship between husband and wife where only one of them becomes a Christian, Luther makes use of the same arguments for re-

---

[46] Luther, *Wochenpredigten über Matth. 5—7. 1930—32*, W. E., XXXII. 379; Luther, *Eine predigt vom Ehestand. 1525*, W. E., XVII (i). 28; Luther, *Von Ehesachen. 1530*, W. E., XXX (iii). 241; Luther, *Wochenpredigten über Matth. 5—7. 1530—32*, W. E., XXXII. 377; Luther, *Matth. 18—24 in Predigten ausgelegt. 1537—40*, W. E., XLVII. 318—19.

[47] Both E. Friedberg and G. E. Howard express themselves to the effect that there are contradictions in Luther's statements on marriage and divorce, but it appears to the present writer that they theologically disappear in the light of Luther's differentiation between the kingdom of God and the kingdom of the world. E. Friedberg, *Das Recht der Eheschliessung in seiner Geschichtlichen Entwicklung*, p. 157; G. E. Howard, *A History of Matrimonial Institutions*, p. 387.

[48] Luther, *Wochenpredigten über Matth. 5—7. 1530—32*, W. E., XXXII. 379. Luther, *Vom ehelichen Leben. 1522*, W. E., X (ii). 289; Luther, *Wochenpredigten über Matth. 5—7. 1530—32*, W. E., XXXII. 379; Luther, *Von Ehesachen. 1530*, W. E., XXX (iii). 241.

marrying as mentioned above. Quoting 1 Corinthians VII. 15: "But if the unbelieving depart, let him depart. A brother or a sister is not under bondage in such cases", Luther categorically states that the believing spouse is free to marry again[49], just as if the unbelieving party were dead[50].

In the two treatises just quoted, as well as in his sermon on marriage, 1530, and his sermon on Matthew v, Luther goes a step further in the practical application of his exegesis. If the husband is such a rascal that he, contrary to the Bible, leaves wife and children, then he is no better than a gentile or unbeliever and deserves no less punishment than the worst adulterer[51]. Since the Apostle Paul permits the believing spouse to marry again, Luther sees no reason why the same principle should not apply when a husband deserts his wife and family[52].

Within the same category falls the case where a wife, not because of sickness but because of stubbornness, will not render the conjugal duty as mentioned by the Apostle Paul, 1 Corinthians VII. 3–4. If after warning and counsel she continues in her stubbornness, then the husband should let a Vashti go and take an Esther, just as King Ahasuerus did[53].

It has been noticed how strongly Luther emphasized marriage as being a *res sacra*, and how this influenced his concept of divorce. However, Luther also refers to marriage as a secular affair, and it will therefore be necessary to see if this idea conflicts with his first concept, and how it influences his exegesis of the divorce texts.

In Luther's discussion of the non-sacramental concept of marriage as expressed in *The Babylonian Captivity of the Church*, he attacks the Papacy, which, in spite of calling marriage a sacrament and denying divorce, yet makes so many exceptions that marriage is no longer a *res sacra*. Luther agrees that there may be specific circumstances which justify exceptions to the rule, but these have to be judged by principles based on a true knowledge of the gospel. Since the Pope does not possess the gospel, Luther claims that when two learned and pious men agree in the name of Christ and make their opinion known in the spirit of Christ, then their judgement is better than any councils[54]. Furthermore, the Pope had usurped the God-given power and

---

[49] Luther, *Bab. Capt., L. W.*, XXXVI. 106.
[50] Luther, *Das siebend Kapitel aus der Epistel S. Pauli zu den Chorinthern. 1523, W. E.*, XII. 123.
[51] Luther, *Wochenpredigten über Matth. 5–7. 1530–32, W. E.*, XXXII. 380.
[52] Luther, *Bab. Capt., L. W.*, XXXVI. 106.
[53] Luther, *Vom ehelichen Leben. 1522, W. E.*, X (II). 290.
[54] Luther, *Bab. Capt., L. W.*, XXXVI. 106.

authority of the state which includes the right to deal with marriage problems. Luther assigns the state to deal with marriage matters[55].

If all were Christians, then no government, with its power of the sword, would be necessary[56], but since the world at large cannot be ruled by the gospel, then secular power is a necessity[57]. God has ordained two kinds of rulership in the world just as there are two kinds of people, namely, those governed by God's Word and the Holy Spirit, and the unbelievers[58]. Commenting on the Pauline divorce text Luther states that in the Old Covenant was found a spiritual and secular, or an inward and outward government. In the New Covenant the government rules the secular world[59]. The secular estate is a divine order, and the office of the emperor, king, magistrate, etc. is a divine gift[60], and all ruling estates are to be considered as God's servants[61]. Accordingly, the Church should be obedient to the government[62].

Luther refers to the marriage estate as a secular thing like clothes, food, and housing, and it is therefore subjugated to the secular government. In the same connection he makes reference to 1 Corinthians VII and states that for the Christian there is no need of a secular government, but regarding the unbeliever, the secular sword has to render its function[63]. In other words the Christian, who lives within the realm of the gospel, is in the spiritual kingdom, and his marriage is a *res sacra*, not needing the correcting and punishing sword of the secular power. It is therefore very significant that when Luther, in a discussion, brings together marriage and the magistrate, it is most often in connection with some punitive measures which ought to be taken because someone's marriage falls below or basically contradicts the *res sacra* concept. In Luther's comment on the divorce logion in Matthew V he also refers to the marriage estate as a secular institution, but this is in connection with the problem of divorce[64]. Turning to Mat-

---

[55] Luther, *An den christlichen Adel deutscher Nation von des christlichen Standes Besserung. 1520, W. E.*, VI, 404—69.
[56] Luther, *Von weltlicher Oberkeit. 1523, W. E.*, XI. 249—50.
[57] Luther, *Predigten des Jahres 1525, W. E.*, XVII (I). 149.
[58] Luther, *Von weltlicher Oberkeit. 1523, W. E.*, XI. 251.
[59] Luther, *Das siebend Kapitel aus der Epistel S. Pauli zu den Chorinthern. 1523, W. E.*, XII. 118. See also: Luther, *Epistel S. Petri gepredigt und ausgelegt. 1523, W. E.*, XII. 327—31.
[60] Luther, *Predigten des Jahres 1534, W. E.*, XXXVII. 443.
[61] Luther, *Wider die räuberischen und mörderischen Rotten der Bauern. 1525, W. E.*, XVIII. 360.
[62] Luther, *Der 82. Psalm ausgelegt. 1530, W. E.*, XXXI (I). 193.
[63] Luther, *Von Ehesachen. 1530, W. E.*, XXX (III). 205.
[64] Luther, *Wochenpredigten über Matth. 5—7. 1530—32, W. E.*, XXXII. 379.

thew XIX the secular authority is again mentioned because of its importance in connection with divorce[65].

In his preface to John Brenz's book on marriage, 1531, Luther emphasizes the fact that the Pope had usurped the authority given to the secular powers by God. He points out that the secular court is more competent to deal with matrimonial matters than is the papal court[66]. In various marriage problems the counsel of the lawyer and magistrate should be sought and the court should then make a decision, since it has the punitive power[67]. The pastor should seek the advice of the magistrate so that the people do not misuse the Christian liberty in matrimonial matters[68].

In Luther's *Table-talks* are found a great number of references to marriage, and among them several deal with marriage in its relationship to the secular authorities. When this is the case, in nearly all instances the question on counsel and judgement in matrimonial matters is brought up[69]. In the light of Matthew XXII. 21, Romans XIII. 1—7, and 1 Peter II. 13—15, the government has to demand obedience, and it has to decide what is a rightful marriage. In Luther's discussion of divorce and remarriage it was noticed that remarriage was justified by the fact that the adulterer was the same as dead in the eyes of God and in his relationship to the innocent party. Luther even felt that the adulterer deserved capital punishment. Since God has not permitted the Church to use the sword but has granted its power to the magistrate only, the question of divorce must therefore be settled by the secular authority. Thus is revealed a close relationship between Luther's exegesis of the divorce texts and his concept of the role assigned to the secular authorities by God. Furthermore, Luther does not contradict himself when he speaks about the marriage estate as a *res sacra* and also as a secular thing. Reference to both aspects are often found in the same context. According to the very condition of life in this world there must be two aspects: a spiritual and a secular. In his exegesis of the divorce texts he was influenced by both.

The story of the recommendation of Luther and his associates of a second wife for Henry VIII and Philip of Hesse, rather than allowing

---

[65] Luther, *Vom ehelichen Leben. 1522, W. E.*, I (II). 289, 290.

[66] Luther, *Vorrede zu Johann Brenz, Wie in Ehesachen christlich zu handeln sei. 1531, W. E.*, XXX (III). 481—86.

[67] Luther, *Vom ehelichen Leben. 1522, W. E.*, X (II). 290; Luther, *Von Ehesachen. 1530, W. E.*, XXX (III). 243—47.

[68] Luther, *Unterricht der Visitatorn an die Pfarhern ym Kurfurstenthum zu Sachssen*, in section Von Ehesachen, *W. E.*, XXVI. 225.

[69] Luther, *Tischreden, W. E.*, II. 1523, 1734; III. 3267; IV. 3980, 4086, 4345, 4716, 4736; V. 6326, 6458; VI. 6911, 6918.

divorce, is well known[70]. Here it suffices to suggest that the recommendation was not without relation to the principles which formulated Luther's concept of divorce. His conservatism and his conviction that Christ allowed divorce only on grounds of adultery, made him detest divorce. However, in every circumstance Christian liberty, with its exercise of faith and love, seeks to do the best thing possible in order to help the individual, including a person with sexual problems. The tension between the ideals of the kingdom of Christ and the secular society would unavoidably create anomalies because of their different natures. In the secular society laws and recommendations which were not on par with those of Christ had to be given in order that greater evils might be avoided. In such cases times and circumstances would have to be taken into consideration as God also did in the Old Testament. At the time of Luther the recommendation of a second wife was not uncommon[71].

Luther's counsel on divorce was given by one who stood on the battle front in the midst of a formative and formulative period. While it is possible to make his various statements on divorce coherent, it was left to his associates to systematize his teaching. The associates of Luther confirm the outlines and principles which have appeared by examining his thinking in connection with the exegesis of the divorce texts. The exegetical works of Philip Melanchthon and John Brenz will be examined separately. But first it should be noticed that the significance of the reformers' teaching on divorce and the need for bringing their material together are also indicated by several other documents. One of them is the work of Erasmus Sarcerius, 1569. In a tome of three hundred folio pages he brought together, under various headings, statements on marriage matters from about a dozen Protestant theologians[72]. Reference should also be made to a booklet writ-

---

[70] For a discussion of the story and process of Henry VIII's divorce case with Catherine of Aragon see: Gilbert Burnet, *The History of the Reformation of the Church of England*, London, 1681—83, II. II; Preserved Smith, "German Opinion of the Divorce of Henry VIII", *The English Historical Review*, XXVII. 671—81. For a study of the history of bigamy and the story of Philip of Hesse's bigamy see: William Walker Rockwell, *Die Doppelehe des Landgrafen Philipp von Hessen*, Marburg, 1904. This work also deals with Henry VIII's divorce case.

[71] Erasmus, Pope Clemens VII, and Cardinal Cajetan agree that bigamy may be permissible under certain circumstances. See: Rockwell, *Die Doppelehe des Landgrafen Philipp von Hessen*, pp. 304—8; Smith, "German Opinion of the Divorce of Henry VIII", *The English Historical Review*, XXVII. 673.

[72] Erasmus Sarcerius, *Corpvs Ivris Matrimonialis*, Frankfurt, 1569. The most significant theologians quoted in this work are Luther, Melanchthon, Bugenhagen, Brenz, Bucer and Bullinger. This work has little exegetical value as it is only a

ten by John Bugenhagen, 1540. It dealt with adultery and desertion and was dedicated to the Danish King, Christian III[73]. Since Bugenhagen worked in northern Germany and Denmark, this book became important in establishing Protestant principles on divorce in this part of Europe. The book may be considered as an instruction to the King telling him how to deal with matrimonial matters and divorce especially. At the same time it also exhorted the monarch to deal seriously with these matters through civil law-giving, because the judicial decisions in divorce matters had unlawfully been usurped by the Papacy. This book is not an exposition of the divorce texts but expresses Luther's idea of divorce on the grounds of adultery and desertion, the latter including divorce between a believer and an unbeliever. Bugenhagen acknowledged his debt to Luther calling him "my beloved Father in Christ"[74].

Philip Melanchthon

In Philip Melanchthon's comments on the divorce texts which are found in his commentaries on the Gospel of Matthew and 1 Corinthians[75], it is noticeable that he repeatedly emphasizes the indissolubility of the marriage tie as when he writes: "By definition marriage is the legitimate and indissoluble union of one man with one woman."[76] Accordingly, Christ forbade "Mosaic divorces, and referred back to the original institution of marriage: The two shall be one flesh ... This dictum is the law of perpetual marriage, ordaining the perpetual union of one man with one woman, perpetual and indissoluble, and forbidding all union apart from this established institution"[77]. The sinfulness of unchastity in general and fornication and adultery especially, is revealed in God's punishments from the time of the deluge and Sodom down through the history of Israel and the

collection of statements and reprints of sections of works. Furthermore, the important theologians quoted are dealt with in the present study.

[73] John Bugenhagen, *Ehesachen: vom Ehebruch und heimlichem weglauffen*. It was published in Wittenberg. 1540, together with Luther's *Von Ehesachen* and Melanchthon's *De Arbore Consangvinitatis et Affinitatis, siue de Gradibus*.

[74] Bugenhagen, *Ehesachen*, sig. Tɪɪv.

[75] Philip Melanchthon, *Breves Commentarii Matthaeum*, in *Corpus Reformatorum*, XIV, 1847; Melanchthon, *Argumentum et Brevis Explicatio Prioris Epistolae Ad Corinthios*, *Corpus Reformatorum*, XV, 1848; Melanchthon, *De Coniugio*, *Corpus Reformatorum*, XXI, 1854.

[76] Melanchthon, *De Coniugio*, *Corpus Reformatorum*, XXI. col. 1064. See also cols. 601, 602, 920.

[77] Melanchthon, *Comm. Matth.*, *Corpus Reformatorum*, XIV. cols. 603, 920.

gentile world[78]. Melanchthon's first maxim is therefore: "Let married people know, that it is the will of God that marriage ought to be of one man and one woman lawfully and indissolubly united, and that indisputably those who furnish cause for divorce as by adultery or desertion, commit sin."[79]

In view of the fact that Christ renews the original marriage concept, then "the Lord prohibits divorce with one exception, which is adultery"[80]. However, Melanchthon points out desertion as still another cause[81]. The theological ground for this viewpoint is, as for Luther also, the Pauline statement: "But if the unbelieving depart, let him depart. A brother or sister is not under bondage in such cases."[82] A deserter is defined as a person "who out of malice and without just cause leaves the other, and stays away for a long time, as often happens. Very often such are adulterers and adulteresses"[83]. The time element which should elapse before the deserted one could remarry varied with the Christian Roman emperors from two to ten years. Melanchthon is not ready to prescribe any definite time but will leave it to be decided by the secular judge[84].

In the light of 1 Corinthians VII Melanchthon affirms that a Christian should not leave an unbelieving husband or wife[85]. "As the church is able to exist under atheistic kings, so a pious wife can remain with an unbelieving husband."[86] The truth of this is illustrated in the lives of Queen Esther and the pious mother of Augustine as well as Emperor Constantine's sister married to Licinius. It also "harmonizes with Paul's feelings in his dictum: 'I am made all things to all men.'"[87] Furthermore, if the gospel had disrupted marriage, there would have been a cause for scandal, for it would have made all moderate-minded men abhor the gospel. Consequently, Paul asserted that

---

[78] Melanchthon, *Comm. Matth.*, *Corpus Reformatorum*, XIV, col. 920; *De Coniugio*, *Corpus Reformatorum*, XXI. cols. 1064, 1072.

[79] Melanchthon, *Comm. Matth.*, *Corpus Reformatorum*, XIV. col. 602.

[80] Melanchthon, *De Coniugio*, *Corpus Reformatorum*, XXI. col. 1064. See also *Comm. Matth.*, *Corpus Reformatorum*, XIV. cols. 922, 923; *Ad Corinthios*, *Corpus Reformatorum*, XV. col. 1083.

[81] Melanchthon, *Comm. Matth.*, *Corpus Reformatorum*, XIV. col. 603. See also *De Coniugio*, *Corpus Reformatorum*, XXI. cols. 1064; *Ad Corinthios*, *Corpus Reformatorum*, XV. cols. 1083, 1084.

[82] Melanchthon, *De Coniugio*, *Corpus Reformatorum*, XXI. col. 1066.

[83] Melanchthon, *Comm. Matth.*, *Corpus Reformatorum*, XIV. col. 604. See also *De Coniugio*, *Corpus Reformatorum*, XXI. col. 1066.

[84] Melanchthon, *De Coniugio*, *Corpus Reformatorum*, cols. 1066, 1067.

[85] Melanchthon, *De Coniugio*, *Corpus Reformatorum*, XXI. col. 1063.

[86] Melanchthon, *Ad Corinthios*, *Corpus Reformatorum*, XV. col. 1086.

[87] Melanchthon, *Ad Corinthios*, *Corpus Reformatorum*, XV. col. 1086.

marriage ought not to be rent asunder because of differing opinions about God, if only unbelievers do not forsake those who disagree with them[88]. If the latter should be the case, then the unbeliever is considered as a deserter. Thus Melanchthon exegetically justifies desertion to be a second reason for divorce. He does not try to include the Pauline exception in that given by Christ, but states that the one of adultery is given by Christ and the other by Paul[89].

Turning to the question of whether or not any type of sickness would be a legitimate reason for divorce Melanchthon's answer is: "I reply plainly and unequivocably, divorce ought not to be granted on account of sickness, nor should the sick husband be forsaken nor the sick wife be deserted, for this truth must always be held firmly and immovably: 'What therefore God hath joined together, let not man put asunder.'"[90] He most strongly emphasizes that in sickness, even in the case of leprosy, fidelity should be shown to the sick. As later will be noticed, some of the Reformed theologians disagreed with Melanchthon's view concerning those who had leprosy. Therefore the following statement from his pen is pertinent:

Some inhumanly reckon leprosy to be akin to death and are eager to examine if the outward appearance of the person is healthy. But this sophistry is plainly cruel. The dead do not need the help and aid of any other person, but the sick person does. Wherefore, because someone holds fast to true friendship for the sake of attentions, he is not yet as dead. So he is in your care, and the divine law applies to you: no one hates his own flesh. So by the authority of the magistrate a healthy person should be constrained not to desert nor neglect the sick, but to render help to the one who is sick[91].

The only exception given under the category of sickness is that of impotence, and the question of divorce is pertinent only after three years of ineffective medical treatment[92]. If, as is usually the case, impotence existed at the time of marriage, the question is not of divorce in the proper sense of the word[93]. Thus there remain only two Biblical reasons for divorce: adultery and desertion. However, it should be noticed that this regulation pertains only to the kingdom of God or the Church. In the secular society one moves in a different sphere, and because of its nature other regulations are manifested.

---

[88] Melanchthon, *Ad Corinthios, Corpus Reformatorum*, XV. col. 1086.
[89] Melanchthon, *Ad Corinthios, Corpus Reformatorum*, XV. cols. 1083, 1084.
[90] Melanchthon, *De Coniugio, Corpus Reformatorum*, XXI. col. 1069.
[91] Melanchthon, *De Coniugio, Corpus Reformatorum*, XXI. col. 1070.
[92] Melanchthon, *De Coniugio, Corpus Reformatorum*, XXI. col. 1068.
[93] Melanchthon, *Comm. Matth., Corpus Reformatorum*, XIV. col. 605.

Melanchthon follows Luther's concept of the two kingdoms when he discusses cruelty, sorceries, deceitful behaviour and similar cases as legitimate reasons for divorce. Having restated that Matthew xix. 9 grants divorce only on the grounds of adultery, and having referred to the law of the Emperor Theodosius giving other causes for adultery, Melanchthon writes: "And when the Lord expressly stated that in the Mosaic economy divorce was allowed because of hardness of heart, He signified that there was one ruling which was proper for men who are members of the Church, and who want to comply with the Gospel, and another policy for the impious and contumacious, who are unwilling to be restrained by law."[94] God wants the magistrate to be a blessing to the good and a terror to the evil. Those whose morals are above suspicion ought to be given peace and protection[95]. Therefore it is only to be expected that "the magistrate may add certain laws to the divine precepts, not in the least negating them but which are to be administered so that the divine laws may be better observed"[96].

The secular aspect of divorce is reflected in the fact that the only means of punishment granted the Church is that of excommunication, while to the magistrate is given authority and the power of the sword whereby to declare a divorce legal and punish the guilty partner[97]. The guilty should either be executed, expelled from society, or exiled from the locality where the innocent party is living[98].

The marriage tie is severed by the adulterer himself[99] and not by the innocent party, who is free[100]. Therefore, when the judge declares the innocent party free, he should expressly state that he or she may enter another marriage with a clear conscience[101]. When that declaration is made, the innocent party can marry at any time[102]. Melanchthon does not, as does Luther, give any exegetical reasons why the innocent party may marry again. He only lays down the proposition: "If the innocent party was not allowed to marry again, it would be a divorce only in name and not in reality."[103]

---

[94] Melanchthon, *De Coniugio*, *Corpus Reformatorum*, XXI. col. 1068.

[95] Melanchthon, *De Coniugio*, *Corpus Reformatorum*, XXI. col. 1069.

[96] Melanchthon, *De Coniugio*, *Corpus Reformatorum*, XXI. col. 1072.

[97] Melanchthon, *Comm. Matth.*, *Corpus Reformatorum*, XIV. cols. 604, 606; *De Coniugio*, *Corpus Reformatorum*, XXI. cols. 1065, 1073.

[98] Melanchthon, *Comm. Matth.*, *Corpus Reformatorum*, XIV. col. 923; *De Coniugio*, *Corpus Reformatorum*, XXI. cols. 1064, 1065.

[99] Melanchthon, *Comm. Matth.*, *Corpus Reformatorum*, XIV. col. 923.

[100] Melanchthon, *Comm. Matth.*, *Corpus Reformatorum*, XIV. col. 604; *Ad Corinthios*, *Corpus Reformatorum*, XV. cols. 1083, 1084.

[101] Melanchthon, *De Coniugio*, *Corpus Reformatorum*, XXI. col. 1065.

[102] Melanchthon, *De Coniugio*, *Corpus Reformatorum*, XXI. col. 1067.

[103] Melanchthon, *Comm. Matth.*, *Corpus Reformatorum*, XIV. col. 603.

John Brenz

Reference has already been made to John Brenz's book on marriage to which Luther wrote the preface[104]. It may be considered as a manual on matrimonial matters for the pastor, since each chapter closes with a statement to the effect that the pastor ought to adhere to the counsel given. This manual reflects Brenz's exegesis of the logia on divorce in the Gospels of Matthew and Mark. The same may be said of the *Württembergisches Glaubensbekenntniss*[105]. This statement of faith was written by John Brenz under the direction of Duke Christoffer and contains a section on marriage. The *Württembergische Eheordnung*, 1534, had the imprimatur of Brenz[106].

In his exegesis John Brenz follows the general Lutheran line of thought. Marriage as an institution originated at the time of Creation and is indissoluble, and Christ renewed this primeval concept[107]. While Moses allowed divorce for certain reasons, Christ reduced them to one cause, that of adultery[108]. Brenz distinguishes between three types of adultery. Firstly, the one committed in the heart for which the marriage should not be dissolved. Secondly, the one with an unmarried woman which should not sunder the marriage tie at once, and which is considered less offensive than the third, which is adultery with a married woman. In the last case divorce is legitimate, however it should be considered a most serious thing[109]. Desertion is a second reason for divorce, for Paul permits a convert to Christianity to take another wife if he be deserted by his former wife on account of religion[110]. Brenz, as did Melanchthon, also denies divorce for any type of sickness, even leprosy. The exception is impotence, if three years of medical treatment fails to remedy the weakness[111].

It has been noticed that the exegetical reason given for allowing remarriage according to Luther is that the adulterer is as dead, so that, as Melanchthon put it, remarriage would be permitted lest the

---

[104] John Brenz, *Wie inn Eesachen vnnd den fellenn so sich derhalben zütragen nach gotlichem billichem rechten Christlich zuo handeln sey*, n. p., 1531.

[105] *Württembergisches Glaubensbekenntniss*. Also printed in *Evangelische Volksbibliotek*, II, Stuttgart, 1863.

[106] Aemilius Ludwig Richter, *Die evangelischen Kirchenordnungen des sechszehnten Jahrhunderts*, I, Weimar, 1846, 279.

[107] John Brenz, *Opervm Reverendi et Clarissimi Theologi ... In Qvo Continentur Commentarii in tres Euangelistas. In Matthaeum. Marcum. Lucam.* Tübingen, 1582, pp. 165, 167, 510, 511.

[108] Brenz, *Comm.*, pp. 164, 1200; *Eesachen*, sig. DIV.

[109] Brenz, *Comm.*, p. 166.

[110] Brenz, *Comm.*, p. 164.

[111] Brenz, *Eesachen*, sig. EIIIR.

divorce be one in name only. The latter is also mentioned by Brenz[112]. However, he points out a third evidence:

> But from Matthew and Mark it is clear that he who puts away his wife for a trivial cause, and gives her freedom to marry another, he commits adultery, not because he himself takes another, which the law permits, but on account of the repudiation, since the divorced wife commits adultery in marrying another. She who is for a slight cause put away is not yet in God's sight separated from her husband, but remains still under the bond of marriage, wherefore when she is married to another, she becomes an adulteress. And indeed this which is adulterous in man's sight is not so in God's because what the Law permits is held adulterous in the eyes of God. It is not so that a man, who repudiates his wife for a trivial cause, commits adultery because he himself marries another, but because he gives occasion for the repudiated wife to commit adultery. This is borne out in Matthew v, where it says: Whosoever puts away his wife, except for the cause of fornication, causes her to become an adulteress[113].

Brenz strongly emphasizes the Lutheran difference between the secular world and the kingdom of God or that between Law and Grace. God's Word can alone rule the pious Christian, but the magistrate has to rule over both Jews, Christians, Pagans, and Turks, and that must be by law[114]. Moses is called not only a *Doctor Ecclesiasticus* but also a political legislator[115]. He is referred to as a secular magistrate just as the emperor[116]. It should also be noticed that when Paul lays down a second cause for divorce, even though Christ had said that there is only one, then he does so "as an administrator of public morals"[117]. When Christ refers to the law of Moses he thinks of another domain than that of His kingdom and grace, namely, the kingdom of the world where evil is restrained by law. Accordingly, Brenz comments:

> Christ came not to abolish the law itself, that is, to overthrow the external civil customs of the people, and Himself set up new ones, as the Jews thought their Messiah would do. Hypocrites in the Church also dreamed such dreams. He not only did not interfere with Gentile politics when they were consistent with conscience, but even showed everyone by His example that each should remain obedient to the laws of the civil order. As He Himself had obeyed the law of Moses, because He was one of the people of Moses, so it is incumbent on all to obey the laws of his own state or region[118].

---

[112] Brenz, *Eesachen*, sig. D<small>III</small>R, D<small>IIII</small>R, D<small>IV</small>R, E<small>I</small>R.
[113] Brenz, *Comm.*, pp. 350–51.   [114] Brenz, *Comm.*, p. 1198; *Eesachen*, sig. E<small>III</small>R.
[115] Brenz, *Comm.*, p. 165.   [116] Brenz, *Eesachen*, sig. E<small>III</small>R.
[117] Brenz, *Comm.*, p. 165.   [118] Brenz, *Comm.*, p. 1198.

As a prudent and pious legislator Moses had to tolerate the evil of polygamy and the letter of divorce lest worse evils should develop[119].

In view of the secular nature of the Mosaic law-giving, although given by God, it was only reasonable to think that pious Christian emperors had the same prerogatives of law-giving for the same purpose in their society. Those political laws could give other grave reasons for divorce than adultery[120].

The spiritual and secular aspects of the marriage estate, including divorce, were maintained by the Lutheran theologians as reflected in the *Württembergisches Glaubensbekenntniss*. Drafted by Brenz and approved by an evangelical synod it was presented to the Council of Trent in 1552. Article twenty-one deals with marriage. It begins by stating that marriage was ordained by God, and, according to the Apostle Paul, it is called a mystery or, as commonly interpreted, a great sacrament of Christ and His church[121]. However, since marriage belongs to this present life it is a secular affair and belongs under the secular court[122]. In the case of adultery the good bishop and prince should make sure that the persons are legally divorced so that the innocent party can marry again; a liberty which is granted him according to the words of the Lord[123].

Brenz concludes his exegesis of the divorce texts by making a Christological and soteriological observation. Since Christology was the axis of Luther's thought and soteriology the cornerstone of his exegesis, the texts on divorce not exempted, then a more appropriate note to conclude the Lutheran concept of divorce could not be found. Having referred to the fact that Christ came to vindicate the true and genuine meaning of the divine law from the trivialities and fancies of the Pharisees, thus revealing the true nature of sin, Brenz writes: "Christ expounded the law, not that He might involve men in its curse, in which they were fated to perish eternally, but that by revealing and disclosing the curse He might incite men to seek salvation through His Gospel." This was the experience of David when the prophet Nathan came to him and referred to the law: "Thou shalt not commit adultery." David "submitted himself to Christ, and believed that he received remission of sins. Does, from this faith, you say, true remission of sins and salvation come to me? Assuredly, it comes through this faith alone, and that on account of Christ. But may I indulge in all manner of impurity of life because I have remission of sins through faith? By no means"[124].

---

[119] Brenz, *Comm.*, pp. 165, 350.   [120] Brenz, *Comm.*, p. 352.
[121] *Württembergisches Glaubensbekenntniss*, art. 21.
[122] *Württembergisches Glaubensbekenntniss*, art 21.
[123] *Württembergisches Glaubensbekenntniss*, art. 21.   [124] Brenz, *Comm.*, p. 1200.

III. The Reformed Theologians

Huldreich Zwingli

In Zürich the Protestant Reformation began when Huldreich Zwingli opposed the sale of indulgences in 1519, and three years later made the breach with Rome by his first publication, a book written against fasting. His work was carried out at the same time as Luther's, but his life was of shorter duration since he was killed (in the battle of Kappel, 1531) fifteen years before Luther died. In his commentary on the New Testament Zwingli deals with all the logia on divorce except the one in the Gospel of Luke. The annotations on 1 Corinthians were printed in 1528, but those on the Gospels were published posthumously in 1539[1]. Zwingli's exegesis reveals some basic differences as compared with Luther's. The principal one is his contention that when Christ granted divorce on account of adultery, He did not exclude other reasons for divorce or prescribe this only but mentions this as one among many.

Interpreting Matthew v. 32 Zwingli asserts that Christ, in his statement, "whosoever shall put away his wife", had in mind the Jews, who were accustomed to put away their wives for trivial reasons[2]. Therefore, Christ puts a check to this, lest they should indulge their passions too much, but it did not mean that adultery was the sole reason for divorce. There are other evils which are even worse than adultery, as for example, treachery, sorcery, and parricide. By pointing out that it is a hermeneutical principle of the Scriptures that by one example is included a host of similar cases[3], Zwingli answers the

---

[1] For a list of Zwingli's works see: Georg Finsler, *Zwingli-Bibliographie. Verzeichnis der gedruckten Schriften von und über Ulrich Zwingli*, Zürich, 1897. In the present study all references are made to Zwingli's collected works: M. Schuler and J. Schulthess, editors, *Huldrici Zuinglii Opera (Huldreich Zwingli's Werke)*, Zürich, 1828–42. Hereafter referred to as *Opera*. The annotations on the New Testament logia on divorce are found in Opera, VI (i). 228–31 (Matthew v. 32); VI (i). 345–47 (Matthew xix); VI (i). 516–18 (Mark x); VI (ii). 153–56 (1 Corinthians vii).

[2] Zwingli, *Opera*, VI (i). 228.   [3] Zwingli, *Opera*, VI (i). 228.

question: Why did the Lord mention only adultery and not the other evils which would legitimize divorce? Through several illustrations Zwingli seeks to prove his point.

In Deuteronomy xix. 1 only one case of manslaughter is given for which the doer may find refuge, and that is if an axe happens to slip from the handle and slay one's comrade. A single instance is given, and from this, other cases may easily be inferred. Thus Zwingli concludes that "whoever slays a person, on whatever occasion with any weapon, if it is clear that it was inadvertent, and without malice, the Lord declares him to be innocent, although He specifically mentions an iron tool"[4]. Next, Zwingli refers to the Anabaptists, who contend that Christ's words, "Swear not at all", make it unlawful to take oaths, and that a Christian cannot stand surety for another person. This is an incorrect assertion because Christ meant by the one statement all kinds of words by which the name of God is profaned in everyday conversation. In this connection Zwingli states his concept of Christ's relationship to the judicial laws of Moses when he writes: "Christ brought nothing new into the law of the fathers, but He made fresh the old commandments, and did away with human traditions."[5]

Turning to Matthew xix. 9 Zwingli develops further the points already mentioned[6]. He first denies the Catholic concept that married people could not be divorced for any cause. Secondly, he refers to those who say that adultery is the only reason for divorce and that death alone can disrupt the marriage tie. Zwingli's exegetical principle is made evident in the following words:

But we do not want, in the way of the Jews, to cling so closely and superstitiously to the mere letter of the law, that we ignore other laws which have been dictated and given in the same spirit. The Lord condemned all trivial divorce of the Jews, but not all putting away. Nor did He exempt one cause, although He mentions only one. This in fact is the way with the Hebrews, that under one instance all like cases, little or bigger, are understood and included. So the least important cause of adultery or fornication is mentioned as it were putting the limit below which no one ought to put away his wife[7].

Zwingli brings forth a few examples to illustrate his assertion. In Leviticus xviii God forbids a man to marry the wife of his brother, but says nothing about a woman marrying the husband of her sister. However, the content of the chapter indicates that the latter is equally illegal. A second reference is made to Deuteronomy xix dealing with

---

[4] Zwingli, *Opera*, VI (1). 229.
[5] Zwingli, *Opera*, VI (1). 230.
[6] Zwingli, Opera, VI (1). 345—47.
[7] Zwingli, *Opera*, VI (1). 345.

a fortuitous manslaughter. Divorce on account of impotence is not expressly mentioned in so many words in the Scriptures. However, in the light of the Apostle Paul's words, "if they cannot contain, let them marry: for it is better to marry than to burn", impotence seems a legitimate cause for seeking a divorce. Further, Paul admitted divorce in the case of unequal marriage, if either party forsook the other because of a professed difference of faith. Moses was not commanded but allowed to give the people the right to issue a letter of divorcement because of their frailty. In the light of the Gospel other exceptions are permitted. Men, for example, are treated with more toleration, and women with more modesty and affection[8].

The question of the right understanding of law as related to marriage and divorce is Zwingli's main theme in his exposition of the divorce text in the Gospel of Mark. He introduces his comments with the following statement:

> When laws are multiplied, circumstances gradually deteriorate. But where piety, faith, and love are, there is least need for laws. Wherefore, when the Jews subverted the law of God, Moses was constrained to permit a bill of divorcement. But, first, this law of Moses was without doubt so wide, that it could be used in the greatest and most serious cases. Then evil people can abuse good laws, and each began to put his wife away for trifling reasons[9].

When the Pharisees therefore asked Christ: "Is it lawful for a man to put away his wife for every cause?", they hoped either that His answer would make Him hated by the mob if He spoke against abuse, or that He might appear to condemn the law of Moses if He spoke against transgression of the law. However, Christ avoided both pitfalls. When He said that a man shall "leave father and mother, and cleave to his wife", then it was "a mandate of the Lord, that no one should put away his wife"[10]. On the other hand, when Christ said that divorce was allowed for fornication, then according to Zwingli it should be perceived in the following manner: "Laws ought to be more widely and largely understood. He who gives permission for divorce because of fornication or adultery, without doubt will not refuse it for greater reasons."[11]

Zwingli's comments on 1 Corinthians VII did not add anything to what he had already said, or subtract from it either. He shares the common Protestant concept of connecting the words of Christ and Paul, allowing divorce and remarriage if man or wife is an unbeliever[12].

---

[8] Zwingli, *Opera*, VI (I). 345.
[9] Zwingli, *Opera*, VI (I). 516.
[10] Zwingli, *Opera*, VI (I). 516.
[11] Zwingli, *Opera*, VI (I). 516.
[12] Zwingli, *Opera*, VI (II). 153—57.

In his exposition of Matthew xix. 9 Zwingli sums up his understanding of Christ's attitude toward divorce, attributing the following words to Him: "My Spirit makes for moderation, and shuns all contumacy. I am light, and I came to restore all things to their primeval condition."[13] The reference to the primeval condition does not necessarily mean the same to Zwingli as it did to Luther, namely only the status in Eden. Commenting on the time referred to in Christ's words, "from the beginning it was not so" (Matthew xix. 8), Zwingli writes: "Without doubt, while piety, charity, and the fear of God flourished among men in the days of Abraham, Isaac, Jacob, etc..."[14] In other words, in his answer to the Pharisees, Christ goes back to the time before the Jews abused good laws. This interpretation is in harmony with the statement of Zwingli already referred to, namely, that "Christ brought nothing new into the law of the fathers, but He made fresh the old commandments, and did away with human traditions."

Considering the creation and institution of marriage, Zwingli states when God united man and woman to become one, it would be contrary to God's law for either to desert or forsake the other[15]. Further, the dignity of matrimony is illustrated in the relationship between Christ and His Church (Ephesians v. 32). Marriage is referred to as a "sacrament"[16], not in a general sense, but sanctified in Christ and the Church, as Paul bears witness[17]. It is "more than a sign of the unity of the church with Christ (for to signify or to be a type does not sufficiently express the sense and force of it), but it is a sacrament, and it is evident that it is holier and more than a sign"[18]. No doubt the only case in which Luther and Zwingli used the word sacrament with the same connotation was in their *res sacra* concept of matrimony.

In 1525 certain regulations were formulated regarding matrimonial matters, and in them guidance is given on the question of divorce. Zwingli is the main author of the document, and it reflects his interpretation of the divorce texts. It first mentions the common concept of the reformers that divorce is allowed in case of public adultery, and, when it has been confirmed by the court, the innocent party is free to marry again. When a person commits adultery with the purpose of entering into a new marriage, he should be excommunicated by the pastor, and the civil authorities should punish him, remembering the punishment prescribed by the Mosaic law. Reasons other than adultery are given for divorce. If a person cannot render the conjugal duty on account of impotence or other bodily weaknesses, divorce is

---

[13] Zwingli, *Opera*, VI (1). 345.   [14] Zwingli, *Opera*, VI (1). 516.
[15] Zwingli, *Opera*, VI (1). 344.   [16] Zwingli, *Opera*, VI (1). 344.
[17] Zwingli, *Opera*, VI (1). 516.   [18] Zwingli, *Opera*, VI (1). 517.

permissible, but first after a year's probation during which time the bodily weakness is made evident. For threatening of life, mental sickness, desertion and similar cases, no definite rule could be laid down for divorce, but the judge has the right to decide each case on its own merits[19].

Only the secular authorities could make a divorce valid since they alone could make the marriage legal. Commenting on Christ's words, "What therefore God hath joined together", Zwingli writes: "Therefore God marries, when the contracting parties are joined together in accordance with the ordinance and will of God, and the rites of the nation and the civil code. Hence they follow human, not divine tradition who say that mutual agreement is the only thing necessary for marriage."[20] The magistrate is the minister of God. "Hence those who abide by those laws, God marries them. Those who go against those laws, or whatever those laws condemn, God does not sanction their marriage."[21] In this connection it should be noticed that in December, 1526, the city of Zürich created a domestic relations court, the so-called Zürcher Ehegericht[22]. Regulations were laid down telling how to deal with adultery and other marriage problems. Zwingli was no doubt the inspiration behind this matrimonial tribunal, which was of a theocratic nature. Its historical significance will be noticed later.

A final example further illustrates Zwingli's concept of divorce matters. The answer of Luther and Melanchthon to Henry VIII on his request for advice regarding a divorce from Catherine of Aragon has been mentioned. Henry VIII was troubled over the fact that he had married his brother's wife which was forbidden by the Mosaic law. Luther and Melanchthon asserted that the law of Leviticus XVIII. 16 and XX. 21 was not a legitimate ground for divorce, because it was done away with. Therefore, they reluctantly recommended bigamy. Zwingli was also asked for counsel, and in harmony with his reference to Leviticus XX. 21 in his exegesis of Matthew XIX. 9[23] he reaffirmed that marriage with a brother's wife was forbidden according to divine

---

[19] Zwingli, *Opera*, II (II). 356—59. "Ordnung und ausehen, wie hinfür zu Zürich in der statt über eelich sachen gericht soll werden." May 10, 1525. See also "Züricher Chorgerichtsordnung" in Aemilius Ludwig Richter, *Die evangelischen Kirchenordnungen des sechszehnten Jahrhunderts*, Weimar, 1846, I. 21—22.

[20] Mark x. 9; Zwingli, *Opera*, VI (I). 517.

[21] Zwingli, *Opera*, VI (I). 517.

[22] "Ordnung und satzung von ei(ne)m ersamen R. der stadt Zürich von wegen der straf des ebruchs und unelicher biwonung" (Dec. 15, 1526), printed in Emil Egli, *Actensammlung zur Geschichte der Zürcher Reformation in den Jahren 1519—1533*. Zürich, 1879. Nr. 1087, pp. 521—23.

[23] Zwingli, *Opera*, VI (I). 345.

law. Thus the King's marriage with Catherine was invalid. This opinion, with a discussion of the various relevant texts, was written in a letter dated August 17, 1531, in answer to a letter from Oecolampadius asking for Zwingli's advice[24]. After learning about the opposite advice from the Lutheran reformers, Zwingli reaffirmed his opinion in another letter[25]. He also opposed a resort to polygamy and was thus in accord with Oecolampadius, who in another letter thanking Zwingli for his message of August 17, referred to Luther's advice and wrote: "God forbid that in this we should obey Mohammed more than Christ."[26] In his comments on 1 Corinthians VII Zwingli states: "It is according to the law, and constitution of God, that each has his own wife, and her alone, for God said: 'The two shall be one flesh.' For if at sometime in derogation of the law, one man should have many wives, the law is not abrogated."[27]

Zwingli's aversion to polygamy is adequately revealed by the fact that a certain citizen was condemned to be beheaded for the crime on April 30, 1527, and no doubt with the approval of Zwingli. After the death of Zwingli a case is recorded where a man thought it better to plead guilty to adultery than to polygamy[28].

In evaluating the different exegetical results of Luther and Zwingli it should be observed that the "fundamental difference between the two reformers lay perhaps in the starting points of their thinking. Where Luther says, 'How shall I be saved?' Zwingli says, 'How shall my people, my nation, be saved?'"[29] Luther was indeed interested in his country and Zwingli in the individual soul; however, Zwingli's influence in Zürich indicates a rather theocratic standpoint such as that found in the Old Testament. His view does not mean however that Zwingli was less Christological than Luther. Theoretically or legally the church of Zürich was under the magistrate, but practically she was the moving influence in the city, and Zwingli himself was considered as the *prophet*. Zwingli sought to make real the principle that nothing is more conducive to the exercise of secular authority than the teaching of Christ[30]. Luther left it to the lawyer and the

---

[24] Zwingli, *Opera*, VIII. 631—32. Letter LXIII, "Oecolampadius Zuinglio", Aug. 13, 1531.

[25] Gilbert Burnet, *The History of the Reformation of the Church of England*, London, 1681—83, I. II. 93—94.

[26] Zwingli, *Opera*, VIII. 634. Letter LXVI, "Oecolampadius Zuinglio", Aug. 20, 1531.

[27] Zwingli, *Opera*, VI (II). 153.

[28] Egli, *Actensammlung*, Nr. 1174, p. 541; Nr. 1941, p. 851.

[29] Jaques Courvoisier, *Zwingli, A Reformed Theologian*, London, 1964, p. 17.

[30] Zwingli, "Von göttlicher und menschlicher gerechtigkeit", 1523, *Opera*, I. 447.

magistrate to work out the matters of divorce, since the main function of the church was to hold up the *res sacra* concept of marriage. In his quest for the universal kingship of Christ Zwingli sought to permeate the secular government in a most practical way with the principles of the Bible as he understood them. Accordingly, the laws and regulations, including discipline and punishment, which should guide the magistrate in cases of divorce and other marriage problems, had to be in harmony with the teaching of Christ. No doubt this is the basic motivation behind the hermeneutic principles which guided Zwingli in his interpretation of the divorce texts. Thus his approach was different from that of Luther.

It has been pointed out that the Zürcher Ehegericht was the real ancestor of the Genevan Consistory[31]. Calvin's Geneva became the cradle of Presbyterianism and Puritanism with their theory of social ethics, which was based upon the Bible and which was brought into relationship with the universal kingdom of God; yet, the roots must be traced back to the Zürcher Ehegericht inspired by Zwingli. Seen in historical perspective Zwingli's exegesis of the New Testament logia on divorce and its practical application thus becomes very significant.

Heinrich Bullinger

At the death of Zwingli it was only to be expected that his mantle should fall upon Heinrich Bullinger. His inaugural sermon on December 23, 1531, so impressed the people that they seemed to hear the voice of Zwingli. In Bullinger's interpretation of the New Testament divorce texts the voice of Zwingli was also echoed as he applied the hermeneutical principles of his predecessor.

In his commentaries upon the New Testament Bullinger confines himself mainly to the exposition of Matthew XIX. 9, even though he deals with all the logia on divorce[32]. One of his specific objectives is to discredit those who would permit polygamy, even as an excuse for preserving a marriage. Doing this, Bullinger emphasizes that Christ,

---

[31] Walther Köhler, *Zürcher Ehegericht und Genfer Konsistorium*, Leipzig, 1932—42.

[32] Heinrich Bullinger, *In Sacrosanctvm Iesu Christi Domini nostri Euangelium secundum Matthaeum, Commentariorum libri* XII, Zürich, 1542; *In Sacrosanctvm Euangelium Domini nostri Iesu Christi secundum Marcum, Commentariorum lib.* VI, Zürich, 1545; *In Lvcvlentvm et sacrosanctum Euangelium domini nostri Iesu Christi secundum Lucam, Commentariorum lib.* IX, Zürich, 1546; *In Omnes Apostolicas Epistolas, divi videlicet Pavli* XIIII. *et* VII. *canonicas, commentarii,* Zürich, 1537.

in his answer to the Pharisees, "purged the marriage bond from many errors, and referred back to the primeval divine institution. He denounced the abuses which had grown up and the evil customs which the centuries had brought in"[33]. Having referred to Christ's words that man "shall cleave to his wife: and they twain shall be one flesh"[34], he made several statements to the effect that if those who argued about polygamy in former days had observed the words of Christ, they would not have begun to permit a man to have several wives. Bullinger expresses his amazement that some "Christians who began in the Spirit, now want to be corrupted by the flesh, and choose to follow Abraham in his polygamy, rather than in his righteous deeds"[35]. Next, he exhorts all to study the evangelical doctrine lest they should give offence by these strange opinions and so bring the gospel into despite, or they should begin to follow this unfortunate teaching with the enticement of carnal living[36]. Thus Bullinger strongly underlines what Zwingli already has said on this point.

Commenting on the permission given by Moses to issue a letter of divorcement, Bullinger states: "What Moses propounded when he gave a letter of divorce, he did not do in antagonism to the law of God, but he conceded it as permission and a dispensation."[37] The Jews had misunderstood this permission and used it for trivial reasons. Accordingly, Bullinger writes: "It is seen that Moses permitted this, not for any trivial cause, but for intolerable evil, which from the beginning would disrupt the marriage."[38] This is the situation Christ faced when He answered the Pharisees, and therefore He spoke against the practice of issuing a letter of divorce.

Bullinger follows Zwingli when he interprets Christ's words to include causes other than adultery.

The Lord replies, not for any cause you please and not for a lesser reason than fornication or adultery. He included in fornication equal or more serious reasons. Certain types of these are listed in the law of Justinian. Likewise the words of our Lord, he who marries a divorced person, are not to be taken absolutely, but in this manner: he who rashly for whatever reason that pleases him, puts away his wife, and illegitimately takes another, commits adultery. If anyone slavishly adheres to the letter of this which our Lord says to us, let him note what Paul says, by the Spirit of God, in 1 Corinthians VII. He permitted separation openly if the wife were neglected and deserted by her infidel husband[39].

---

[33] Bullinger, *Matth. Comm.*, sig. 178R.
[34] Bullinger, *Matth. Comm.*, sig. 178R, 178v.
[35] Bullinger, *Matth. Comm.*, sig. 179R.   [36] Bullinger, *Matth. Comm.*, sig. 179R.
[37] Bullinger, *Matth. Comm.*, sig. 178v.
[38] Bullinger, *Matth. Comm.*, sig. 179v.   [39] Bullinger, *Matth. Comm.*, sig. 179v.

Two other references, made by Bullinger to the same effect, should also be noticed. Having referred to the husband-wife bond as similar to that between Christ and the Church he writes: "And a bond so indissoluble ought not to be broken for any commonplace reason or fancies, but only for most serious and intolerable causes."[40] In his comments on 1 Corinthians VII he makes this remark: "For the Lord in the Gospel permits divorce, but for certain causes, of which uncleanness of adultery is not the least."[41]

A certain point in Bullinger's exegesis was later taken up by Milton[42]. Bullinger emphasizes that Christ restored marriage to the primeval ideal. This ideal we have already referred to as the *res sacra* concept. The letter of divorce was permitted only as a dispensation for a certain time and for certain causes which were not to be considered lightly, but of intolerable evil. Christ did not abolish divorce, but forbad His followers to obtain an easy divorce as did the Jews. Therefore, He made the regulation that divorce was permissible only on account of adultery, which in the opinion of Bullinger became a measuring rod whereby to decide the gravity of a certain marriage situation and the validity of a possible divorce for other reasons than adultery. Milton raises the question whether or not there was any difference between the principle involved in the Mosaic letter of divorce, when correctly used, and divorce on account of adultery or equally grave reasons. As will be noticed in Milton's discussion of the divorce texts, his contention is that Christ did not in principle abolish the letter of divorce, but only the misuse made of it by the Jews.

In his comment on Luke XVI. 16—18 Bullinger points out that Christ sought to admonish "the Pharisees and the whole Jewish nation, that they might observe not merely the external meaning of the law but might penetrate into the faith itself, which is the sum and aim of the law and the prophets". In his explanation of 1 Corinthians VII he does not add anything new or different as compared with other Protestant expositors[43]. In his exegesis of the divorce texts Bullinger twice makes reference to a further explanation in his book *Der christliche Ehestand*, and the same is done in one of his sermons[44]. It will therefore be necessary to turn to this work.

The beginning of Bullinger's writing on Christian matrimony goes back to his stay and teaching in the Cistercian Convent at Kappel.

---

[40] Bullinger, *Matth. Comm.*, sig. 179v.

[41] Bullinger, *Apost. Epist.*, p. 168.

[42] See p. 130 ff. below.

[43] Bullinger, *Lucam Comm.*, sig. 102v. Bullinger, *Apost. Epist.*, pp. 168—69.

[44] Bullinger, *Matth. Comm.*, sig. 178R, 179v; Heinrich Bullinger, *The Decades of Henry Bullinger* (Parker Society), Cambridge, 1849—52, V. 511.

Der christliche Ehestand is listed among the books he worked on during the years from 1523 to 1528[45], but the publication first took place in 1540, as he himself writes[46]. The book is a well-prepared manual on marriage relations, the subject matter being divided into twenty-five short chapters. The concept of marriage and divorce, as pointed out in his commentaries, is here systematized, but reference will be made only to those specific points which have a bearing on the concept of divorce.

In his opening paragraph Bullinger refers to Christ's words about the primeval origin and God-given purpose of marriage[47]. A threefold purpose is expressed: that children might be produced, that fornication might be avoided, and that husband and wife might "be one flesh"[48]. Husband and wife should be as eye, ear, mouth, hand, and foot for one another[49]. It should be noticed that Bullinger not only mentions a corporal and religious unity as being of fundamental importance, which Luther and his associates also did, but he strongly emphasizes oneness of mind, disposition, or temper[50]. The significance of the latter was taken up by Milton and developed to the point where he contended that if divorce was permissible for impotence, then it was equally well justified for incompatibility of mind and temperament.

Bullinger does not directly refer to marriage as a sacrament, but his remarks, based on Ephesians v. 32, reveal that he has the same concept as already expressed by Luther and Zwingli[51]. The question of whether or not the laws of Leviticus xviii and xx are still valid is answered affirmatively, asserting that the judicial laws were given to God's people of old in order that they might become an example for all nations. A reference is made to the law that no one should marry his brother's wife[52]. Bullinger was thus in agreement with Zwingli in the advice given to Henry VIII. He also expresses himself in words similar to those of Oecolampadius when the latter writes to Zwingli after Luther's advice of bigamy was given to Henry VIII. Bullinger writes that those who allow more than one wife follow the law of

---

[45] Heinrich Bullinger, *Diarium*, printed in *Quellen zur Schweizerischen Reformationsgeschichte*, II, Basel, 1904, p. 15.

[46] Bullinger, *Diarium*, p. 27.

[47] Heinrich Bullinger, *Der christliche Ehestand*, Zürich, 1854, p. 1; Matthew xix. 3—9.

[48] Genesis i. 28, 1 Corinthians vii. 1—2, Genesis ii. 24.

[49] Bullinger, *Ehestand*, p. 35. See also pp. 1—7, 31—35.

[50] Bullinger, *Ehestand*, pp. 10, 6, 88.

[51] Bullinger, *Ehestand*, p. 2.

[52] Bullinger, *Ehestand*, p. 24. See also pp. 20—26.

Mohammed rather than that of Christ[53]. Bullinger's great disagreement with those who held a contrary opinion was noticed in his comments on Matthew XIX. 9. He discusses the awfulness of fornication in chapter XIII and makes reference to a number of Bible texts dealing with this sin and its consequences[54]. The next chapter points out that the punishment for adultery, among both the Israelites and other nations, was the death penalty[55]. Regarding the adulteress to whom Christ said, "Neither do I condemn thee"[56], Bullinger asserts that Christ with this answer preserved the judicial sentence for the judge[57]. Furthermore, Bullinger follows the example of Luther when he argues that the innocent party in a divorce has the right to remarry because the law states that the one party is free when the other is dead. This is the case when one has committed adultery, for the law prescribed that he should die[58].

The last chapter deals directly with the question of divorce. Bullinger recognizes that the knowledge of divorce regulations belongs to the judge; yet, he mentions these matters for the common reader as an exhortation. He characterizes divorce as a medicine for the sake of men and the betterment of the marriage estate; however, it is an awful and deplorable medicine. Husband and wife should do all they can to avoid its use, but if the circumstances make its application necessary, the final decision rests with the magistrate, who should also do his best in an attempt to unite the couple again. Failing this, the Lord Himself had given fornication and adultery as legitimate reasons for divorce, but this cause did not exclude similar and greater offences. Paul allowed divorce between a Christian and an unbeliever, and the Christian God-fearing emperors, as for example Constantine, Theodosius, and Justinian, allowed divorce for other offences than adultery. From this, each thinking person should realize that marriage was given for the honour and dignity of man and not for his disgrace and ruin[59].

An evaluation of Bullinger's exegesis of the New Testament logia on divorce would not be complete without noticing how his interpretation is reflected in some of his sermons[60]. In a sermon on the seventh commandment Bullinger emphasizes that marriage was instituted "to the end that man's life might be pleasant, sweet, and thoroughly

---

[53] Bullinger, *Ehestand*, p. 8.   [54] Bullinger, *Ehestand*, pp. 44—52.
[55] Bullinger, *Ehestand*, pp. 52—60.   [56] John VIII. 11.
[57] Bullinger, *Ehestand*, p. 60. so sprach Jesus: 'So verdamme ich dich auch nicht.' Denn mit dieser Antwort hat er den Richtern das Urtheil vorbehalten.
[58] Bullinger, *Ehestand*, p. 140.
[59] Bullinger, *Ehestand*, pp. 137—41.   [60] Bullinger, *Decades*.

furnished with joys sufficient". Of the three objectives for which marriage was instituted: to preserve mankind, to avoid fornication, and to be a help for one another, the last is mentioned first in order to stress the purpose of a "pleasanter and more commodious" life[61]. As will be noticed later, the idea of mutual compatibility is further developed by Martin Bucer. The bond of wedlock is called "indissoluble and everlasting, that is to say, such a knot as never can be undone"[62]. The death penalty for adultery is again referred to, and regarding the adulteress mentioned in the Gospel of John, Bullinger writes:

Our Saviour did not come into the world to be a judge, but a saviour; neither did he in any place usurp the right of the sword. Who, therefore, will make any marvel at it, to see the adulteress not condemned by him to be stoned to death? Yet he said: 'Hath no man condemned thee?' as if he minded not to have resisted the law, if judgement had once passed upon her. For he came not to be a patron to adulterers, nor to break the law, but to fulfil it[63].

Bullinger's exegetical use of the judicial laws of Moses has been noticed. One of his sermons deals with these. He calls them "the most ancient, and very fountains of all other good laws which are to be found almost in all the world", and mentions that "the judicial laws were with wonderful faith and diligence set out of God by the ministry of his servant Moses; and God is not wont to reveal any thing to mankind with so precise and exquisite diligence, unless it do directly tend to mankind's great commodity"[64]. Regarding the divorce law he writes:

Divorcements and separations were permitted by the law in the twenty-fourth chapter of Deuteronomy, for nothing else but for the hardness of the Jewish people's hearts, and for the avoiding of some greater inconvenience; to wit, lest peradventure any man should poison, strangle, or otherwise kill the woman, his wife, which he hated, when he could by none other means rid his hands of her. And they that were in that manner divorced might at their pleasures be married to others[65].

A reference to the sermon on the seventh commandment is made in one dealing with institutions of the Church among which "wedlock is not to be accounted least"[66]. While Bullinger grants the magistrate the "authority to execute the sword upon evildoers . . . and that a

---

[61] Bullinger, *Decades*, II. 397.
[62] Bullinger, *Decades*, II. 403.
[63] Bullinger, *Decades*, II. 413–14.
[64] Bullinger, *Decades*, III. 218, 217.
[65] Bullinger, *Decades*, III. 228.

magistrate is very necessary for the church in respect of his office"[67], he also states that the matters should not be decided by "unbelieving judges: therefore the church of God hath very well appointed a court to try matters of matrimony". This is obviously a reference to the matrimonial court established by the city of Zürich on the initiative of Zwingli. Bullinger states that this court "must judge in matters and causes of matrimony according to right and equity, or rather according to God's laws and the rule of honesty"[68]. These statements indicate the theocratic attitude of Bullinger and confirm the suggestion that the *Zürcher Ehegericht* is the ancestor of the Genevan Consistory.

Bullinger writes that he has nothing more to write than Erasmus had written in his *Annotations* and the beloved Martin Bucer in his commentary on the Gospels[69]. Since the exegesis of Erasmus has been considered, it would be appropriate to turn to the Strassburg reformer.

Martin Bucer

The sources for an examination of Bucer's interpretation of the New Testament logia on divorce are his *Enarrationes* or commentary on the synoptic Gospels and the work *De Regno Christi*. The former was published in 1527, at a time when Luther's exegesis on the divorce texts was already well-known, but none of the commentaries of the Reformed theologians were as yet printed. *De Regno Christi* was first published thirty years later, in 1557, too late to have influenced the writings of Luther's associates and the Swiss reformers in their interpretations. The exception would have been Beza. In view of the publication of the writings of many of the reformers during this thirty year period, it seems advisable to examine each of Bucer's works separately, so that any possible change or development in his own concept and any possible reciprocal influences between him and the other reformers may be ascertained.

Bucer's Commentary on the Gospels

Bucer was one of the foremost exegetes of the Reformation period[70]. In his comments on the Psalms he mentions two of his exegetical prin-

---

[66] Bullinger, *Decades*, V. 509. [67] Bullinger, *Decades*, V. 509.
[68] Bullinger, *Decades*, V. 511.
[69] Bullinger, *Apost., Epist.*, p. 168; *Matth. Comm.*, sig. 179v.
[70] For a full bibliography of Bucer's works see: F. Mentz, *Zur 400 jährigen*

ciples. Firstly, he kept himself away from the use of the allegorical interpretation because it could impair the authority of the Scriptures. Secondly, since the Apostles followed the historical sense very closely in the treatment of their subjects, the same should be done by the expositors[71]. In this he had John Colet as his example[72], indicating the humanistic influence in his life.

The commentary on the synoptic Gospels was mainly an exposition of the Gospel of Matthew with references to parallel passages in the other two Gospels[73]. Thus his exegesis of the divorce texts is found in his comments on Matthew xix. 9, except for a few remarks on Matthew v. 32. His basic attitude toward divorce is that it should be abhorred in the greatest possible way. It should not be permitted except under the greatest necessity, because it is quite odious to nature[74].

In interpreting the passages of Scripture dealing with divorce, we should not cling to the individual words, but we should consult and compare other passages, so that we see what Christ did in that particular instance, and make a careful search of what in every case harmonizes with the primeval institution of God. When that is done, then the Christian should most willingly advance what is most consistent with truth and right living. Also, we should keep in mind the wonderful dignity of matrimony of which God is the author, for He Himself unites those who come together in marriage[75].

The concept of the two kingdoms has a fundamental bearing upon Bucer's exegesis. Having pointed out that adultery should be considered a capital crime, he refers to those who think that since Christ did not punish the adulterous woman, therefore this punishment is abolished. However, such persons do not understand Christ's words to Pilate: "My kingdom is not of this world." Christ exhorted the adulteress to repent and did not prohibit the punishment. "By no means therefore can this law about punishing adultery be considered neutralized here. Christ acquiesced to the kingdom of this world the external

---

Geburtsfeier Martin Butzer's. Bibliographische Zusammenstellung der gedruckten Schriften Butzer's, Strassburg, 1891.

[71] Martin Bucer, *Sacrorvm Psalmorvm Libri Quinque*, Strassburg, 1532, sig. IIIv.

[72] Martin Bucer, *Enarratiovm in Evangelia Mattaei, Marci, & Lucae, libri duo*, Strassburg, 1527, p. 7.

[73] A new edition of Bucer's *Enarrationvm in Evangelia Matthaei, Marci, & Lucae* was printed in 1530, a combination of his expositions of the synoptic Gospels and the Gospel of John. It is this edition which is quoted in the present study: Martin Bucer, *Enarrationes perpetvae in sacra qvatvor evangelia, recognitae nuper & locis compluribus auctae*, Strassburg, 1530.

[74] Bucer, *Enarrationes*, sig. 153v.

[75] Bucer, *Enarrationes*, sig. 154R.

kingdom of Rome, and the Mosaic legal system, and whatever else was constituted for public peace and probity." The kingdom of heaven is defined as "the kingdom of those who believe in Him, in which no one, unless he had repented from his sins and yielded himself to the good will of God, is welcomed"[76]. The secular authority is "to be solemnly warned by all who love the kingdom of Christ, that they should know that they received their authority from God Himself, and not from the Pope, and they must have the approbation of God as they exercise this power"[77].

Since Christ affirmed that His kingdom was not of this world, His answer to the Pharisees regarding divorce has to be understood as indicating "only what the elect might be permitted to do about divorce, that is what is upright and pleasing to God, and not at all to state anything about controlling evils"[78]. This was the principle Paul had in mind when he said: "For what have I to do to judge them also that are without?"[79] Therefore, Christ wished to teach the pious "this only, that there should be the closest union among those who were married by God's institution, and so putting away of the wife was not allowable, except for the reason of adultery, and the one who committed adultery sinned against marriage; however many excuses he made, the marriage was wickedly broken up"[80]. Christ "showed that the lax readiness of divorce which the Jews allowed, should be truly alien to the pious people, who know themselves to be united by the Lord, and cleave mutually to one another in closest union"[81]. Furthermore, "there is no impulse which the Lord cannot help us to control. Hence I affirm that whoever puts away his wife except for the cause of fornication does not remove the offence, but makes it more grievous. So the result is, that she who is put away becomes an adulteress, and he who marries her is an adulterer"[82].

Making a clear demarcation between the two kingdoms, Bucer asserts, on the one hand, that Christ gave adultery as the only cause for divorce; yet, on the other hand, He did not abolish the Mosaic law of divorce[83]. Adultery is not only an offence "against the law of God, but also against that of Caesar"[84]. Where there are impious people with hardness of heart, there is a need for consulting the magistrate. The magistrate should be thankful that the law of divorce given to the Jews is also in effect today. This fact does not contradict the dictum:

---

[76] Bucer, *Enarrationes*, sig. 152R.
[77] Bucer, *Enarrationes*, sig. 153R.
[78] Bucer, *Enarrationes*, sig. 153R.
[79] 1 Corinthians v. 12.
[80] Bucer, *Enarrationes*, sig. 153R.
[81] Bucer, *Enarrationes*, sig. 153v.
[82] Bucer, *Enarrationes*, sig. 54R.
[83] See Bucer's comments on Matthew v. 32 in *Enarrationes*, sig. 53v—54R.
[84] Bucer, *Enarrationes*, sig. 152.

"What therefore God hath joined together, let not man put asunder", for it is God who separates through the law, those who in their hearts are already parted. It is permitted in order that greater evil may be avoided[85]. Further, in regard to Christ's answer to the Pharisees: "let not man put asunder", He had not the magistrate in mind, but the question before them was "whether or not a husband in particular was free to put away his wife for any cause he wished, just or unjust. To this He replied that man should not divorce"[86]. It is a different matter when there is separation due to hardness of heart, and hatred and execration arise between the two in heart, for then the magistrate should permit divorce for the innocent wife. Evidently he does not separate those who were joined together by God, but he keeps those who are now separated in heart from greater danger[87]. Thus the law is a defence for the innocent and punishment for the transgressor[88].

While Bucer acknowledged that the question of divorce is under the jurisdiction of the magistrate, still he felt that it is a Christian responsibility to appeal to the secular authorities that they should exercise their God-given power, usurped by the Roman Pontiff, and govern so that God might be honoured. "The Christian magistrate should know all the external matters that are demanded of him that he tries public causes honestly and to the glory of God, nor should it be unseemly for him to deal with matters which Moses permitted among God's people. That is God's will. Oh, that our holy state may be governed as it was in the time of Moses."[89] Bucer also expresses himself to the effect that "the magistrate neither has less need than in Moses' time to use his power as he pleases"[90]. Bucer no doubt has in mind that Moses, as one who had secular authority, had to decide what was best under the given circumstances, keeping in mind the original purpose of marriage. This was just what Christian emperors, such as Theodosius and Justinian, did. They made divorce a public matter and allowed it only for certain valid reasons. Bucer lists these reasons, and they amount to about twenty. For the man they include various crimes, such as homicide, poisoning, falsifying, robbery, spying, etc.[91]. The wife could be divorced if she visited the theatre or circus, etc., against her husband's will[92].

From this it appears that Bucer gives the state quite a scope for causes permitting divorce. It is true that other reformers refer to the laws of the Christian emperors, but it is rather in order to endorse a

---

[85] Bucer, *Enarrationes*, sig. 150v–151v. [86] Bucer, *Enarrationes*, sig. 150v.
[87] Bucer, *Enarrationes*, sig. 151R. [88] Bucer, *Enarrationes*, sig. 151R.
[89] Bucer, *Enarrationes*, sig. 151R–151v. [90] Bucer, *Enarrationes*, sig. 150v.
[91] Bucer, *Enarrationes*, sig. 152v. [92] Bucer, *Enarrationes*, sig. 152v.
[93] Bucer, *Enarrationes*, sig. 152v.

principle. They do not spell out the many causes for which divorce was permitted; thus there appears to be a difference of emphasis. Referring to the divorce law of Theodosius and Justinian, Bucer says that in the name of religion it deserves much praise, for it promoted public equity and honesty, and it should be maintained in part as agreed upon[93]. Some may argue that if the magistrate allows divorce and a second marriage, then many marriages which were firmly established may be broken up. But the reply is that the magistrate acts in accordance with his office, and divorce is granted only because those marriages have already become sacrilegious[94].

How a state should be governed according to Christian principles generally, and in marriage matters especially, is the topic of *De Regno Christi*, which calls for an examination.

De Regno Christi

On the invitation of Archbishop Cranmer, Bucer went to England in April, 1549, and there he died two years later. During this period he wrote his work *De Regno Christi* and in 1550 dedicated it to the young King Edward as a token of appreciation[95]. However, it was first printed in Basel, 1557[96].

The aim of this work was to reveal the nature of the kingdom of Christ and to point out the ways and means whereby it could be established[97]. The book was esteemed by theologians in England and elsewhere, reflected in the fact that it was translated into French[98] and German[99]. Nearly a century after its dedication to King Edward VI, John Milton translated into English great sections of it dealing with marriage and divorce[100]. The Latin edition is composed of

---

[94] Bucer, *Enarrationes*, sig. 153R.
[95] Burnet, *The History of the Reformation of the Church of England*, II. I. 156.
[96] Martin Bucer, *De Regno Christi Iesu seruatoris nostri*, Basel, 1557.
[97] An analysis of *De Regno Christi* has been made by W. Pauck, *Das Reich Gottes auf Erden*, Berlin, 1928.
[98] Martin Bucer, *Deux Livres dv Royavme de Iesvs Christ Nostre Savvevr*, n. p. 1558.
[99] Martin Bucer, *Vom Reich Christi vnsers Herren vnd Heilands, Wie das selbige von allen Christlichen Oberkeiten anzustellen, vnd ins werck zubringen seye*, Strassburg, 1563. A rare copy of this edition is found in Bibliothèque du Consistoire, Colmar, France.
[100] Martin Bucer, *The Ivdgement of Martin Bucer, concerning Divorce*, London, 1644, printed in *The Works of John Milton*, New York, 1931, IV. 1—61. This translation by Milton is quoted. Where Milton has not translated Bucer, reference is made to *De Regno Christi*.

two hundred and forty-nine folio pages, and nearly one third of the book deals with marriage matters and divorce especially. Thus a prominent place is given to the problem of divorce in that needed reformation which should make the nature of the state exemplify the kingdom of Christ. In Bucer's treatment of the subject matter a change is noticeable in his interpretation of the divorce texts.

Emphasizing that matrimony belongs to the civil domain, which has unjustly been invaded by the popes, Bucer appeals to the King for the constitution of laws by which "mariages, according to the will of Christ, be made, maintain'd, and not without just cause dissolv'd"[101]. When interpreting the divorce texts in order to ascertain Christ's teaching, one should keep four self-evident principles in mind. The first axiom is that Christ was the mediator of the law of Deuteronomy XXIV. 1, and "what the Lord permitted to his first-borne people, that certainly he could not forbid to his own among the Gentils". Wherever the same urgent causes are present, and human nature has not changed, there the same permissions may be applied, "when the discipline of the church and Magistrate hath tri'd what may be tri'd"[102].

The second self-evident truth is that the Lord "took not on him either to give new laws in civil affairs, or to change the old". Christ came to preach the gospel with its message of repentance and forgiveness, therefore

> those who put away thir wives without any just cause, were not toucht with conscience of the sin, through misunderstanding of the law, he recall'd them to a right interpretation, and taught that the woman in the beginning was so join'd to the man, that there should be a perpetual union both in body and spirit: where this is not, the matrimony is already broke, before there be yet any divorce made or second mariage[103].

The third and fourth axioms point out two hermeneutical principles. The narratives of the Evangelists should be taken together when they are treating the same subject or incident, and the briefer narratives of other Gospels should be harmonized with the fuller accounts and interpreted with reference to other passages of Scripture relating to the same matter. To validate this principle Bucer draws on several narratives recorded in the synoptic Gospels[104]. Thus when the Lord in two places in Matthew most clearly allowed a concession about divorce, namely, in the case of adultery, then the same should be added to the words and replies of the Lord as recorded in Mark and Luke[105].

---

[101] Bucer, *Divorce*, p. 22. [102] Bucer, *Divorce*, pp. 34—37.
[103] Bucer, *Divorce*, p. 37. [104] Bucer, *De Regno Christi*, pp. 149—53.
[105] Bucer, *De Regno Christi*, p. 160.

Christ's words, "What therefore God hath joined together, let not man put asunder" (Matthew xix. 6) have to be evaluated in the light of the primary purpose of marriage as recorded in Genesis II. Bucer emphasizes more strongly than Bullinger the importance of spiritual and affectional unity. In the latter he was surpassed only by Milton. Reference has been made to Bucer's statement of a perpetual union not only of body but also of mind; where that unity is disrupted, marriage is already broken before any divorce has become a fiat. Accordingly, "the proper and ultimate end of mariage is not copulation, or children, for then there was not true matrimony between Joseph and Mary the mother of Christ, nor between many holy persons more; but the full and proper and main end of mariage, is the communicating of all duties, both divine and humane, each to other, with utmost benevolence and affection"[106]. This statement reflects his suggestion regarding the marriage service that the third cause listed in the exhortation, mutual assistance, ought to have the first place[107]. This prime characteristic of marriage is constituted in a unity not only of body "but in mind also, with such an affection as none may be dearer and more ardent among all the relations of mankind, nor of more efficacy to the mutual offices of love, and loyalty"[108]. Discussing whether to permit the annulment of a promise of marriage Bucer underlines the same thought.

> And as there is no true mariage between them, who agree not in true consent of mind, so it will be the part of the godly Magistrates to procure that no matrimony be among thir Subjects, but what is knit with love and consent ... [God's] ancient people had power, yea a precept, that who so could not bend his mind to the true love of his wife, should give her a bill of divorce, and send her from him, though after carnal knowledge and long dwelling together. This is anough to authorize a godly Prince in that indulgence which he gives to the changing of a Contract ... it should be a Princes care that matrimony be so joyn'd, as God ordain'd; which is, that every one should love his wife with such a love as Adam exprest to Eve[109].

While Bucer did not say in so many words that incompatibility of mind is a legitimate cause for divorce, his arguments followed to a logical conclusion would lead to such an assertion as seen in the writings of Milton. Having listed genuine love, communion of true religion, the wife's being a helpmate, and conjugal relationship as necessary qualities for true marriage, he draws the following conclusion:

---

[106] Bucer, *Divorce*, p. 47.
[107] Martin Bucer, *Scripta Anglicana*, Basel, 1577, p. 488.
[108] Bucer, *Divorce*, pp. 46—47.   [109] Bucer, *Divorce*, p. 26.

"Hence it follows according to the sentence of God, which all Christians ought to be rul'd by, that between those who either through obstinacy, or helples inabilitie, cannot or will not perform those repeated duties, between those there can be not true matrimony, nor ought they to be counted man and wife."[110] Leprosy, impotence, and mental diseases are lawful causes for divorce, even when contracted during marriage. If the cause lies with the wife, the state should take care of the woman and any children she may have[111]. The death penalty is strongly advocated as the punishment for adultery[112].

In his commentary on the New Testament Bucer states that Christ gave adultery as the only one cause for divorce, but, making a sharp distinction between the two kingdoms, he advocates the use of the Mosaic laws on the secular level. The same distinction he has in mind in the beginning of his discussion of divorce in *De Regno Christi*. "I confess that the civil laws of Moses and ceremonies given to the people of old do not apply to our liberties, given us by Christ, for they concern external circumstances and elements of the world. But no laws can be more upright, just, and salutary than those which God Himself ordained (if only they are applied in the sense God gave them, in our affairs and actions) in eternal goodness and wisdom."[113] As Bucer proceeds in his discussion he states that there are those who hold a different view, namely, that the exception mentioned by the Lord covers other reasons than fornication. No doubt he has in mind Zwingli and Bullinger. He asks the question, whether the cause of fornication covers a general concession for divorce. Bucer does not answer the question directly, as did Zwingli and Bullinger, by saying that Christ by the one exception concealed other causes. He rather infers that Christ would allow other reasons[114]. "To this question, if we retain our principles already laid, and must acknowledge it to be a cursed blasphemy, if we say that the words of God doe contradict one another, of necessity we must confesse that our Lord did grant divorce, and mariage after that for other causes besides adultery, notwithstanding what he said in Matthew."[115] If it can only be proved that one other cause than adultery is found lawful, then the above assertion is correct. Bucer finds that in 1 Corinthians VII. 15[116].

As statements for lawful divorce Bucer brings together the texts of Deuteronomy XXIV. 1, Malachi II. 14, Matthew XIX. 9 and 1 Corinthians VII. 15 as being of equal value. "That God changes not his

---

[110] Bucer, *Divorce*, p. 48.
[111] Bucer, *De Regno Christi*, pp. 180–82.
[112] Bucer, *De Regno Christi*, pp. 156–59.
[113] Bucer, *De Regno Christi*, p. 129.
[114] Bucer, *De Regno Christi*, p. 154.
[115] Bucer, *Divorce*, p. 42.
[116] Bucer, *Divorce*, p. 42.

minde, dissents not from himself, is no accepter of persons; but allows the same remedies to all men opprest with the same necessities and infirmities; yea, requires that wee should use them. This he will easily perceave, who considers these things in the Spirit of the Lord."[117] That the words, "For the woman which hath an husband is bound by the law to her husband so long as he liveth", are no argument against divorce, is asserted by Bucer by referring to the previous verse: "Know ye not, brethren, (for I speak to them that know the law,) how that the law hath dominion over a man as long as he liveth?"[118] The Israelites "knew no law of God but that by Moses, which plainly grants divorce for several reasons. It cannot therefore be said that the Apostle cited this generall example out of the law, to abolish the several exceptions of that law, which God himself granted by giving authority to divorce"[119].

The Lord has further commanded that the civil laws should be observed. They may vary from country to country, but each person should follow the customs of the land in which he lives. In the eyes of God marriage is dissolved by the laws of the country[120]. Bucer also refers to divorce by mutual consent:

It was permitted also by Christian Emperours, that they who would divorce by mutuall consent, might without impediment. Or if there were any difficulty at all in it, the law expresses the reason, that it was only in the favour of the children, so that if there were none, the law of those godly Emperours made no other difficulty of a divorce by consent. Or if any were minded without consent of the other to divorce, and without those causes which have bin nam'd, the Christian Emperours laid no other punishment upon them then that the husband wrongfully divorcing his wife should give back her dowry, and the use of that which was call'd Donatio propter nuptias; or if there were no dowry nor no donation, that he should then give her the fourth part of his goods. The like penalty was inflicted on the wife departing without just cause. But that they who were once maried should be compell'd to remain so ever against thir wills, was not exacted. Wherin those pious Princes follow'd the law of God in Deut. 24. 1. and his expresse charge by the Profet Malachy to dismisse from him the wife whom he hates. For God never meant in mariage to give a man a perpetuall torment, instead of a meet help. Neither can God approve that to the violation of this holy league (which is violated as soon as true affection ceases and is lost), should be added murder, which is already committed by either of them who resolvedly hates the other, as I shew'd out of 1 John [III] 15. Who so hateth his brother is a murderer[121].

---

[117] Bucer, *Divorce*, p. 43.
[119] Bucer, *Divorce*, p. 40.
[121] Bucer, *Divorce*, pp. 51—52.

[118] Romans VII. 1, 2.
[120] Bucer, *Divorce*, pp. 43, 48—52.

Another statement to the same effect should be noticed: "And hence is concluded, that matrimony requires continuall cohabitation and living together, unlesse the calling of God be otherwise evident; which union if the parties themselves dis-joyn either by mutuall consent or one against the others will depart, the marriage is then brok'n."[122]

In the closing pages Bucer re-emphasizes that none of the mentioned causes for granting divorce disagrees with Christ's words stating only the cause of adultery. His final declaration is that all that he has written is in harmony with God's law and the teaching of Christ[123].

Bucer is generally considered as one who sought to soften sharp points of differences between the Lutheran and Reformed theologians. His *ecumenical* attempts are reflected in the discussion of the Lord's Supper both on the Continent and in England. In his interpretation of the divorce texts it seems that Bucer sought to bridge the Lutheran and the Zwingli-Bullinger exegeses. In his commentary he followed Luther's distinction between the two kingdoms and in his exposition of Christ's words he stated that they allowed only one cause for divorce. However, he emphasized more strongly than Luther that the state should be governed according to the Old Testament. This is confirmed by the fact that Bullinger, his exegesis being influenced by a rather theocratic concept and being different from Luther's, expressed his debt to Bucer. Milton also noticed this emphasis in Bucer's commentary. In his translation of *De Regno Christi* he refers to Bucer's teaching on this point in the latter's commentary and inserts a quotation from Bucer's comments on Matthew v. 32[124]. In *De Regno Christi* Bucer implies that Christ, in spite of the words in Matthew, allowed other reasons for divorce than adultery. Thus he seeks to balance between the Lutheran interpretation, which he himself applied in his commentary, and the Zwingli-Bullinger exegesis which asserted that Christ by the one exception covered other causes. In reality Bucer adhered to the exegesis of the Zürich Reformers in *De Regno Christi*, since he equalizes the two divorce texts of the Old Testament with those of Matthew xix. 9 and 1 Corinthians vii. 15. It is interesting to notice that when Burnet outlines the teaching of *De Regno Christi* in a few sentences, his statement on Bucer's divorce concept is that Bucer thought a lawful divorce "might be made for Adultery, and some other reasons"[125].

In his theocratic application of the divorce texts Bullinger went further than Bucer in the latter's commentary, but in *De Regno Christi* Bucer applied the divorce texts in a more liberal way than

---
[122] Bucer, *Divorce*, p. 46.   [123] Bucer, *Divorce*, pp. 54–59.
[124] Bucer, *Divorce*, p. 24.
[125] Burnet, *The History of the Reformation of the Church of England*, II. i. 156.

Bullinger. It seems that allowance should be made for a reciprocal influence. A progressively liberal interpretation is evident from Luther through Zwingli and Bullinger to Bucer, and even in Bucer's own two writings. That this comparison and conclusion of Bucer's exegesis is plausible, is sustained by the fact that while contemporaries esteemed the basic ideas of *De Regno Christi*, yet his exposition of the divorce texts was considered too liberal.

In a letter written by John Burcher to Henry Bullinger and dated June 8, 1550, Burcher writes about the progress of the Reformation through the writings and ministry of John Hooper. A few other items are mentioned, and one of these is Bucer's attitude toward divorce as expressed in some discussions. Burcher has a certain resentment against both Bucer and Fagius[126], which should be taken into consideration when he speaks about Bucer. His statement regarding Bucer's concept of divorce, while somewhat exaggerated, nevertheless reflects to some degree Bucer's liberal views as compared with other reformers and the impression his thoughts may have made on some. Burcher writes: "Bucer is more than licentious on the subject of marriage. I heard him once disputing at table upon this question, when he asserted that a divorce should be allowed for any reason, however trifling; so that he is considered, not without cause, by our bishop of Winchester as the author of the book published in defence of the Landgrave."[127]

The translator of the French edition of *De Regno Christi*, published in 1558, a year after the original Latin edition, found it necessary to point out in the preface that Bucer had a somewhat different viewpoint from that of other theologians. The writer expresses his own and Calvin's great regard for Bucer. Because of Bucer's outstanding learning as a theologian the former had decided to translate *De Regno Christi*. His comments on Bucer's concept of divorce are thus given by one who admires and respects Bucer and not by a critic such as Burcher. He writes:

Furthermore he deals with marriage and divorce, and this in such a complete way that he equals any other person of our time concerning this subject, which shows his great diligence, versatility and profound knowledge. If also he differs from the opinion and way of thinking of some learned and excellent personalities who had a clearer view of the truth and have approached the true meaning of the Scriptures more fully, especially concerning the intentions of the Saviour with reference to marriage and divorce:

---

[126] *Original Letters Relative to the English Reformation* (Parker Society), Cambridge, 1846–47, Letter CCCXI, II. 662–63; Letter CCCXII, II. 665–67.

[127] *Original Letters*, II. 665–66. The reference to "the Landgrave" means Philip of Hesse.

yet he wished to admonish the reader not to be troubled or offended by such diversity and to adhere always to the conclusions and rules practised in our day, in this respect, by the better reformed churches, according to the resolution made by several good servants of God still living, who pay attention to everything written in the word of God and to the most appropriate meaning in analogy to the faith. Doubtlessly Bucer would have yielded to their opinion, it being the most holy and veritable one, if the Lord had not taken him away from this world after the accomplishment of his work, and if he had given him the opportunity to discuss the matter with them, and he would not have been ashamed to take back and revoke that which he had proclaimed, just like St. Augustine and other excellent men being bent on truth[128].

In a letter from Johann Flinner to Conrad Hubert dated Heidelberg, August 25, 1557, the same caution is expressed regarding Bucer's teaching on divorce. Johann Flinner, 1520—78, was a strict Lutheran minister and had worked as pastor in Augsburg, Heidelberg, Münster, and Strassburg. During the year 1551 he was in Denmark. Conrad Hubert, 1507—77, was deacon at St. Thomas, Strassburg, 1531—68, and was the real editor of *De Regno Christi*. Hubert wished to dedicate it to the King of Denmark, who had invited Bucer, 1549, to come to Copenhagen. Flinner, who was Hubert's colleague at Strassburg, 1553—56 and 1559—77, had been in personal contact with the Danish King, 1551, and was asked by Hubert to send the book with the dedication to the King. This gave occasion to Flinner to criticize the dedication and show how he himself would have formulated it. Flinner writes that in *De Regno Christi* there are things which do

---

[128] Martin Bucer, *Deux Livres dv Royavme de Iesvs Christ Nostre Savvevr*, sig. iiiir—v. Au surplus, il traitte du mariage, & du diuorse, autant amplement qu'auteur qui ait escrit de nostre temps, en quoy lon pourra facilement voir sa grande diligence, futilité, & profond sauoir. Mais d'autant qu'il est different de l'opinion & intelligence de plusieurs sauans & excellens personnages, qui ont de plus pres regardé la verité, & plus approché du vray sens de l'Escriture, & de l'intention du Seigneur, en ce poinct du mariage, & du diuorse: i'ay bien voulu admonnester le lecteur, de ne se troubler & offenser en telle diuersité, ains de se tenir tousiours à la conclusion & arrest qui est auiourd'huy practiqué en ceste matiere aux Eglises mieux reformées, suiuant la resolution qu'en ont donnée plusiers bons seruiteurs de Dieu encore viuans, qui ont du tout regard à ce qui est exprimé en la parole de Dieu, & au sens plus conuenable à l'analogie de la foy. Et ne doute point de ma part, que Bucer n'eust adheré a leur opinion, comme la plus saincte & plus veritable, si le Seigneur ne l'eust retiré de ce monde tantost apres auoir fait cest'oeuure, & luy eust donné l'oportunité de conferer auec eux, & n'eust eu honte de retracter & reuoquer ce qu'il auoit ia mis en auant, non plus que sainct Augustin, & autres bons personnages, desquels le desir est tousiours de viser droit au but de verité.

not agree with the common doctrines, such as, for example, Bucer's discussion on divorce, and suggests that they should be mollified. Since the book was published posthumously, the thought was expressed that the author might have been willing to alter some parts and not leave them so crude[129]. In other words Flinner feels that some words of caution should have been expressed in the preface, just as it has been noticed that the translator of the French edition did.

Among the Lutheran and Reformed theologians whose writings are being considered, Beza is the only one who wrote on marriage and divorce after the publication of *De Regno Christi*. However, as will be noticed, his exegesis was not influenced by Bucer. In his treatise on divorce he refers to some of Bucer's arguments concerning marriage and divorce and makes this comment: "But as to Doctor Bucer, a man of pious memory, I am constraint to dissent a great deal in this argument."[130] It would be correct to accept this statement as expressing Beza's general opinion of Bucer's interpretation of the divorce texts by the fact that Beza's exegesis differs from that of Bucer and opposes it to a very large degree. Martin Bucer's view of divorce, as expressed in *De Regno Christi*, was not accepted by his contemporaries at large. The real heir of Bucer is first found in Milton a century later.

Pietro Martire Vermigli

Pietro Martire Vermigli, 1500—62, was dedicated by his father to the Dominican Saint, Peter Martyr (d. 1252). By the name of the latter he is commonly known as a Reformed theologian. Influenced by the writings of Erasmus, Bucer and Zwingli, he became a Protestant. From 1542—47 he lectured at the University of Strassburg. Here he was closely associated with Martin Bucer, as well as in England where he taught at Oxford. At the accession of Queen Mary he returned to

---

[129] "Johann Flinner an Conrad Hubert, Heidelberg 25. 8. 1557." Archive St. Thomas, Strasburg 156, no. 111. Cum quaedam in libro sunt quae non cum doctrina vulgari consentiunt, ut vel solus articulus de divortio est, hoc revera aliquo modo praevenire debueratis, vel saltem lenire, dicendo, si forsan difficilia aut paradoxa videri possent, quasi non concordarent cum aliis doctoribus ... denique librum esse posthumum, ab ipso authore non editum, qui procul dubio omnibus satisfecisset atque forsitan quaedam mutasset, vel non ita nude invulgasset. I am indebted to M. Jean Rott of the Library of Strassburg for bringing this letter to my attention.

[130] Theodore Beza, *Tractatio De Repvdiis et Divortiis*, Geneva, 1573, p. 200. D. Bucerus autem (piae memoriae vir, sed a quo in hoc quidem argumento cogor in multis dissentire) duobus aliis multo in speciem vehementioribus argumentis nititur.

Strassburg, but from 1556 to the end of his life he was a professor at Zürich[131].

Peter Martyr's first lectures at Oxford were on the First Epistle to the Corinthians, but his commentary on this epistle was printed posthumously in 1567, as most of his other commentaries were. His comments on the seventh chapter are the main source for an examination of his exposition of the divorce texts[132].

A French pastor in London, Robert Masson, brought together in four books all the works of Peter Martyr which had been published. The title is *Loci communes*, 1576, and its content is arranged after the pattern of Calvin's *Institutes*. Its significance for Protestant thought is indicated by its being published in several editions and in an English translation, 1583[133]. Its subject matters are dogmatical, ecclesiastical, and ethical, and include a discussion of the marriage institution with related sociological and ethical problems. The section on divorce is largely a reprint of his commentary on 1 Corinthians VII. 10—11. Considering his association with Bucer and Bullinger and his intimate knowledge of their thinking on divorce, it is significant to notice his more conservative attitude.

In discussing the divorce question a difference in motivation appears between those who hold that unity of mind and spirit is a basic objective in marriage and those who hold that procreation is the basic objective. Whereas Bullinger emphasized the former and Bucer placed it first, Peter Martyr held the latter view. Of course, this did not mean that he and others, such as the Lutheran reformers, placed exclusive stress upon the conjugal relationship, relegating the principle of unity and harmony to a place of no significance; however, the evaluation of the divorce problem is bound to be related to the basic orientation of the theologian as to the objectives of marriage.

---

[131] For the life and works of Peter Martyr see: C. Schmidt, *Peter Martyr Vermigli. Leben und ausgewählte Schriften*, printed in *Leben und ausgewählte Schriften der Väter und Begründer der reformirten Kirche*, Elberfeld, 1858, VII. Philip McNair, *Peter Martyr in Italy: an Anatomy of Apostasy*, Oxford, 1967.

[132] Peter Martyr, *In selectissimam D. Pauli priorem ad Corinthios epistolam*, n. p., 1567 (British Museum Library Catalogue). Another edition was published in Zürich in 1572. Peter Martyr, *In Selectissimam D. Pavli Priorem ad Corinthios Epistolam*, Zürich, 1572.

[133] Peter Martyr, *Loci communes. Ex variis ipsius authoris libris in unum volumen collecti, & quatuor classes distributi*. London, 1576 (British Museum Library Catalogue). The British Museum Library Catalogue lists Latin editions printed in 1576, 1583, 1656. The University of Basel Library Catalogue lists editions printed in 1580, 1587, 1613. Peter Martyr, *The Common Places of . . . Peter Martyr, diuided into foure principall parts: with a large addition of manie theologicall and necessarie discourses, some never extant before*, London, 1583.

Referring to the time of creation Peter Martyr states that then the only reason for marriage was that of procreation. Later, when man was exposed to the danger of fornication, marriage also became a means to avoid this sin[134]. Discussing the question of impotence, which is considered a legitimate reason for divorce together with desertion, Peter Martyr refers to some who say that if the man makes known his impediment beforehand, he may contract a marriage and the woman should remain with him, but Martyr states: "But what maner of marriage will that be, when it is done neither for procreation of children, neither for avoiding of whoredom?"[135]

Finally, in his section on marriage Peter Martyr brings attention to Justinian's definition of the same, as "a coniunction of man and woman, an inseparable conuersation of life, and a communicating of the lawe of God and man". But "this definition must be made perfect by the holie scriptures. Wherefore we must saie, that this coniunction of man and woman, was instituted by God, for the increasing of children, for the taking awaie of whoredome, and that thereby the life of man might haue helpes and commodities"[136].

By the words of Christ it is plainly declared "that a diuorce ought not to be doone, vnlesse it be for the cause of adulterie... And Paule (by whom Christ speaketh) excepteth another thing; namelie, if one of the married persons, in that he is an infidell, will not dwell with the other being faithfull"[137]. Accordingly, "it appeereth, that the sentence of Christ, wherein he onelie excepteth whooredome, was not compleat: seeing the apostle here added another"[138]. Of the recorded words of Christ the shorter readings of Mark x. 11–12 and Luke x. 18 should be read in the light of the longer readings of Matthew v. 32 and xix. 9[139]. The easy way by which the Jews and Gentiles divorced their wives is being opposed by the words of Christ. Not that the law of Deuteronomy xxiv. 1 and the words of Malachi ii. 14 were not endorsed by God: "For the Lord would not, that hatred and enimitie should be reteined in so naere fraendship," but now "Christ calleth vs home vnto the first institution. For insomuch as now, the spirit is more plentifull, and grace more abundant; men ought to vse greater patience and charitie towards their wiues, and not so to deale against them, as they should reject them for euerie cause. In like maner there is required of the wiues a greater obedience and modestie"[140].

---

[134] Martyr, *Common Places*, p. 418.　[135] Martyr, *Common Places*, p. 467, par. 73.
[136] Martyr, *Common Places*, p. 418.
[137] Martyr, *Common Places*, p. 457, par. 53.
[137] Martyr, *Common Places*, p. 465, par. 70.
[139] Martyr, *Common Places*, p. 463, par. 65.
[140] Martyr, *Common Places*, p. 457, par. 52.

Having laid down these basic principles, Peter Martyr recognizes that he faces two problems. First, it is mentioned that "if thou shalt find at this daie, among Christians, such as be so hard-harted, and so obstinate in reteining of hatred and enimitie in wedlocke, as they be not onelie equall to the Jewes, but also go beyond them therein? Seeing then the disease is all one, why is not the same remedie left?"[141] Second, "as touching the cause of adulterie, which Christ excepted, some doubt whether that be the onelie cause; and they are bold to saie, that Christs meaning was to comprehend therin all other wickednesse, which is either equall, or more heinous than adulterie: and they saie that the maner of the holie scriptures is, that in one cause rehearsed, they include others like vnto it"[142].

In answering the first question Peter Martyr clearly endorses the Lutheran concept of the two kingdoms, for he affirms "that they, which be of such sort, be strangers from Christ: wherfore we commit them to the Common-weale, to determine of them as it shall seeme most expedient. For when they cannot be amended by the church, let vs count them for Ethniks and Publicans: let vs deale with them by the ciuill lawes"[143]. Although marriage is instituted by God, "yet, as touching the circumstances, it hath manie things belonging vnto the ciuill lawes and customes"[144]. It should be noticed that Peter Martyr expresses himself to the effect that the magistrate should be careful and moderate when he issues divorce laws. He writes:

We must praie therefore, and by all meanes intreat the magistrate, that he being faithfull, will determine herof; and that he will applie his lawes to the word of God. And it must be foreseene, that it be so determined, as a windowe be not set open to horrible offenses, whereby matrimonies are in manie places rashlie dissolued. And on the other part they must take heed, least while they will defend a dioursement so made, whereof the holie scriptures neuer giue anie testimonie, that the bond of wedlocke still remaineth (the husband and the wife being seuered, and so seuered, as they cannot dwell togither;) I saie heed must be taken, that no occasion be giuen vnto fraile lusts, and companie of harlots[145].

Realizing Peter Martyr's rather conservative attitude as compared with Bucer, it is understandable that he could say: "But of this I maruell offentimes with my selfe, how it came to passe, that Valentinian, Theodosius, and Justinian, otherwise most christian princes, partlie made lawes themselues of diuorsements, and partlie by their authori-

---
[141] Martyr, *Common Places*, p. 457, par. 53.
[142] Martyr, *Common Places*, p. 457, par. 54.
[143] Martyr, *Common Places*, p. 457, par. 53.
[144] Martyr, *Common Places*, p. 458, par. 56.
[145] Martyr, *Common Places*, p. 459, par. 56.

tie confirmed them which were made of old; and that such lawes were not openlie withstood by the most godlie bishops, which liued in those daies." The answer which Peter Martyr gave himself is that they rather condescended into the use of divorce for other reasons than mentioned in the New Testament in order to avoid greater evil in the secular society. For the same reason the Christian magistrate is justified in using divorce as a medicine[146]. He expresses himself in these words:

Neither ought this to trouble vs much, that in the old testament, a bill of diuorsement was permitted for euerie cause; seeing now Christ draweth the matter into so streict a roome: this is no cause, why thou shouldest thinke him to be against the decrees and lawes of his father. But this thou must consider, that in those daies, the same lawe of giuing a bill of diuorsement, which was ordeined in the 24. of Deuteronomie, was ciuill: and Christ dealt not as touching the ciuill affaires. They, which gouerne a Common-weale, appoint themselues such a scope, as if two euils or discommodities be offered, the lesse must be permitted, lest they should fall into the greater[147].

That the divorce law of Deuteronomy was a civil law and in no way on par with the words of Christ is also substantiated by the fact that we have no record telling us that any good man in Old Testament times made use of the divorce law[148]. Peter Martyr's interpretation, that the New Testament allowed only two reasons for divorce, would of course, as compared with Bucer's, make his view of divorce more serious even for the magistrate, who, in a different sphere than the kingdom of God, was allowed to follow the principle involved in the divorce laws of the Israelites and the Christian emperors.

In the second problem faced by Peter Martyr, namely, that some "dare to say" that Christ in the one cause included equal and worse causes, there is no doubt that he has in mind Zwingli's interpretation. He refers to the case of manslaughter, Paul's exception, the exceptions made by Christian emperors, and the general agreement that impotence and desertion are valid reasons for divorce, which are mentioned by those who substantiate the above interpretation. It will be remembered that these are the main arguments used by Zwingli. But Peter Martyr's assertion is: "And yet neuertheless Christ excepted onelie the cause of adulterie."[149] Having further referred to the many exceptions for allowing divorce made by the popes and emperors, he agrees that "it appeereth, that it was not so straitlie judged, that the same onlie

---

[146] Martyr, *Common Places*, p. 459, par. 57.
[147] Martyr, *Common Places*, p. 463, par. 66.
[148] Martyr, *Common Places*, p. 464, par. 67.
[149] Martyr, *Common Places*, p. 458, par. 54.

cause, which Christ dooth expresse, maketh a diuorse"[150]. However, "this (as I have declared) is the opinion of some, which although it be not wicked, and perhaps it can not easilie be confuted: yet for my part, as I will all my hart imbrase those causes, which be expressed in the scriptures; so can I hardlie indure, that diuorsement should stretch beyond these bonds"[151]. This seems to suggest that Peter Martyr in his heart of hearts is convinced that he has proved his point, but since his exposition differs from the Zwingli-Bullinger-Bucer concept, then in an indirect way he tries by this last statement to preserve a cordial relationship with his associates in spite of exegetical differences.

When Christ permitted divorce for the cause of adultery, He had in mind more than just a separation from board and bed. The Lord spoke to the Hebrews, and they could only understand His words to mean a divorce which broke the previous marriage tie and gave permission to remarry. They asked about something they were accustomed to, and Christ's answer must be interpreted in relationship to that historical situation[152].

The contention of later Roman Catholic writers that marriage is a sacrament can be accepted only if the term is understood in its widest sense, which in other instances means holy; but then there would not only be two or seven sacraments but an infinite number. "But if thou wilt drawe the name of a sacrament to those things, which not onelie betoken spirituall things, but also are vsed to be doone by certeine words, and of which there is a commandement extant, that they should be doone: in this sense thou canst not appoint matrimonie [to be a sacrament]." The unity between Christ and the Church cannot prove that the tie between husband and wife can under no circumstances be severed for Christ "made a diuorse from the synagog, and hath coupled our church vnto him". The words: "What therefore God hath joined together, let not man put asunder," are not made void by a divorce according to God's word, for in such cases "it is God which divideth, and not men: forsomuch as he, by his word, hath giuen this power"[153].

At great length Peter Martyr treats the history of punishment for adultery[154] and finds that among the Hebrews and the heathen nations capital punishment was enforced, but later Roman law and canon law were more lenient. His own conviction is that the death penalty ought to be used. He admits "that those ciuill lawes, giuen by

[150] Martyr, *Common Places*, p. 458, par. 54.
[151] Martyr, *Common Places*, p. 458, par. 55.
[152] Martyr, *Common Places*, p. 459, par. 58.
[153] Martyr, *Common Places*, p. 462, par. 63, 64.
[154] Martyr, *Common Places*, pp. 482–95.

Moses, doo no more bind vs than the ceremoniall doo. The ceremonies tooke effect till the comming of Christ. The ciuill lawes had their vse so long as the Common-weale did last; they were conuenient for that people". However, he says: "But I dare to take vpon me to saie, that it were conuenient, that the iustice, which is to be seene in those lawes, should not be neglected, but should be imbraced of magistrates as a profitable thing."[155] The law was no longer a "thou must" in a theocratic sense, but within the secular society it would be advisable for the magistrate to follow it. Within the sphere of the kingdom of God another law operates, namely God's grace. It has been noticed that Peter Martyr emphasizes that in the New Covenant "the spirit is more plentifull and grace more abundant". Accordingly, a Christian should be willing to endure things which were cause for divorce under the Mosaic law[156]. While he speaks about capital punishment he does not neglect to deal with the principles operating within the kingdom of Christ, for in terms of God's forgiving grace and mercy he speaks at some length about reconciliation of husband and wife, even after adultery has been committed[157].

In his exegesis of the divorce texts Peter Martyr follows the pattern of the Lutheran theologians rather than that of Bullinger and Bucer in his work *De Regno Christi*. This he does in spite of his close association with both men.

John Calvin

The denial of marriage as a sacrament has a prominent place in Calvin's discussion of matrimony and is the main item dealt with in his section on marriage in the *Institutes of the Christian Religion*[158]. His contention is that only when the correctness of this denial is understood, could his exegesis of the divorce texts be appreciated. The

---

[155] Martyr, *Common Places*, p. 495, par. 38.
[156] Martyr, *Common Places*, p. 457, par. 52.
[157] Martyr, *Common Places*, pp. 495—97.
[158] In his first edition, *Christianae Religionis Institutio*, 1536, Calvin makes a denunciatory attack on the Roman Catholic sacramental concept including the one *de matrimonio*. His treatment of the latter is retained unaltered in the later editions except for minor changes in wording. In the later editions the title was altered to read: *Institutio Christianae Religionis*. For Calvin's discussion *de matrimonio* in the 1536 edition see Calvin, *Corpus Reformatorum*, I. 192 ff.; ed. 1539—1554 see *Corp. Reform.*, I. 1097 ff.; ed. 1559 see *Corp. Reform.*, II. 1089 ff. Translation according to John Calvin, *Institutes of the Christian Religion*, II, Grand Rapids, Mich., 1957, 646—49.

assertion that marriage is a sacrament because it "is a good and holy ordinance of God", is confuted by the fact that "agriculture, architecture, shoemaking, and shaving, are lawful ordinances of God; but they are not sacraments". In order to institute a sacrament it is required, "not only that it be a work of God, but that it be an external ceremony appointed by God to confirm a promise. That there is nothing of the kind in marriage, even children can judge". To the argument that it is a sign of a sacred thing, Calvin replies: "If by the term sign they understand a symbol set before us by God to assure us of our faith, they wander widely from the mark. If they mean merely a sign because it has been employed as a similitude", then all the parables in the New Testament will be so many sacraments.

It is equally wrong to use the words of Paul, Ephesians v. 32, to adduce that the name of sacrament is given to marriage, since the text only speaks about the spiritual unity between Christ and His Church as "a great mystery". What actually has misled the Roman Catholic Church is the word sacrament. They "have been deceived by the doubtful signification of a Latin word, or rather by their ignorance of the Greek language. If the simple fact had been observed, that the word used by Paul is Mystery, no mistake would ever have occurred". This error is clearly revealed by the fact that in 1 Timothy III. 9, 16, and Ephesians III. 9, the Vulgate translates the same Greek word as *mystery*. Another contradiction, observed by Calvin, is that marriage had been deprecated by the Church in comparison with celibacy. "How absurd is it to debar priests from a sacrament!"[159]

In terms similar to those already expressed, Calvin refutes the sacramental concept of marriage as expressed in the *Augsburg Interim Declaration of Religion*. He points out that the error of the sacramental idea leads to another, namely that marriage is not dissolved on account of adultery, but is only a separation from board and bed. This is a perversion of Christ's words and should be considered a serious fault, since it involves the salvation of husbands who dismiss their adulterous wives. Calvin writes:

Our impartial moderators bind them to a perpetual celibacy. What if they need a wife? No help for it; they must just fret on and atone for another's crime with the destruction of their soul. Thus a Christian man will be forced either to cherish adultery and swallow the dishonour of an unchaste wife, or be cruelly subjected to perpetual disquietude, if the gift of continence be not

---

[159] Calvin, *Institutes*, II. IV. XIX. 646—49. See also Calvin's exposition of Ephesians v. 32 in Calvin, *Corp. Reform.*, LI. 226—27; Translation according to *Commentaries on the Epistles of Paul to Galatians and Ephesians*, Grand Rapids, Mich., 1948, pp. 322—26.

bestowed upon him. While they provide so ill for miserable consciences, shall we aid their inhuman tyranny by their assent?[160]

How Calvin understood Christ's words about divorce, as compared with the interpretation of the other Protestant theologians, is made evident from his commentary on a harmony of the synoptic Gospels and his comments on 1 Corinthians VII[161]. His interpretation comes close to Luther's but in the practical application of his exegesis he is more rigid. This is no doubt due to the rather theocratic nature of the government of Geneva, where Christ's logia on divorce is considered as law.

The outcome of Christ's discussion with the Pharisees was that "a fixed law was laid down as to the sacred and indissoluble bond of marriage". It is not a new law, since Christ took it "for granted that, when God at first instituted marriage, he established a perpetual law, which ought to remain in force till the end of the world. And if the institution of marriage is to be reckoned an inviolable law, it follows that whatever swerves from it does not arise from its pure nature, but from the depravity of men"[162].

The primeval creation of matrimony, in which God joined man and wife so they became "one flesh", is assumed by Christ "as an admitted principle ... and therefore he who divorces his wife tears from him, as it were, the half of himself. But nature does not allow any man to tear in pieces his own body"[163]. The marriage tie is more sacred than the bond which unites parents and children, and it is to remain inviolate[164]. In its origin marriage is a divine institution, and "among the offices pertaining to human society, this is the principal, and as it were the most sacred"[165].

---

[160] John Calvin, "Vera Christianae Pacificationis et Ecclesiae Reformandae Ratio", printed in Calvin, *Corp. Reform.*, VII. 640. Translation according to John Calvin, *Tracts and Treatises*, III, Grand Rapids, Mich., 1958, 189—343.

[161] Calvin's expositions of the New Testament divorce texts are found in *Corpus Reformatorum*, LXXIII. 180 (Matthew v. 32); LXXXIII. 527—33 (Matthew XIX. 3—11; Mark x. 2—12); XLIX. 400—427 (1 Corinthians VII). Translation according to John Calvin, *Commentary on a Harmony of the Evangelists, Matthew, Mark, and Luke*, I—II, Grand Rapids, Mich., 1949. John Calvin, *Commentary on the Epistles of Paul the Apostle to the Corinthians*, I, Grand Rapids, Mich., 1948.

[162] Calvin, *Commentary on Matthew, Mark, and Luke*, II. 378, 381.

[163] Calvin, *Commentary on Matthew, Mark, and Luke*, II. 378. See also p. 380.

[164] Calvin, *Commentary on Matthew, Mark, and Luke*, I. 293; II. 378—79, 383. *Commentary on Corinthians*, I. 238.

[165] See Calvin's exposition of Genesis II. 24, *Corp. Reform.*, XXIII. 50—51; translation according to Calvin, *Commentaries on the First Book of Moses called Genesis*, I, Grand Rapids, Mich., 1948, 136.

The law which Christ laid down in his discussion with the Pharisees took also into consideration the question regarding the "liberty of divorce" as practised by them. It "was settled" by Christ's endorsing one exception for divorce; namely, that of fornication or adultery. "The bond of marriage is too sacred to be dissolved at the will, or rather at the licentious pleasure, of men. Though the husband and the wife are united by mutual consent, yet God binds them by an indissoluble tie, so that they are not afterwards at liberty to separate. An exception is added, "except on the account of fornication"[166]. It should be noticed that while marriage is established by mutual consent, it cannot be absolved by the same.

Reference is made to "those who search for other reasons" for divorce than adultery. Such "ought justly to be set at nought, because they choose to be wise above the heavenly teacher". Sickness, even leprosy and whatever calamity there may come, does not justify divorce. Here Calvin no doubt has in mind the interpretation of Zwingli, Bullinger, and Bucer. Referring to those who have a different view from his own, Calvin expresses his own conservative position:

> They say that leprosy is a proper ground for divorce, because the contagion of the disease affects not only the husband, but likewise the children. For my own part, while I advise a religious man not to touch a woman afflicted with leprosy, I do not pronounce him to be at liberty to divorce her. If it be objected, that they who cannot live unmarried need a remedy, that they may not be burned, I answer, that what is sought in opposition to the word of God is not a remedy. I add too, that if they give themselves up to be guided by the Lord, they will never want continence, for they follow what he has prescribed. One man shall contract such a dislike of his wife, that he cannot endure to keep company with her: will polygamy cure this evil? Another man's wife shall fall into palsy or apoplexy, or be afflicted with some other incurable disease, shall the husband reject her under the pretence of incontinency? We know, on the contrary, that none of those who walk in their ways are ever left destitute of the assistance of the Spirit[167].

After Christ had given his explanation on marriage and divorce, the disciples' answer implied: "If the case of man be so with his wife, it is not good to marry." In his comments on this statement Calvin again underlines that as long as the wives remain chaste, the husbands "are compelled to endure everything rather than leave them". God has instituted "marriage for the general advantage of mankind, though it may be attended by some things that are disagreeable, it is not on that account to be despised. Let us therefore learn not to be

---

[166] Calvin, *Commentary on Matthew, Mark, and Luke*, II. 378; I. 293; See also II. 383.

[167] Calvin, *Commentary on Matthew, Mark, and Luke*, II. 383.

delicate and saucy, but to use with reverence the gifts of God, even if there be something in them that does not please us". It should also be kept in mind that since the fall of man "marriage began to be a medicine, and therefore we need not wonder if it have a bitter taste mixed with its sweetness". When marriage has first been entered upon then "let us hope that he [God] will give us aid should matters go contrary to our expectations"[168].

It is pointed out that in actuality Christ did not have to make any exception to the sacred and indissoluble tie of marriage, since such an exception was made superfluous by the mere fact that it had been decreed that adultery should be punished by death. The exception was given in order to secure the freedom of the innocent party, for "among a corrupt and degenerate people, this crime remained to a great extent unpunished; as, in our own day, the wicked forbearance of magistrates makes it necessary for husbands to put away unchaste wives, because adulterers are not punished". In this connection it is mentioned "that the right belongs equally and mutually to both sides, as their is a mutual and equal obligation to fidelity. For, though in other matters the husband holds the superiority, as to the marriage bed, the wife has an equal right"[169].

Calvin was strongly opposed to any form of polygamy, and he does his best to show from Scripture that even in Old Testament times it was a sin. As will be noticed later, this has a bearing upon his interpretation of Deuteronomy XXIV. 1 and Malachi II. 14, 16, and in turn upon the divorce texts of the New Testament.

When God created Eve as a wife for Adam, He gave him only one wife. "It remains, therefore, that the conjugal bond subsists between two persons only, whence it easily appears, that nothing is less accordant with the divine institution than polygamy."[170] Lamech, who introduced bigamy, was "a cruel man, destitute of all humanity". The corruption of lawful marriage proceeded from the house of Cain and Lamech "in order that polygamists might be ashamed of the example"[171]. In the story of Jacob's courtship Calvin strongly condemns both Laban and Jacob. In this connection reference is made to Malachi II with the comment: "Therefore the Lord, by Malachi, pro-

---

[168] Matthew XIX. 11; Calvin, *Commentary on Matthew, Mark, and Luke*, II. 385, 386; *Commentary on Corinthians*, I. 240.

[169] Calvin, *Commentary on Matthew, Mark, and Luke*, II. 384. See also Calvin, *Tracts and Treatises*, III. 301.

[170] Calvin's exposition of Genesis II. 24, *Corp. Reform.*, XXIII. 50–51; *Commentary on Genesis*, I. 136.

[171] Calvin's exposition of Genesis IV. 19, *Corp. Reform.*, XXIII. 50–51; *Commentary on Genesis*, I. 136.

nounces divorce to be made more tolerable than polygamy."[172] Abraham might have been excused as he was not motivated by lust but sought to fulfil God's promise. Yet, he had to send Hagar away with her son, and he suffered great heartache[173].

The question ought to be asked: Did Calvin remain consistent to his interpretation of only one cause for divorce? The answer is: in practice, no, but from an exegetical and theological point of view, yes. He admits three other grounds, namely, impotence, extreme religious incompatibility, and desertion. The *Ecclesiastical Ordinances*, first proposed in 1545, but adopted by the Little and Large Councils, 1561, mention these three causes together with the one of adultery[174]. His permission for granting divorce between a believer and an unbeliever is based, as would be expected, upon 1 Corinthians VII. 15. Calvin strongly expresses the two points involved in the Pauline permission. "The first is, that the believing party ought not to withdraw from the unbelieving party, and ought not to seek divorce, unless she is put away. The second is, that if an unbeliever put away his wife on account of religion, a brother or a sister is, by such rejection, freed from the bond of marriage." In other words the wife has been driven away by the husband, because of the latter's hatred to God, and she is thus deserted. The Pauline exception thus includes desertion. Theologically the Apostle's allowance is justified by the fact that

... he sets at liberty a believing husband, who is prepared to dwell with an unbelieving wife, but is rejected by her, and in like manner a woman who is, without any fault on her part, repudiated by her husband; for in that case the unbelieving party makes a divorce with God rather than with his or her partner. There is, therefore, in this case a special reason, inasmuch as the first and chief bond is not merely loosed, but even utterly broken through[175].

A practical illustration of the Pauline exception is the case of Galeazzo Caraccioli, Marquis of Vico in Naples, to whom Calvin dedicated his commentary on 1 Corinthians. Accepting the Protestant faith, he had to leave his estate, wife, and children on account of the Inquisition and came to Geneva in 1551. His wife, being a Catholic, declined to follow him after several invitations. Even when a place of residence was found, where both could practise their religion, she

---

[172] Calvin's exposition of Genesis XXIX. 27, *Corp. Reform.*, XXIII. 403–04; *Commentary on Genesis*, II. 133.

[173] Calvin's exposition of Genesis XXI. 14, *Corp. Reform.*, XXIII. 303–04; *Commentary on Genesis*, I. 547–48.

[174] Calvin, "Ordonnances", *Corp. Reform.*, X. 110–14.

[175] Calvin, *Commentary on Corinthians*, I. 240, 244. See also I. 241, 244, 245.

refused. Then Caraccioli's marriage was dissolved and he remarried in 1560[176].

Calvin, like Luther, considered marriage to have as its primary purpose procreation, and since the Fall to provide a medicine against fornication[177]. While the wife was given as a helpmate for the husband, Calvin does not speak about marriage as a mutual companionship as Bullinger and Bucer do. Therefore, in the very nature of matrimony, a marriage properly considered has never been established where one of the partners cannot render the conjugal duty. Consequently in such a case there cannot be a divorce in the proper sense of the word. The first provision in the *Ordinances* for the dissolution of marriage mentions such an annulment.

For what causes a marriage may be declared null:
If it happens that a woman complains that he who has taken her in marriage is malformed by nature, being unable to have intercourse with his wife, and this is proved true by confession or examination, the marriage shall be declared null. The wife shall be declared free and the man forbidden to misuse any woman further.

Likewise, if the man complains of not being able to cohabit with his wife because of some fault in her body, and she does not wish to permit it to be remedied, after the truth of the matter has been found out the marriage shall be declared null[178].

Turning to the question of why Moses had allowed a letter of divorce, Calvin answers that he gave this permission as a restraining power because of the wickedness of the people, but the sad fact was that "the Jews falsely imagined that they discharged their whole duty toward God, when they kept the law in a national manner, so whatever the national law did not forbid, they foolishly supposed to be lawful". It should be understood that "national laws are sometimes accommodated to the manners of men: but God, in prescribing a spiritual law, looked not at what men can do, but at what they ought to do. It contains a perfect and entire righteousness, though we want ability to fulfil it". Thus Moses "did not lay down a law about divorces, so as to give them the seal of his approbation, but as the wickedness of men could not be restrained in any other way, he applied what was the most admissible remedy, that the husband should, at least, attest to the chastity of his wife". The letter of divorce thus became "a sort of testimonial of freedom, so that the woman was afterwards free from

---

[176] John T. McNeill, *The History and Character of Calvinism*, New York, 1957, p. 184.

[177] Calvin, *Commentary on Corinthians*, I. 221, 225.

[178] Calvin, "Ordonnances", *Corp. Reform.*, X. 110.

the yoke and power of the husband". Calvin sees in the granting of divorce the application of the principle of the two kingdoms, as "political and outward order is widely different from spiritual government"[179]. When Calvin's comments on the letter of divorce, as recorded in the Gospels, are brought into relationship with his comments on Deuteronomy xxiv. 1 and Malachi ii. 14, then it appears that his exegesis on this point is somewhat different from those theologians' already considered.

The pivot around which Calvin's interpretation of the two mentioned texts moves, is the opinion that God in view of the sacredness and indissolubility of marriage preferred divorce "to polygamy, since it would be a more tolerable condition to be divorced than to bear with a harlot and a rival". In other words Calvin's concept seems to be that the permission to issue a letter of divorce is not given just so that a man, because he hates his wife, can send her away, but that the letter of divorce includes and cannot be separated from the most likely possibility or already accomplished fact that he has sought conjugal relationship with another. Since God had only meant one wife for each man, then of two evils divorce was to be preferred to polygamy. At the same time the wife was not obliged to live under intolerable circumstances so contrary to the original marriage institution, but she was free. The husband, who wrote the letter, made himself an adulterer by signing it, because he had dissolved a sacred and inviolable bond. His wife was free because of the husband's adultery. These points seem to be the arguments in Calvin's interpretation of Deuteronomy xxiv. 1, thus harmonizing this text with Christ's words of only one exception[180].

In his comments on Deuteronomy xxiv. 1 Calvin makes reference to Malachi ii. 14. In the interpretation of this text he clarifies what has appeared to be his understanding of the letter of divorce. For several of the interpreters, which have been or will be considered, the words of Malachi corroborate the interpretation of Deuteronomy xxiv. 1. On this point Calvin is in agreement with Zwingli and Bullinger but not with their interpretation. His emphasis is again placed upon the sacredness of marriage. The violation of the marriage pledge destroys "the very order of nature; for there can be ... no chastity in social life except the bond of marriage be preserved, for marriage, so to speak, is the fountain of mankind". It is "superior to all human

---

[179] For the discussion of the letter of divorce see: Calvin, *Commentary on Matthew, Mark, and Luke*, I. 292; II. 381—82.

[180] Calvin's exposition of Deut. xxiv. 1—4, *Corp. Reform.*, XXIV. 657—58; translation according to Calvin, *Commentaries on the Four Last Books of Moses Arranged in the Form of a Harmony*, III, Grand Rapids, Mich., 1950, 93—94.

contracts", and its tie "is indeed in all cases inviolable". He applies the question of the Prophet Malachi to the creation, "Has God not made one?", when God could have given Adam two or three wives, but he gave him only one. In his comments on the original marriage institution as recorded in Genesis II, Calvin refers to Malachi II. 14 to show that this Prophet recognized the first institution to be "a perpetual and inviolable law"[181]. Since Calvin's interpretation of Malachi is significant for the understanding of his exegesis of the divorce texts, the following statement must be quoted at length.

But before we proceed farther, we must bear in mind his [Malachi's] object, which was, to break down all those frivolous pretences by which the Jews sought to cover their perfidy. He says, that in marriage we ought to recognise an ordinance divinely appointed, or, to speak more distinctly, that the institution of marriage is a perpetual law, which it is not right to violate: there is therefore no cause for men to devise for themselves various laws, for God's authority is here to be regarded alone; and this is more clearly explained in Matt. XIX. 8; where Christ, refuting the objection of the Jews as to divorce, says, 'From the beginning it was not so'. Though the law allowed a bill of divorce to be given to wives, yet Christ denies this to be right, — by what argument? even because the institution was not of that kind; for it was, as it has been said, an inviolable bond. So now our Prophet reasons, Has not God made one? that is, 'consider within yourselves whether God, when he created man and instituted marriage, gave many wives to one man? By no means. Ye see then that spurious and contrary to the character of a true and pure marriage is everything that does not harmonise with its first institution'[182].

Calvin thus brings together Malachi and Christ by pointing out that they both refer to the original marriage estate. As Christ, so also the Prophet sought to call "the attention of the Jews to the true character of marriage". In no way whatsoever does Calvin refer to a letter of divorce for reasons other than adultery. Through the Prophet "God compares polygamy and divorce" and he says "that polygamy is the worse and more detestable crime". The following statement confirms the suggestion regarding Calvin's understanding of the letter of divorce.

---

[181] Calvin's exposition of Deut. XXIV. 1, *Corp. Reform.*, XXIV. 658; *Commentaries on Four Last Books of Moses*, III. 94. Calvin's exposition of Gen. I. 27, *Corp. Reform.*, XXIII. 28; *Commentary on Genesis*, I. 97. Calvin's exposition of Malachi II. 14—15, *Corp. Reform.*, XLIV. 452, 454; John Calvin, *Commentaries on the Twelve Minor Prophets*, V, Grand Rapids, Mich., 1950, 552, 553, 557.

[182] Calvin's exposition of Malachi II. 15, *Corp. Reform.*, XLIV. 454, *Commentaries on the Minor Prophets*, V. 556—57.

This then is the reason why the Prophet now says, If thou hatest, dismiss; not that he grants indulgence to divorce, as we have said, but that he might by this circumstance enhance the crime; and hence he adds, For he covers by a cloak his violence. Some interpreters take violence here for spoil or prey, and think that the wife is thus called who is tyrannically compelled to remain with an adulterer, when yet she sees a harlot in her house, by whom she is driven from her conjugal bed: but this is too strained and too remote from the letter of the text. The Prophet here, I doubt not, shakes off from the Jews their false mask, because they thought that they could cover over their vice by retaining their first wives[183].

Insisting upon the indissolubility of the marriage tie, Calvin states: "We indeed know that repudiation, properly speaking, had never been allowed by God; for though it was not punished under the law, yet it was not permitted." To this statement the editor of Calvin's English translation has made the remark, that in view of Deuteronomy xxiv. 1 and Matthew xix. 9, it "is not strictly correct"[184]. Read in its context and with Calvin's full discussion in mind, the above statement made by him rather confirms the suggestion already made that even among the Israelites only one cause for divorce was allowed. Seen in the light of Calvin's interpretation of the two texts under discussion, Christ's answer to the Pharisees regarding "the liberty of divorce", which they thought Moses allowed, must be understood in the following way: because of the circumstances Moses had been compelled to allow divorce, but it was implied that it was only granted for adultery. The plausibility of this conclusion is substantiated by the following. Calvin's statement "that repudiation, properly speaking, had never been allowed by God", was not a slip as has been suggested, but must be accounted for by the emphasis he places upon the primeval institution as a perpetual law, and that the question of divorce does not belong to the kingdom of God. However, in the same context he agrees that the Prophet allowed divorce, but no mention is made of reasons other than adultery. Calvin was opposed to the Zwingli-Bullinger concept that Christ's exception covered causes other than adultery. They based this concept partly upon their interpretation of Deuteronomy xxiv and Malachi ii, asserting that divorce was permitted for a certain justifiable hatred. Calvin's exposition of Malachi ii clearly indicates his opposition to this interpretation.

---

[183] Calvin's exposition of Malachi ii. 16, *Corp. Reform.*, XLIV. 457; *Commentaries on the Minor Prophets*, V. 560–61.

[184] Calvin, *Corp. Reform.*, XLIV. 456; *Commentaries on the Minor Prophets*, V. 559.

Theodore Beza

In the exegesis of the texts under consideration the relationship between Calvin and Beza is comparable to that between Zwingli and Bullinger. Beza is guided by the same motives as his predecessor and applies the hermeneutical principles of the latter. He systematizes and amplifies the exegetical results of Calvin.

Beza's annotations to his Greek and Latin New Testament show great erudition and are the primary source for examining his exegesis; the Greek text, Beza's translation, and the Vulgate are printed in three parallel columns. The first edition was printed in 1565 and republished in 1571. A new and enlarged edition was printed in 1582; the title page names it "tertia editio"[185]. The latter was reprinted several times[186]. The second source for an understanding of Beza's concept of divorce is a treatise written on this subject, 1567, and referred to in his *Annotations* of 1582[187].

Commentary on the New Testament

The question about capital punishment for adultery has a direct bearing upon Beza's interpretation of the divorce texts. In his interpretation of Matthew v. 32 he expresses himself to the effect that the exception mentioned by Christ was added, because at that time the observation of the law of stoning for adultery had been neglected by the Jews, otherwise the exception would have been needless[188]. Beza expresses the same thought in his exegesis of the other divorce texts, except in Mark, where he observes however that Moses did not give a precept for putting away wives but rather provided for wives against the husbands' hardness of heart[189]. Since adultery was punished by death, then there was actually no reason to mention an exception, as is the case in the rendering given by Luke. His opinion is that the same law should still be applied, "then there would be no place for this question of divorce among Christians"[190]. Beza's basic understanding of the logia on divorce could therefore be thus defined: The marriage tie is indissoluble and divorce is not allowed; however, an ex-

---

[185] Theodore Beza, *Nouum Testamentum ... Annotationes*, n. p., 1582.

[186] For a list and description of Beza's works see: Heinrich Heppe, *Theodor Beza. Leben und ausgewählte Schriften*, printed in *Leben und ausgewählte Schriften der Väter und Begründer der reformirten Kirche*, Elberfeld, 1861, VI.

[187] Beza, *Annotationes*, part I. 121 (1 Corinthians VII. 10).

[188] Beza, *Annotationes*, part I. 23 (Matthew v. 32).

[189] Beza, *Annotationes*, part I. 176 (Mark x. 5).

[190] Beza, *Annotationes*, part I. 283 (Luke XVI. 18).

ception is made in the case of adultery because the civil authorities do not apply the law of capital punishment. Theoretically there is really no divorce, as the adulterer should be considered as dead.

The meaning of law, as used within the framework of his theocratic or bibliocratic concepts, led him to the same interpretation. Commenting on the letter of divorce in Matthew XIX, he makes the following observation: "Civil laws, if they have been well constituted, prescribe nothing which God prohibits, and prohibit nothing which God prescribes, but by the wickedness of men many things up to now are allowed to pass which cannot be completely justified, and these are the things which are said to be permitted by the laws."[191] The implication is that "these things" are actually not permitted by law. This point is illustrated with reference to usury, which Christian charity prohibits, but which, on account of commerce, many magistrates cannot see themselves prohibiting. The question is asked: "Can then usury be legalized with good conscience?" The answer is: "Assuredly it can hardly be lawful. Rules of conscience should be sought, not from civil laws, but from the word of God."[192] With this illustration in mind Beza turns to the question of divorce laws, saying: "So in fact the Lord, condensing civil laws through Moses, did not allow divorce, for that would have been contrary to Himself."[193] Beza, in common with the other Reformed theologians, seeks to harmonize Christ's logia on divorce with the Mosaic lawgiving, but Beza, as did Calvin, derives a strict concept from both. However, he states: "But for those for whom it was impossible to keep their wives, he prescribed that they should give a bill of divorce." But this permission was not considered as a law for "doubtless it was advised as a counter against the hardness and cruelty of husbands". Furthermore, in the eyes of God such husbands were considered as adulterers[194]. Thus Beza harmonizes Deuteronomy XXIV. 1 with Christ's logia on divorce, and so doing he follows the hermeneutical principles of Calvin.

In 1 Corinthians VII. 11 Paul does not speak about legitimate divorce[195]. In verse fifteen the subject is desertion of an unbeliever who has no intention of returning. Beza expresses his disagreement with those who think that Paul expressed a second cause for divorce in this verse. "Nor in fact did Paul (as some think) while he so spoke, add anything to the dictum of Christ, Who made adultery the only cause for divorce. In this statement neither did he grant divorce to anyone,

---

[191] Beza, *Annotationes*, part I. 87 (Matthew XIX. 8).
[192] Beza, *Annotationes*, part I. 87 (Matthew XIX. 11).
[193] Beza, *Annotationes*, part I. 87 (Matthew XIX. 11).
[194] Beza, *Annotationes*, part I. 87 (Matthew XIX. 11).
[195] Beza, *Annotationes*, part II. 114 (1 Corinthians VII. 11).

but the person who deserts is condemned, and the one who is deserted is given counsel, who not only did not seek divorce but even tried very much to avert it."[196] For a further discussion of the divorce texts Beza makes reference to his treatise on divorce[197], which is examined in the following paragraphs.

Tractatio De Repudiis et Divortiis

In his treatise on divorce Beza seeks to prove the exegetical and theological correctness of the proposition "that marriage can rightly and with good conscience be dissolved by adultery on account of Christ's words on the subject"[198]. At the same time he presents the basic arguments brought against it. Since he is a third generation Protestant theologian his presentation of the various pros and cons becomes to some degree a summary of the exegetical arguments brought forth during more than half a century.

Christ's words, "and whosoever shall marry her that is divorced committeth adultery", were used as an argument against divorce by suggesting that "if the bond may be completely dissolved, a man of this kind cannot be said to commit adultery". Beza replies: "Exception assigned to the first member [see the first part of the verse] is added also to the latter. For if a man dismisses his wife without the excuse of adultery causes her to commit adultery, it follows that he whose wife has been put away because of adultery does not cause her to commit adultery."[199] In the same connection Beza meets the objection that the exception is not mentioned by Mark and Luke, with the common Protestant answer that the shorter rendering should be explained by the longer, since Christ does not contradict Himself.

While the indissolubility of the marriage tie is confirmed by Christ's words, "What therefore God hath joined together, let not man put asunder", Beza denies that they apply to divorce for adultery. The law of capital punishment and Christ's exception make God, and not man, the author of divorce for adultery[200]. In Romans VII. 2–3 Paul does not discuss divorce and its causes but points out that a widow can with good conscience remarry[201]. Paul does not bring the question of divorce for adultery into connection with 1 Corinthians VII. 10–11, but speaks here only about disagreements which happen

---

[196] Beza, *Annotationes*, part II. 115 (1 Corinthians VII. 15).
[197] Beza, *Annotationes*, part II. 114 (1 Corinthians VII. 10).
[198] Theodore Beza, *Tractatio De Repvdiis et Divortiis*, Geneva, 1573, p. 178.
[199] Matthew v. 32; Beza, *De Divortiis*, p. 179.
[200] Beza, *De Divortiis*, p. 180.   [201] Beza, *De Divortiis*, p. 181.

because of dissensions and quarrels[202]. Some think that in every instance a second marriage should be classified as polygamy, but in the case of adultery this could not be so as the adulterer should be considered as nonexistent[203]. Marriage is a sacrament only when understood in the widest meaning of the word, and can therefore not be included among the invisible signs of grace[204]. Accordingly, the sacramental concept of marriage is not a valid reason for denying remarriage in the case of divorce for adultery. Even though it is true that Fabiola did penance, and the canons denied remarriage, Beza's reply is: "There were many blemishes in the very old Canons to which that dictum of the Apostle must be opposed: 'He who is not able to contain, let him marry.'"[205] The severity of these canons was not accepted by all, since Origen, Ambrose, and Jerome excused marriages of this kind[206]. Beza concludes these observations by restating his basic opinion that the adulterer should be punished by the magistrate, "then no place was left for these questions"[207].

The axiom of 1 Corinthians VII. 15 is that the term bondage expresses the obligations of marriage[208]. When it is therefore said that the believer is not "under bondage", then it is understood that he is released from these obligations. This however does not invalidate Christ's words regarding adultery as being the only exception. Neither should it be defined, as some do, as an additional reason for divorce, justified by the fact that Christ Himself spoke through Paul. Beza writes: "I prefer to answer that nothing was absolutely added by Paul to the dictum of Christ."[209] Two points are brought forward by Beza in order to validate this assertion. Christ was asked about marriage by the Jews who, through their circumcision, held the same profession of faith. He did not deal with unequal marriages. Since Paul spoke about the latter he did not add anything to Christ's reply[210]. The main reason presented in order to substantiate this interpretation is that the faithful spouse was not allowed to divorce the unfaithful. It was the faithful partner who was deserted by one who had no intention of returning. Beza's conclusion is the same as that expressed by Luther and Calvin. He says: "How can any fault be found in her, who is definitely rejected because of hatred to the true religion? Hence it was evidently iniquitous for the dismissed person to bear the blame of the impious deserter, as if she remains yoked to the arbitrament of the impious deserter."[211] Regarding the same he further writes: "It is

---

[202] Beza, *De Divortiis*, p. 182.
[203] Beza, *De Divortiis*, p. 183.
[204] Beza, *De Divortiis*, p. 184.
[205] Beza, *De Divortiis*, p. 184.
[206] Beza, *De Divortiis*, pp. 184—86.
[207] Beza, *De Divortiis*, p. 193.
[208] Beza, *De Divortiis*, p. 215.
[209] Beza, *De Divortiis*, p. 216.
[210] Beza, *De Divortiis*, p. 217.
[211] Beza, *De Divortiis*, p. 218.

not a question as to whether divorce should be sought, but whether after divorce has been illegitimately made by the unbeliever, it would be lawful for the believer to follow the dictates of conscience... What if the unbeliever desert the believer? It will be imputed to the unbeliever (says the Apostle) that he is an adulterer if he consorts with another person, though not legitimately divorced."[212]

Examining the exegesis of Calvin it was noticed that he brought the letter of divorce and also 1 Corinthians VII. 15 into relationship with adultery. Likewise, Beza does not think of desertion by the unbeliever without the latter having "consort with another person". Thus understood it is again confirmed that Paul does not add to the words of Christ. Furthermore, there was no reason why so many should be offended by this teaching, since the canonists themselves do not prohibit new marriages in case of desertion[213]. In his discussion of desertion Beza reveals a conservative view concerning remarriage. For example, if an absentee did not desert with an evil mind, the Church of Geneva had decreed that the deserted person should lament not merely for five years but for a full ten year period[214]. Beza's strict view is also applied when it comes to the question whether civil law can allow other causes for divorce than those expressed in God's word. It has been noticed how other reformers refer to the civil laws of the Christian emperors in order to justify divorce for other reasons than adultery, either within the sphere of the kingdom of the world, as Luther did, or within a theocracy, as done by Bullinger and Bucer. Beza's reply is: "I strongly oppose this."[215] The reason why the magistrate is obliged to intervene in the case of divorce, is that the exception of adultery mentioned by Christ actually should have suffered capital punishment[216].

Having stated that the laws of divorce must be sought in the word of God alone[217], he asks two questions where the answers are implied and confirmed by the statements already made. First, "But I ask whether, if at the universal forum of conscience, there can by human laws be any excuse for straying one iota outside the word of God". Next, "Whether in fact it can be right for the magistrates in anything to go beyond the law of Moses?"[218] Beza realizes that bishops of old did not oppose the imperial laws, and many during his own time favoured these laws, but in the light of his exegesis his own opinion is: "It is not a question as to what was done, but what should be done."[219] In a final observation he no doubt has in mind the Zwingli-

---

[212] Beza, *De Divortiis*, pp. 226, 227.
[213] Beza, *De Divortiis*, pp. 227–28.
[214] Beza, *De Divortiis*, p. 242.
[215] Beza, *De Divortiis*, p. 243.
[216] Beza, *De Divortiis*, p. 245.
[217] Beza, *De Divortiis*, p. 245.
[218] Beza, *De Divortiis*, p. 246.
[219] Beza, *De Divortiis*, p. 247.

Bucer interpretation. He writes: "Finally I say it is false that any crime can be found which is equal to adultery, nor yet worse ... Anyone can be idolatrous, a heretic, impious, and yet remain a valid husband. But no one can be an adulterer and a husband, that is to be one flesh of two kinds."[220]

---

[220] Beza, *De Divortiis*, p. 249.

IV. English Expositors

Early English Reformers

William Tyndale, Thomas Cranmer, and John Hooper had a common fate in that they all suffered martyrdom during the early phase of the English Reformation. Tyndale died as a martyr on the Continent, 1536, two years after Cranmer had been enthroned as Archbishop in Canterbury. Hooper died by fire for his Protestant faith in 1555 and Cranmer likewise the following year. While they had martyrdom in common, their life experiences were different, making their individual contributions to the English Reformation distinct and representative of the various avenues through which reform was accomplished. Tyndale sought to smuggle the tenets of the Reformation into England from exile. Cranmer, in his subservience to Henry VIII, only moved as far as the latter allowed. Hooper, on the dissolution of the monasteries and the issuing of the repressive Six Articles, 1539, left England and first returned permanently from Zürich in the beginning of Edward's reign. In many respects he became the first Puritan divine. In the writings of these three men the history of the interpretation of the divorce texts during the reigns of Henry VIII and Edward VI is illustrated and made evident.

William Tyndale

Eager to make an English translation of the New Testament from the Greek, but unable to have it published in England, Tyndale sought refuge on the Continent from 1524 until his death in 1536. His translation was published in 1525, and two years later followed the treatise, *The Obedience of a Christen man, and how Christen rulers ought to governe*. Matrimony is one of the many subjects Tyndale deals with in this work.

Marriage is ordained by God to be an estate in which husband and wife mutually serve one another "with all love and kindness". It was given as a remedy against fornication and for the purpose of procreation, but it cannot be called a sacrament in view of the fact that it does not signify a promise. If marriage should be considered a sacrament because it is employed as a similitude between Christ and the Church, then all other similitudes of the New Testament would become sacraments. In the same treatise criticism is also made of the Roman Catholic impediments of relationship and of spiritual relationships. The grades and lineage are extended further than prohibited by the law of Leviticus xviii, and spiritual relationships included persons taking part in the baptism of a child[1].

The question of whether or not Henry VIII could be divorced from Catherine of Aragon because she had been his deceased brother's wife, is dealt with by Tyndale in *The Practyse of Prelates*, 1530. While Leviticus xviii. 16 forbids a person to marry his brother's wife, Deuteronomy xxv. 5 commands that if a deceased husband has no children, then the brother should marry the widow. For Tyndale it is evident that Moses only forbade a man to take his brother's wife as long as the latter was alive; consequently, Leviticus xviii. 16 gave no Scriptural justification for a divorce between Henry VIII and the Queen. Tyndale states that he is not able to find a lawful cause for divorce either by his own reasoning, in Scripture, or from learned divines. Tyndale published his opinion in the same year in which the other reformers privately answered the request made to them regarding counsel on this point. He did this so that he might discharge his conscience and in order "that any man should cast me in the teeth in time to come, when this old marriage were broken, and a new made, why I had not spoken rather [earlier]?"[2]

Tyndale's interpretation of Christ's logia on divorce is found in his exposition of the Sermon on the Mount. His exegesis is a comprehensive usage of the basic arguments used by Luther. While Moses had allowed the letter of divorce on account of extreme necessity, the Israelites had abused the law by putting away their wives for any light reason, but Christ restored the original marriage estate taking away all causes for divorce except that of adultery. By the law of Moses the adulterer was declared dead, thus the innocent party was without all question free. By bringing 1 Corinthians vii. 15 into relationship with 1 Timothy v. 8, "But if any provide not for his own, and specially for those of his own house, he hath denied the faith, and is worse than an infidel," Tyndale points out desertion as a second

---

[1] William Tyndale, *The Obedience of a Christen man, and how Christen rulers ought to governe*, printed in *Doctrinal Treatises* (Parker Society), Cambridge, 1848, pp. 254, 245.

[2] William Tyndale, *The Practyse of Prelates. Whether the kinge's grace maye be separated from hys quene, because she was his brother's wyfe*, printed in Expositions and Notes (Parker Society), Cambridge, 1849, p. 332.

cause for divorce. However, it appears that he cannot think of desertion without adultery being involved. He writes: "For what right is it that a lewd wretch should take his goods, and run from his wife without a cause, and sit by a whore, yea, and come again after a year or two (as I have known it) and rob his wife of that she hath gotten in the mean time, and go again to his whore?" If husband and wife should separate because "the one cannot suffer the other's infirmities, they must remain unmarried"[3].

Among the reformers' written statements on marriage and divorce, those of Tyndale, Bucer, and Zwingli come closest to Luther in sequence of time. For the most part Tyndale's theology reflects that of Luther, and the influence of Lutheranism, which came to England through the vehicle of Tyndale's New Testament and his other writings, included Luther's interpretation of the divorce texts.

Thomas Cranmer

Two events in which Cranmer was deeply involved mark out his interpretation of the divorce texts in a historical setting. In 1540 he understood the words of Christ to mean only separation from board and bed, but eight years later he interpreted them to mean a complete dissolution of the marriage tie.

Strype records that "it was ordinary to annul Marriages, and divide Man and Wife from each other, who it may be had lived long together, and had Children in Wedlock". Divorce was made under the "pretence of some Pre-contract or Affinity: Which by the Pope's Law required a Divorce". In other words it was the usage of the impediments, which, as it had been noticed, both Erasmus and Luther attacked, that called for a reform. "These Divorces the Arch-bishop highly disliked; and might probably have laid before the King the great Inconveniences, as well as Scandal, thereof." This led Henry VIII, 1540, to issue an act forbidding these divorce practices[4].

Cranmer was also troubled about the things he had heard from Germany regarding divorce, the possibility of a second marriage, and even bigamy. Regarding these questions he wrote a letter to Andreas Osiander, dated December 27, 1540. He introduces the letter by emphasizing the seriousness of the subject for "those who profess the truth of the Gospel". He refers to the report that the German reformers allowed the noblemen to have concubines but not the priests, and that Melanchthon had been present as a bridesman at the wed-

---

[3] William Tyndale, *An Exposition uppon the v. vi. vii. chapters of Matthew*, printed in *Expositions and Notes*, pp. 54, 55.

[4] Strype, *Memorials of Thomas Cranmer*, I. xx. 80.

ding of Philip of Hesse. However, his main concern is the permission to enter a new marriage after divorce. He writes: " ... what can possibly be alleged in your excuse when you allow a man after a divorce, while both man and woman are living, to contract a fresh marriage." Cranmer himself finds that the Scriptures are against this practice, "as will be seen from Matthew XIX., Mark X., Luke XVI., Romans VII.; 1 Cor. VII.: from which passages it is clear that, according to the institution of the apostles, and therefore of Christ himself, one person ought to be joined in matrimony with one person, and that persons so joined together cannot again contract marriage until the death of one of the parties shall have happened". The same is substantiated by the history of the Church. In other words Cranmer maintains the exegesis of the Catholic theologians. In this connection it should be remembered that Edward Lee, who had attacked the exegesis of Erasmus, was Archbishop of York from 1531 until his death in 1544[5].

During the latter part of the year 1540 Cranmer composed some questions and answers concerning the sacraments and the appointment and power of bishops and priests. In his discussion of the sacraments he denies the validity of seven sacraments: "The determinate number of seven sacraments is no doctrine of the scripture, nor of the old authors."[6] Marriage is defined in the general sense as a mystery:

> Of matrimony also I find very much in scripture, and among other things, that it is a mean whereby God doth use the infirmity of our concupiscence to the setting forth of his glory, and increase of the world, thereby sanctifying the act of carnal commixtion between the man and the wife to that use; yea, although one party be an infidel: and in this matrimony is also a promise of salvation, if the parents bring up their children in the faith, love, and fear of God[7].

During the second year of Edward VI's reign Cranmer reversed his exegesis of the divorce texts. This was occasioned by a restudy of Christ's teaching in connection with the case of William Parr as reported by Burnet[8]. William Parr, in 1547 created Marquis of Northampton, had married Anne Bourcher, daughter of the Earl of Essex. Anne was later convicted of adultery, but the divorce "according to the Law of the Ecclesiastical Courts was only a separation from Bed

---

[5] For Cranmer's letter to Osiander see: Thomas Cranmer, *Miscellaneous Writings and Letters of Thomas Cranmer* (Parker Society), Cambridge, 1846, pp. 406, 407. For Edward Lee's attack on Erasmus see pp. 27—29 above.

[6] Cranmer, *Miscellaneous Writings and Letters*, p. 115.

[7] Cranmer, *Miscellaneous Writings and Letters*, p. 116.

[8] Gilbert Burnet, *The History of the Reformation of the Church of England*, II. London, 1683, 56.

and Board". The suggestion was made that consideration should be given to what might be done to the innocent party in a divorce case. However, during the reign of Henry VIII no further decision was reached. Burnet tells us: "So in the beginning of King Edward's Reign, of the 7th. of May, a Commission was granted to the Archbishop of Canterbury ... to try whether the Lady Anne was not by the Word of God so lawfully divorced, that she was no more his Wife, and whether thereupon he might not marry another Wife. This being a new Case, and of great importance, Cranmer resolved to examine it with his ordinary diligence." As time passed and no counsel came from the commission, the Marquis entered a second marriage on January 28, 1548. The commission considered this as a "great scandal, since his first Marriage stood yet firm in Law". Defending himself Parr expressed the conviction "that by the Word of God he was discharged of his tye to his former Wife; and the making Marriages indissoluble was but a part of the Popish Law, by which it was reckoned a Sacrament". He further thought "that the condition of this Church was very hard, if upon Adulteries, the innocent must either live with the Guilty, or be exposed to temptations to the like sins, if a separation was only allowed, but the bond of the Marriage continued undissolved". Since he had married before any decision had been made by the commission, it was ordered that he should be separated from his second wife until a report was presented. This decision indicates that it was indeed a completely new concept that a second marriage should be allowed to the innocent party in the case of adultery. When the commission finally presented its report, its findings were that a second marriage was permissible. Since this report is significant in the history of the interpretation of the divorce texts in England, the exegetical arguments should be quoted at length.

Christ condemned all Marriages upon Divorces, except in the Case of Adultery; which seemed manifestly to allow them in that Case. And though this is not mentioned by St. Mark, and St. Luke, yet it is enough that St. Matthew has it. Christ also defined the state of Marriage, to be that in which two are one flesh; so that when either of the two hath broken that Union, by becoming one with another Person, then the Marriage is dissolved. And it is oft repeated in the Gospel, That married Persons have power over one anothers Bodies, and that they are to give due benevolence to each other; which is plainly contrary to this way of separation without dissolving the Bond. St. Paul putting the case of an Unbeliever departing from the Partner in Marriage, says, The Believing Party, whether Brother or Sister, is not under Bondage in such a case: which seems a discharge of the Bond in case of Desertion: and certainly Adultery is yet of a higher nature[9].

---
[9] Burnet, The *History of the Reformation of the Church of England*, II. 57.

These exegetical results reflect the influence of Luther and Erasmus especially. The main points, which were brought against them on the other side, are also mentioned together with a reply.

But against this was alledged on the other side, That our Saviours allowing Divorce in the Case of Adultery was only for the Jews, to whom it was spoken, to mitigate the cruelty of their Law, by which the Adulteress was to be put to death: and therefore he yielded Divorce in that Case, to mitigate the severity of the other Law. But the Apostle writing to the Gentile Christians, at Rome, and Corinth, said, The Wife was tied by the Law to the Husband, as long as he lived. And that other general Rule, Whom God has joyned together let no Man put asunder, seems against the dissolving the Bond. To this it was answered, That it is against separating as well as dissolving: that the Wife is tied to her Husband; but if he ceaseth to be her Husband, that tie is at an end: That our Saviour left the Wife at liberty to divorce her Husband for Adultery, though the Law of Moses had only provided, That the Adulterous Wife, and he who defiled her, were to die, but the Husband who committed Adultery was not so punishable; therefore our Saviour had by that Provision declared the Marriage to be clearly dissolved by Adultery[10].

The Ancient Fathers had also been examined and reference is made, among others, to Tertullian, Jerome, and Chrysostom, as well as to the civil laws of the Christian emperors as having allowed a second marriage. The report says that all these points "were collected by Cranmer, with several very important Reflections on most of the Quotations out of the Fathers". The findings of the commission were sent to some "learned men ... and they returned their Answer in favour of the second Marriage"[11]. Thus through a renewed study of the divorce texts and the Fathers Cranmer officially sanctioned divorce and remarriage in the case of adultery. However, it should be noticed that this permission was not granted by the ecclesiastical court to which such matters belonged. The recommendation of the royal commission, allowing William Parr to remarry, had to be sanctioned by Parliament, as the ecclesiastical court, being guided by the old canon law, could issue only a separation from board and bed.

John Hooper

While on the Continent Hooper lived in various Reformed cities. In Strassburg he met his future wife, and they were married in Basel, 1546. From March of 1547 he lived in Zürich for two years in close association with Bullinger. In spite of his friendship with Bullinger

---

[10] Burnet, *The History of the Reformation of the Church of England*, II. 57.
[11] Burnet, *The History of the Reformation of the Church of England*, II. 58.

his exegesis of the divorce texts, as found in his commentaries, resembles that of Peter Martyr and Bucer, but both of these men were indebted to Luther. Hooper's interpretation of the logia on divorce is found in connection with his comments on the Seventh Commandment. His *A Declaration of the Ten Holy Commandments of Almighty God* was first printed in a foreign edition, 1549, and the following year a new edition was published in London[12].

Having referred to Christ's words in Matthew v. 32 and xix. 9, as well as Mark x. 11—12, Hooper asserts that "Christ saith, there is no lawful cause to dissolve matrimony, but adultery". He further confirms that the act of adultery dissolves the marriage tie, and the innocent party, whether husband or wife, has the right to enter a new marriage[13]. Categorically he denies any other cause for divorce than fornication: "I will not entreat of other causes of divorcements than fornication, because my book maketh no mention of any other."[14] Regarding Christ's comments on Deuteronomy xxiv. 1, Hooper again asserts the *only-one-exception* interpretation:

> But for the frowardness of conditions, or tediousness of manners, men should not separate their wives, neither from bed, neither from board; much less marry another. He or she that cannot with wisdom amend the displeasant and crooked manners of his or her mate, must patiently bear them; remembering, if Christ command us to be of such a tolerancy and patience to endure the obloquy and injuries of all men though they be our enemies; how much more the morosity and injuries of a domestical companion! A hard cross! But patience must lighten it, till God send a redress[15].

Hooper also makes reference to the Pauline exception and explains the Apostle's word in the common Protestant way. The conclusion is therefore that "the Lord, Matt. v. xix. giveth licence for adultery to divorce and marry again; and Paul for infidelity"[16]. Hooper had expressed equality of man and woman in divorce matters, and according to his own words he met opposition on this point. The opposition may have been rather strong as he defends this position in great de-

---

[12] John Hooper, *A Declaration of the Ten Holy Commandments of Almighty God*, printed in *Early Writings of John Hooper* (Parker Society), Cambridge, 1843, pp. 249 ff. For a discussion of the various editions see p. 253.

[13] Hooper, *A Declaration of the Ten Holy Commandments, Early Writings*, pp. 378, 379, 382.

[14] Hooper, *A Declaration of the Ten Holy Commandments, Early Writings*, p. 382.

[15] Hooper, *A Declaration of the Ten Holy Commandments, Early Writings*, p. 386.

[16] Hooper, *A Declaration of the Ten Holy Commandments, Early Writings*, p. 385.

tail. Under all circumstances it indicates that he went further than many of his English colleagues[17].

The Influence of the Continental Reformers

The influence of the Continental reformers is reflected in the writings of Tyndale and Hooper, and this also includes Cranmer from the beginning of the reign of Edward VI. The various influences from the outside should be noticed in the historical evaluation of the interpretation of the English divines.

Continental Writers

Having received a copy of Erasmus' New Testament, 1516, Colet makes this comment in his reply: "Your new edition is bought with avidity, and read everywhere here. There are many that approve and admire your studies, others that disapprove and find fault."[18] Those who disapproved had the power during the reign of Henry VIII, but at the accession of Edward VII the interpretation of Erasmus came to the forefront. William Parr's self-defence and the commission's report indicate an acquaintance with Erasmus. The significance of Erasmus' influence is made evident by the fact that the English edition of the *Paraphrases* was published in London, 1548, and not long afterward followed his annotations on 1 Corinthians vii, also in English. Cranmer himself prescribed that a copy of *The Paraphrase of Erasmus* should be placed in each parish[19].

Through Tyndale the interpretation of Luther reached England in 1527, and Luther's own comments on 1 Corinthians vii, which contain a lengthy discussion of the divorce question, were translated into English, 1529[20].

The influence of Bullinger reached England directly through his own writings. *Der christliche Ehestand* was translated into English, and the first edition was printed in 1541, a year after the first German edition. Between 1541 and 1575 seven different editions were printed in England and two of these twice[21]. The influence of the volume

---

[17] Hooper, *A Declaration of the Ten Holy Commandments, Early Writings*, pp. 382–84.

[18] Nichols, *The Epistles of Erasmus*, II. 286. Epistle 411, "John Colet to Erasmus" (June 20, 1516).

[19] See p. 24 above.   [20] See p. 69 above.

[21] The book was translated into English by Miles Coverdale and prefaced by

upon English domestic-conduct books has been established[22]. In December 1586 the Convocation, under the direction of Archbishop Whitgift, issued regulations for the purpose of securing a better educated ministry. One of these prescribed that each minister should possess a copy of Bullinger's *Decades* either in Latin or in English[23].

Bucer's and Peter Martyr's personal presence in England from 1549, as a response to Cranmer's invitation, has already been mentioned. While *De Regno Christi* was first published in 1557 and Peter Martyr's commentary on 1 Corinthians in 1567, both posthumously, yet the interpretations of both men were known in England during the latter part of Edward's reign. The *Loci communes* of Peter Martyr was printed in an English translation, 1583[24]. When the Marian exiles returned in the beginning of Elizabeth's reign, many came back imbued with the theology of Geneva. Thus all the different interpretations of the divorce texts, as they have been noticed on the Continent, found their way into England.

The Reformatio Legum Ecclesiasticarum

During the year 1534, when Henry VIII made his break with Rome complete, a commission was appointed to frame a new set of ecclesiastical laws which should reverse and replace the old existing canon laws. The work seems to have been completed in 1545—46, but it never received the official sanction of the King, no doubt due to the opposition by Gardiner and other Roman Catholic bishops, who considered such an enterprise as an innovation[25]. No copy of these revised laws is

---

Thomas Becon. The printers published it in the name of the latter no doubt in order to increase the sale. For the story of the English edition see: Thomas Becon, *Early Works* (Parker Society), Cambridge, 1843, p. 29, n. 2; *Original Letters Relative to the English Reformation* (Parker Society), Cambridge, 1846—47, II. 422 ff.

[22] Alfred Weber, *Heinrich Bullingers "Christlicher Ehestand", seine zeitgenössischen Quellen und die Anfänge des Familienbuches in England.* Leipzig, 1929.

[23] Bullinger, Decades, I. VIII; V. XXVII—XXXI, XX. During the time of Whitgift there appeared three editions in English in 1577, 1584, and 1587. The Latin Decades were printed separately during the years 1549—51, and some of them were immediately translated into English. In a letter dated at London, June 6, 1566, John Abel writes to Bullinger telling him that he has received the *Decades Bullingeri* and adds: "In this book all the articles of our christian faith are fully declared and set forth, and it is comforting, and agreeable, and instructive to me to read it." "John Abel to Henry Bullinger", Letter XLIX in *The Zurich Letters*, Second Series (Parker Society), Cambridge, 1845.

[24] See p. 89 above.

[25] Strype, *Memorials of Cranmer*, I. xxx. 132—33.

in existence, but they are generally considered to be different from those formulated during the next reign, when Edward VI appointed a commission for the establishment of a new code of ecclesiastical laws. The commission was composed of thirty-two members: eight bishops, eight divines, eight laymen, and eight lawyers[26]. In letters to Bullinger written during the year 1552, Peter Martyr and Martin Micronius tell Bullinger about the work of the commission and express the hope that the new laws are expected to obtain the sanction of the Parliament and that the present opposition may be ineffectual[27]. While the report of the commission was a result of the work of the whole committee, it seems that Archbishop Cranmer and Peter Martyr carried the main responsibility[28].

The *Reformatio Legum Ecclesiasticarum* does not enter into any exegesis of the divorce texts, but the regulations laid down in the section "De Adulteriis et Divortiis" reflect the exegesis of the Continental reformers. The main points can be listed as follows: In the case of adultery the innocent party may contract a new marriage; however, reconciliation should be hoped for. No one can on his own authority divorce his wife, not even in the case of adultery. The sentence has to be given by the ecclesiastical judge. Divorce is legitimate on account of desertion, and after a period of two or three years the deserted is permitted to remarry. Deadly hatred and the offence of violent treatment can in the end bring about divorce. Small contentions are not a justifiable reason for divorce, neither can chronic ill health dissolve marriage. Separation from board and bed should be abolished, being contrary to the teaching of Scriptures[29].

The work was completed before the end of Edward's reign, and Cranmer was eager to have the reformed canon law adopted, but the record reads: "Who [Cranmer] with indefatigable Pains had been, both in this and the last King's Reign, labouring to bring this Matter about, and he did his part, for he brought the Work to perfection. But it wanted the King's Ratification, which was delayed, partly by Business, and partly by Enemies."[30] During the reign of Mary the religious situation was turned into reverse, but when Elizabeth came on the throne the report of the commission was read in Parliament, but no action was taken. The next and final step in the history of the new ecclesiastical laws took place in 1571. John Foxe, the martyrologist,

---

[26] Strype, *Memorials of Cranmer*, II. xxvi. 271; II. xxxv. 299.

[27] *Original Letters*, Letter CCXXXVI, II. 503; Letter CCLXVII, II. 580.

[28] John Foxe, ed., *Reformatio Legvm Ecclesiasticarvm*, London, 1571. Reprinted Oxford, 1850. See preface by Edward Cardwell, p. VI.

[29] Foxe, *Reformatio Legvm Ecclesiasticarvm*, pp. 50–58.

[30] Strype, *Memorials of Cranmer*, II. xxvi. 271.

was commissioned with the permission of Archbishop Parker to edit this new edition. He and other progressive reformers worked and hoped for a more thorough Reformation in line with the new ecclesiastical injunctions[31]. Foxe wrote a preface to the 1571 edition which in content was the same as the one produced by Cranmer during Edward's reign. The acceptance of these ecclesiastical laws was discussed in Parliament. "But it made no progress. The Queen, averse to all interference of the Commons in ecclesiastical matters, had conceived an especial displeasure against the individuals by whom the measure was recommended."[32] The Queen's opposition to the acceptance of the *Reformatio Legum Ecclesiasticarum* also meant, as it will be noticed, an official rejection of the Protestant interpretation of the divorce texts.

Anglican and Puritan Exposition

Before examining the interpretation of the New Testament logia on divorce from the time of the Elizabethan Settlement to John Milton at the beginning of the Puritan Revolution or the English Civil War, a few preliminary observations, which have a direct bearing upon this examination, should be made. The first deals with the preservation of the medieval canon law, and the second with the question of biblical scholarship.

The failure of replacing the old canon law with the *Reformatio Legum Ecclesiasticarum* meant that the former laws remained intact. Thus the official standard of the Church of England was the doctrine of the indissolubility of the marriage tie, and in the case of adultery only separation from board and bed was permissible. In *Of the Laws of Ecclesiastical Policy,* 1593, Richard Hooker makes no reference to divorce whatsoever, but in his discussion of marriage he mentions that man and woman "were of necessitie to bee linked with some straight and insoluble knot"[33]. In the history of the marriage institution during the period under discussion, it is recognized that the official view of the Church of England regarding divorce differed not at all from the Roman Catholic Church. Marriage matters belonged to the ecclesiastical courts, and the impediments with their loopholes remained. The state of affairs continued as it had been before, but

---

[31] For a study of John Foxe's theological and reformatory views see: Viggo Nörskov Olsen, "The Concept of the Church in the Writings of John Foxe", London, Ph. D. thesis, 1966.

[32] Foxe, *Reformatio Legvm Ecclesiasticarvm,* p. XI.

[33] Richard Hooker, *Of the Lawes of Ecclesiastical Politie,* London, 1617, V. LXXIII. 397.

alongside the old Roman Catholic practices are found the promulgation of the Protestant interpretations of the divorce texts. However, in the question as to whether or not marriage is a sacrament, a definite break was made with late medieval teaching. The Edwardian Articles or the Forty-two Articles of Religion, 1553, and the Thirty-nine Articles of 1563 and 1571, assert that there are only two sacraments ordained by Christ; the other five, including marriage, cannot be counted as sacraments of the gospel[34].

From the time of the Christian humanists an increased interest in biblical studies was manifested, and the fruitage was seen in a great number of Bible commentaries by both Catholic and Protestant scholars in the various countries on the Continent. In England no theologian of reputation produced any work of this sort. The reason for this is no doubt twofold. The combined linguistic studies of Hebrew, Greek, and Latin were almost nil in English colleges and universities as compared with the Continent. Furthermore, the struggle and controversies between Catholics and Anglicans and between the latter and the Puritans concerning basic principles and policies absorbed the energies of the theologians, the Cartwright-Whitgift controversy being a notable example[35]. The interpretation of the divorce texts can therefore not be found in commentaries but to a large degree must be sought within the polemic writings published after the failure of getting new ecclesiastical laws accepted, or after the greater hostility to the Puritan movement was manifested when Whitgift became Archbishop, 1583. It will be observed that those who justify divorce in the case of adultery limit the causes to adultery and desertion. The other reasons for divorce given in the *Reformatio Legum Ecclesiasticarum* do not seem to have been included. The interpretation of the divorce texts can thus be characterized as conservative in accordance with the general mood of the Elizabethan Settlement. However, from a theological point of view the reason is no doubt the influence of the *only-one-exception* exegesis of Calvin and Beza. From an exegetical point of view the English divines do not add anything new when compared with the Continental writers. The recording of the examination of their interpretation can therefore be confined to a comprehensive view of the general scope and aspect of its history and principles.

While the Anglican and Puritan divines opposed one another on basic policies and principles, they were united in a common front

---

[34] "The Thirty-nine Articles of Religion", art. xxv. in *Creeds of Christendom*, ed. Philip Schaff, III, New York, 1931, pp. 502–3. See also I. 614–15.

[35] For a study of the history of the Bible and commentaries, etc., during the Reformation period see the article by Basil Hall, "Biblical Scholarship: Editions and Commentaries", in *The Cambridge History of the Bible*, ed. S. L. Greenslade.

against Roman Catholicism. In the literature aginst the latter some of the divines found opportunity to advocate the Protestant interpretation of the divorce texts. The Catholic Rheims Version of the New Testament was published in 1582, and six years later the Archbishop of Colchester, George Wither, wrote *A View of the Marginal Notes of the Popish Testament* in which he criticized the former[36]. The following year a better known refutation was printed by William Fulke, Master of Pembroke Hall, Cambridge[37]. This work had been begun by Thomas Cartwright, but Fulke finished it. Fulke was one of twenty-five theologians appointed in 1582 to hold dialogues with Roman Catholics concerning points of controversy. Of the two replies Fulke's is the more comprehensive, but both assert that the act of adultery severs the marriage tie and that remarriage is then permissible. The indissolubility of marriage, as advocated by Roman Catholic theologians in the light of their interpretation of Ephesians v. 32, Romans VII. 2, 1 Corinthians VII. 10—11 and the shorter readings of Mark x. 12 and Luke XVI. 18, as over and against the exception mentioned by Matthew, is opposed by Wither and Fulke with the common Protestant exegesis.

John Raynolds, president of Corpus Christi College, Oxford, held a prominent position at the Hampton Court conference, 1603—04. He represented the Puritans and was chosen to be a member of the committee which should work on a new English translation of the Bible. He was a Greek scholar, and it is thought that he actually initiated the plan for a new version. He died in 1607, but his treatise, dealing with the interpretation of the New Testament logia on divorce, was published posthumously, 1610. The title indicates that it was written as a defence of the interpretation of the Reformed Churches. At the same time it is a confutation of a Latin treatise of Cardinal Robert Bellarmine and another one by an anonymous author. The four chapter headings point out the scope of his discourse:

The first Chapter.

The state of the question betwene the church of Rome, & the reformed churches being first declared, the truth is proved by scripture: That a man having put away his wife for her adulterie may lawfully marrie another.

---

[36] George Wither, *A View of the Marginal Notes of the Popish Testament, translated into English by the English fugitiue Papists resiant at Rhemes in France*, London [1588].

[37] William Fulke, *The Text of the New Testament of Iesvs Christ, translated ovt of the vulgar Latine by the Papists of the traiterous Seminarie at Rhemes ... Whereunto is added the Translation out of the Original Greeke, commonly vsed in the Church of England, with a Confvtation*, London, 1589.

The second Chapter.
The places of scripture alleaged by our adversaries to disprove the lawful liberty of marriage after divorcement for adulterie are proposed, examined, & proved not to make against it.

The third Chapter.
The consent of Fathers, the second pretended proofe for the Papistes doctrine in this point, is pretended falsly: & if all be weighed in an even balance, the Fathers checke it rather.

The fourth Chapter.
The conceits of reasons urged last against vs are oversights proceeding from darknesse, not from light: & reason itself, dispelling the mist of Popish probabilities, giveth cleare testimonie with the truth of Christe[38].

Raynold's treatment of the subject matter indicates that when he seeks to defend the "Ivdgment of the Reformed churches", his method is the Calvin-Beza exegesis.

In the continued controversy with Rome Francis White, Bishop of Carlisle, took an active part and wrote a reply, 1618, to Thomas Worthington, president of the English Catholic college in Douay. In his attack on the Reformation Worthington had made insinuations regarding Luther's moral concepts saying: "His lust and incontinencie is prooued by his words and confession, He giueth counsell: If the wife will not, or cannot, let the maid come." White's answer is that Worthington has divorced the statement from its context. Luther had said that if a woman denies to render the conjugal duty and after admonition continues to be obstinate, then she should be considered a kind of deserter and as such liable to be divorced. The implication seems to be that White would agree to divorce for adultery and desertion proper, but not for any other reason, for concerning the statement of Luther he writes: "Now although this opinion of his concerning diuorce, be not so iustifiable: yet the Papists do shamefully abuse him, in detorting his words to a giuing libertie to adulterie and dishonestie, which he neuer intended."[39]

Reference should be made to two authors who deal with matrimony as an institution. The first, William Perkins, 1558—1602, is mentioned by John Milton in his first discourse on divorce[40], and he seems to

---

[38] John Raynolds, *A Defense of the Iudgment of the Reformed churches. That a man may lawfullie not onelie put awaie his wife for her adulterie, but also marrie another*, London, 1610, sig. Aɪᴠ.

[39] Francis White, *The Orthodox Faith and Way to the Chvrch explaned and ivstified: In Answer to a Popish Treatise*, London, 1617, pp. 353, 354.

[40] John Milton, *The Doctrine & Discipline of Divorce Restor'd to the good of both Sexes, From the bondage of Canon Law, and other mistakes, to the true*

suggest the radical idea found in Milton, that it is permissible to divorce for grave mental incompatibility. Perkins was known for his Puritan leanings and his opposition to all Roman Catholic practices. His work, *Christian Oeconomie*, appeared in a Latin edition in 1590 and in an English translation in 1609. Perkins advocates the broader concept of divorce as expressed in the *Reformatio Legum Ecclesiasticarum*. Thus in addition to adultery, desertion, and long absence, hateful dealing is mentioned as a justifiable cause for divorce as "when dwelling together, they require of each other intolerable conditions"[41]. The second, Henry Smith, 1550—91, was likewise Puritanically inclined. He is the author of *A preparative to mariage*, in which he writes: "The disease of marriage is adultery, and the medicine heerof is Diuorcement... If they might be seperated for discord, some would make a commodotie of strife; but nowe they are not best to be contentius, for this Law will holde their noses together, til wearines make them leaue strugling, like two spaniels which are coupled in a chain, at last they learne to goe together, because they may not goe a sunder."[42]

The writings of Joseph Hall and Henry Hammond, two of John Milton's contemporaries, should be noticed as they represent the Puritan concept after Milton had presented his *radical* interpretation. They confirm the conservative Reformed exegesis of Calvin and Beza as already expressed by earlier writers.

Joseph Hall was Bishop of Exeter and Norwich from 1627 and 1641 respectively, in spite of his Puritan sympathies. In his discussion of the divorce question he makes his own position clear and at the same time challenges Milton's interpretation.

> Our Saviour hath so punctually decided the case, in his Divine Sermon upon the Mount, that I cannot but wonder at the boldness of any man, who calls himself a Christian, that dares raise a question, after so full and clear a determination from the mouth of Truth itself. Whosoever, saith he, shall put away his wife, saving for the cause of fornication, causeth her to commit adultery: and whosoever shall marry her that is divorced, committeth adultery; Matt. v. 32.

---

meaning of Scripture in the Law and Gospel compar'd. Wherin also are set down the bad consequences of abolishing or condemning of Sin, that which the Law of God allowes, and Christ abolisht not, London, 1644, printed in *The Works of John Milton*, III (II), New York, 1931, p. 470.

[41] William Perkins, *Christian Oeconomie: or, a short survey of the right manner of erecting and ordering a familie, according to the Scriptures . . . Written in Latin . . . and now set forth in the vulgar tongue . . . by T. Pickering*, London, 1609, pp. 101 ff.

[42] Henry Smith, *A preparative to mariage*, London, 1591, pp. 90—91.

Yet I find this, so evident an assertion, checked by two sorts of adversaries: the one, certain wild Novellists, who admit of very slight causes of separation; the other, Romish Doctors, who plead for some other main and important additions to this liberty of divorce ... Woe is me! to what a pass is the world come, that a Christian, pretending to reformation, should dare to tender so loose a project to the public![43]

Bishop Hall deals with all the divorce texts and asserts that Christ allowed divorce for adultery and Paul for desertion with right for the innocent party to remarry. This right was equal for both man and woman. The latter was not the opinion of Henry Hammond, who otherwise holds the same concept as Bishop Hall.

Henry Hammond was made archdeacon of Chichester, 1643, the same year Milton published his first edition of the divorce tract. The following year Hammond's *A Practical Catechism* appeared. The first edition was published anonymously. The twelfth edition was printed in 1684. He asks the following questions relative to divorce.

What doeth Christ now in his Law in this matter of Divorce?

He repealeth that whole Commandment, Deut. 24. 1 and imposeth a stricter yoke on his Disciples. For coming now to give more Grace than the Law brought with it to the Jews, he thinks not fit to yield so much to any considerations, particularly to the hardness of mens hearts, as to allow Christians that liberty, so contrary to the first institution of Wedlock.

Is there no other cause of divorce now pleadable or justifiable among Christians, but that in case of fornication?

I cannot define any, because Christ hath named no other[44].

The question is also asked:

... if there should be found any other cause as great as that, it might be conceived comprehended under that example (named) of fornication: and then I shall be bold to interpose my opinion, that sure, if the wife should attempt to poison or otherwise take away the life of the husband, this would be as insupportable an injury as adultery, and so as fit a cause of a divorce as that[45].

This question expresses the concept advocated by Zwingli and Bullinger. In the reply it is admitted that "an objection of some difficulty" has been proposed. However, it is answered with a denial in harmony with the exegesis of the reformers of Geneva.

In 1653 Hammond published *A Paraphrase, and Annotations upon all the Books of the New Testament: Briefly explaining all the diffi-*

---

[43] Joseph Hall, *The Works of Joseph Hall*, VII, Oxford, 1837, pp. 466—67.

[44] Henry Hammond, *A Practical Catechism*, twelfth edition, London, 1684, pp. 147, 148.

[45] Henry Hammond, *A Practical Catechism*, p. 149.

cult places thereof. He deals with all the logia on divorce and by his exegesis confirms what already has been stated in the Catechism.

While English divines with Puritan leanings supported what can best be characterized as a Genevan exegesis of the divorce texts, the typical Anglican divine adhered to an interpretation which fell within the framework of canon law, only permitting separation from board and bed.

Lancelot Andrewes, successively Bishop of Chichester, Ely, and Winchester, was equally removed from Puritanism and Romanism. He was present at the Hampton Court conference and was one of the members of the committee selected to prepare the Authorized Version. He wrote a discourse, *Against Second Marriage after Sentence of Divorce with a former Match, the Party then living,* 1601. His proposition is: "The Question is, whether upon adultery proved, or sentence recorded, a man be set at liberty, that he may proceed to contract with another."[46] His first argument is:

First, I take the act of adultery doth not dissolve the bond of marriage: for then it would follow, that the party offending would not upon reconciliation, be received again by the innocent to former society life, without a new solemnising of marriage, insomuch as the former marriage is quite dissolved, which is never heard of, and contrary to the practice of all churches[47].

He next states the opinion:

But, in my opinion, second marriages (where either party is living) are not warranted by the word of God. The ground of which opinion is, that one may not in any wise have two wives at once, for by the original institution, there can be but two in one flesh. But a man having one wife already, which, not withstanding she hath profaned marriage with another, is not thereby become the wife of him with whom she now liveth, but remaineth his wife whose first she was, and whose only she can be while she liveth[48].

Andrewes' exegetical arguments are identical to those applied by Roman Catholic theologians. He refers to Romans VII. 2, 1 Corinthians VII. 10—11, Mark x. 11 and Luke XVI. 18. In the light of these texts the exception in Matthew v. 32 and XIX. 9 should be explained.

In the same year that Lancelot Andrewes' discourse was printed, 1601, John Dove, a pastor of London, published his sermon on di-

---

[46] Lancelot Andrewes, *A Discourse, Written by Doctor Andrewes, Bishop of Ely, Against Second Marriage After Sentence of Divorce with a former Match, The Party then Living, in Anno 1601.* Printed in *Two Answers to Cardinal Perron and other Miscellaneous Works,* Oxford, 1854, p. 106.

[47] Lancelot Andrewes, *A Discourse Against Second Marriage,* p. 106.

[48] Lancelot Andrews, *A Discourse Against Second Marriage,* p. 107.

vorce[49]. The text of his sermon is Matthew XIX. 9, and he expresses the opinion that according to Christ's words divorce is under no circumstances lawful. The influence of Beza's theology during this period is indicated in his preface when he states that while he is thankful for much in Beza's writings, he is obliged to differ from him when he differs from Christ. This is the case regarding Beza's interpretation of the divorce texts. Dove's exegesis and arguments follow the same pattern as those of Lancelot Andrewes.

Godfrey Goodman, who became Bishop of Gloucester in 1625, may be characterized as an Anglican with strong Roman Catholic sympathies. In a book, 1616, he deals, among many other things, with the duties of husband and wife, and in this connection he speaks against divorce and a second marriage. The bitterness of his attack upon the Protestant concept of divorce is most evident. He writes:

Thus assuredly the greatest cause of complaint is in the husband, who had the government of his wife, who might in wisdome preuent his owne shame, and should teach her a modest and chaste carriage; but I knowe not what ill spirit hath let them at enmity, whom God hath coupled together: sometimes indeed the streame of the husbands loue, being carried another way, is apt to cast any aspersion vpon his wiues honesty; and then he begins to practise with heretickes, and to commend the law of liberty, that after a diuorse it should be lawfull to marry againe, and againe. Heere you shall see large expositions written in defence thereof, and the opinions of certaine Diuines, Ministers, Pastors, Superintendents of the separated congregations, or the new Churches from beyond the seas, (thus they would seeme to haue a Catholicke consent) together with such bitter invectiues against all superstitious fasts, calling all chastisements of the flesh, sins against the body[50].

Finally, a work by Edmund Bunny should be noticed. Bunny became chaplain to Grindal in 1570, when the latter was Archbishop of York. Later he spent his time travelling in most parts of England as an itinerant preacher; thus, he was well acquainted with the religious life in various parts of the country. He deals with the subject of divorce in a book published in 1610. The title clearly states his concept, *Of Diuorce for Adulterie and Marrying againe: that there is no sufficient warrant so to do*[51]. His exegesis contains no new arguments, but follows the pattern of Andrewes and Dove. However, his preface throws an interesting light over the real situation. He mentions that

---

[49] John Dove, *Of Diuorcement. A Sermon preached at Pauls Crosse the 10. of May. 1601*, London, 1601.

[50] Godfrey Goodman, *The Fall of Man, or the Corruption of Nature proved by the light of our naturall Reason*, London, 1616, pp. 260–61.

[51] Edmund Bunny, *Of Diuorce for Adulterie, and Marrying againe: that there is no sufficient warrant so to do*, Oxford, 1610.

divorce and remarriage actually took place. Having referred to some definite cases, he writes: "And besides those . . . an other there was of more speciall reckoning than they, who so got divorce against his wife also, & married an other."[52] Referring to those of another opinion than he himself held, he writes: "True it is, that many of the learned haue beene, and yet are, of that opinion, & accordingly haue interpreted, and yet doe, such Scriptures as they haue conceived to appertaine therevnto: but it is as true withal, that as many of the learned againe, if not far mo, haue beene, and are, of other opinion, and haue otherwise vnderstoode, & yet doe, those Scriptures aforesaid."[53] Thus Bunny confirms the facts as they gradually have become crystallized from the examination of the writings of the various representative English divines. Canon law was officially maintained, but its loopholes and slackness in its administration made divorce and remarriage possible. The divines themselves were divided in their interpretation of the logia on divorce.

John Milton

At the beginning of the Puritan Revolution and within a month after the Westminster Assembly had convened, July 1, 1643, in order to effect a more thorough reformation of the Church of England, Milton published *The Doctrine and Discipline of Divorce*. A second and much larger edition appeared in February, 1644, with a preface to "The Parlement of England, with the Assembly", in which he makes this appeal: "Yee have now, doubtlesse by the favour and appointment of God, yee have now in your hands a great and populous Nation to Reform; from what corruption, what blindnes in Religion yee know well." He places himself within the great movement for reform as somewhat of a *prophet* when he writes: "Mark then, Judges and Lawgivers, and yee whose Office is to be our teachers, for I will utter now a doctrine, if ever any other, though neglected or not understood, yet of great and powerfull importance to the governing of mankind."[54]

Milton continued his study of the question of divorce and translated large sections of Bucer's *De Regno Christi* dealing with this subject. It was published as a booklet, July, 1644, under the name: *The Iudgement of Martin Bucer concerning Divorce*[55]. In the introduction

---

[52] Edmund Bunny, *Of Diuorce for Adulterie, and Marrying againe*, p. 2.

[53] Edmund Bunny, *Of Diuorce for Adulterie, and Marrying againe*, p. 9.

[54] John Milton, *The Doctrine & Discipline of Divorce*, Works, III (II). 372, 373.

[55] Martin Bucer, *The Ivdgement of Martin Bucer concerning Divorce*, printed in Milton, *Works*, IV.

he tells the reader that he had not read Bucer's work prior to the publication of his own divorce tracts, but was happy to find that Bucer's exegesis was the same as his own. In order to give weight to Bucer's interpretation Milton lists a number of testimonies on behalf of Bucer from well-known reformers, among whom are Calvin, Beza, and Peter Martyr. While these men respected and honoured Bucer, Milton's usage of these references is misleading, since the interpretation of these men, as it has been ascertained, deviated from and even opposed the exegesis of Bucer.

The divorce tracts were greatly opposed, and this caused Milton to write *Tetrachordon*[56] and *Colasterion*[57], both published in 1645. *Tetrachordon* is his major work on divorce, and as its title-page indicates, it seeks to harmonize the Old Testament texts with those of the New Testament in the light of a historical and exegetical study. In a preface addressed to the Parliament he draws a parallel between Bucer's relationship to the Reformation by Edward VI and his own relationship to the Parliament. What was not accomplished then, he hoped would be realized now. He felt himself indissolubly involved within the framework of this movement for reform, which also called for a reappraisal of the marriage estate. This is the historical setting for Milton's re-evaluation of the doctrine of divorce. To this could be added a personal problem.

In May, 1643 (some think a year earlier), Milton was married to Mary Powell, a young lady only half his own age. Shortly after their marriage she left him, and they were first reunited in 1645. It could with good reason be thought that this personal experience led him to write about divorce as he did[58]. However, entries in his *Common-*

---

[56] John Milton, *Tetrachordon: Expositions upon the foure chief places in Scripture, which treat Mariage, or nullities in Mariage. On Gen. 1. 27. 28. compared and explain'd by Gen. 2. 18. 23. 24. Deut. 24. 1. 2. Matth. 5. 31. 32. with Matth. 19. From the 3d. v. to the 11th. 1 Cor. 7. from the 10th to the 16th. Wherin the Doctrine and Discipline of Divorce, as was lately publish'd, is confirm'd by explanation of Scripture, by testimony of ancient Fathers, of civill lawes in the Primitive Church, of famousest Reformed Divines, and lastly, by an intended Act of the Parlament and Church of England in the last yeare of Edvvard the sixth.* London, 1645, printed in *The Works of John Milton*, IV.

[57] John Milton, *Colasterion: A Reply to a Nameles Ansvver against the Doctrine and Discipline of Divorce*, London, 1645, *Works*, IV.

[58] Chilton Powell categorically states that *The Doctrine and Discipline of Divorce* "had no connection whatever with his own domestic life", but Douglas Bush gives his date for Milton's marriage as May, 1642 and suggests the opposite. James Holly Hanford presents the two suggestions and says that it "is an open question how much further one can go in tracing the details of Milton's experience". See: Chilton Latham Powell, *English Domestic Relations 1487–1653*,

Place Book[59] indicate that Milton had begun to study the question of divorce several years before his marriage, and his work *De Doctrina Christiana*[60] reveals that he did not change his ideas. It seems reasonable to think that his teaching on divorce would have been presented without his unhappy personal experience; yet, the latter would make the topic more personal and may account to some degree for the urgency whereby he expresses himself.

The purpose of marriage, as instituted by God in Genesis, is the angle from which the question of divorce should especially be considered. If marriage can be exactly defined, then it will be possible to ascertain "when there is a nullity thereof, and when a divorce"[61]. Its chief end "consisted in the mutual love, society, help, and comfort of the husband and wife, though with a reservation of superior rights to the husband"[62]. The last point Milton explains by referring to the words that in "the Image of God created he him, not them", and Paul substantiates the same[63]. Therefore, "if man be the image of God, which consists in holines, and woman ought in the same respect to be the image and companion of man, in such wise to be lov'd, as the Church is belov'd of Christ, and if, as God is the head of Christ, and Christ the head of man, so man is the head of woman; I cannot see by this golden dependance of headship and subjection, but that Piety and Religion is the main tye of Christian Matrimony"[64].

Because God created man as male and female, the second purpose of marriage is expressed, namely that of generation. However, "the right, and lawfulnes of the marige bed" should be considered "much inferior to the former end of her being his image and helpe in religious society"[65]. The lack of fulfilling either of these two objectives constituted for Milton the basic reason for divorce. Thus he suggests that, while it is a hard thing to dismiss a wife because of barrenness, it would seem justifiable under certain circumstances[66].

Turning to the marriage institution as recorded in Genesis II, Mil-

---

New York, 1917, App. B, p. 230; Douglas Bush, "John Milton", *Encyclopaedia Britannica*, XV, London, 1964, pp. 506—15; James Holly Hanford, *A Milton Handbook*, London, 1934, p. 79.

[59] John Milton, *A Common-Place Book of John Milton, and a Latin Essay and Latin Verses presumed to be by Milton*, Ed. Alfred J. Horwood, London, 1877, pp. 16—17.

[60] John Milton, *De Doctrina Christiana*, I. x, *Works*, XV.

[61] Milton, *Tetrachordon*, *Works*, IV. 100. See also IV. 107.

[62] Milton, *Doctrina*, *Works*, XV. 121.   [63] Milton, *Tetrachordon*, *Works*, IV. 76.

[64] Milton, *Tetrachordon*, *Works*, IV. 79.

[65] Milton, *Tetrachordon*, *Works*, IV. 80.

[66] Milton, *Tetrachordon*, *Works*, IV. 82.

ton considers it as a commentary and exposition of Genesis 1. God had approved all his creation as being good; yet he found it not satisfying that man should be alone. This loneliness was eliminated by giving Adam a companion of spiritual and mental compatibility. From this the conclusion is drawn that "a mariage, wherin the minde is so disgrac't and vilify'd below the bodies interest, and can have no just or tolerable contentment, is not of Gods institution, and therfore no mariage"[67]. When God said that He would make Adam "an help meet", then it was for mutual comfort. Accordingly, Milton grades the objectives of marriage as follows: " . . . first a mutuall help to piety, next to civill fellowship of love and amity, then to generation, so to houshold affairs, lastly the remedy of incontinence."[68] Adam expressed the unity between himself and Eve when he said: "This is now bone of my bones, and flesh of my flesh", but it was not to be understood as "an indissoluble bond of mariage in the carnall ligaments of flesh and bones", for the unity was "not so much in body, as in unity of mind and heart"[69]. Further, the meaning of the words: "Therefore shall a man leave his father and his mother, and shall cleave unto his wife: and they shall be one flesh", was first of all "to shew us the deer affection which naturally grows in every not unnatural mariage, ev'n to the leaving of parents, or other familiarity whatsoever"[70]. However, it does not mean "absolutely without all reason he shall cleave to his wife, be it to his weal or to his destruction as it happens, but he shall doe this upon the premises and considerations of that meet help and society before mention'd"[71].

The key text that expositors generally refer to when establishing the indissolubility of the marriage tie is Christ's reference to Genesis II, that husband and wife "shall be one flesh". The oneness thus expressed can only be considered fulfilled when "the joyning causes" are present and they consist of "fitnes of mind and disposition, which may breed the Spirit of concord, and union between them", as well as "good will, love, help, comfort, fidelity". Thus the unity of the mind and the soul "is neerer and greater then the union of bodies, so doubtles, is the dissimilitude greater, and more dividuall, as that which makes between bodies all difference and distinction". Accordingly, Milton does not hesitate to say that "if the essential form be dissolved, it follows that the marriage itself is virtually dissolved"[72].

---

[67] Milton, *Tetrachordon, Works,* IV. 87.
[68] Milton, *Tetrachordon, Works,* IV. 88, 101.
[69] Milton, *Tetrachordon, Works,* IV. 92, 93.
[70] Milton, *The Doctrine and Discipline of Divorce, Works,* III (II). 478.
[71] Milton, *Tetrachordon, Works,* IV. 94.
[72] Milton, *Tetrachordon, Works,* IV. 97, 98; *Doctrina, Works,* XV. 157.

The unity between Christ and His Church, which is called a mystery, cannot be illustrated by the "one flesh" idea of marriage, unless there is a spiritual and mental unity between husband and wife which is called a mystery by the Apostle Paul. Having brought forth this argument, Milton restates his conclusion that "ther cannot hence be any hindrance of divorce to that wedlock wherin ther can be no good mystery"[73].

The significance Milton places upon the Mosaic letter of divorce, Deuteronomy XXIV. 1, as related to his general notion of law and grace, has also a decisive bearing upon his exegesis of Christ's words on divorce. The permission given by Moses to issue a letter of divorce, when the husband "hath found some uncleanness in her", contained an immutable and moral principle: "This Law, if the words of Christ may be admitted into our beleef, shall never while the world stands, for him be abrogated." He emphasizes that the uncleanness mentioned does not refer merely to fornication as generally stated, but the meaning is "nakednes of any thing"[74]. Thus Milton finds no reason why he should deviate from his general exegesis "which gives us freely that God permitted divorce, for whatever was unalterably distastful, whether in body or mind"[75]. At great length and through rational reasoning Milton seeks to prove that the principle of Deuteronomy XXIV. 1 is a just and immutable law.

The purpose of a law is to guaranty "the liberty and the human dignity of them that live under the Law"[76]. Since no law could go against the primary purpose of its own institution, then neither can it enforce a marriage to continue where no mutual affection binds the partners together. This so much the more since marriage from the beginning had as its aim "the fulfilling of conjugall love and helpfulnes". Even the strongest Christian will despair and fall into temptations if the latter is not present. Where the joining causes of marriage are lacking, such a marriage is already more disrupted than "by a needfull divorce", and is "unpleasing to God, as any other kind of hypocrisie". Just as spiritual and mental distress and disharmony are realized in allowing divorce where the one party is an unbeliever, so the same should be recognized where the marriage is "uncurably unfit". It would be against nature "to prohibit divorce sought for natural

---

[73] Milton, *Tetrachordon, Works,* IV. 100.

[74] Milton, *The Doctrine and Discipline of Divorce, Works,* III (II). 388; *Tetrachordon, Works,* IV. 113–14. See also *The Doctrine and Discipline of Divorce, Works,* III (II). 389; *Doctrina, Works,* XV. 171.

[75] Milton, *Tetrachordon, Works,* IV. 114.

[76] Milton, *Tetrachordon, Works,* IV. 121.

causes"[77]. Furthermore, "all Law is available to som good end, but the final prohibition of divorce avails to no good end, causing only the endles aggravation of evil, and therfore this permission of divorce was givn to the Jews by the wisdom and fatherly providence of God; who knew that Law cannot command love, without which, matrimony hath no true beeing, no good, no solace, nothing of Gods instituting, nothing but so sordid and so low, as to bee disdain'd of any generous person"[78].

Canon law and theologians in general would agree to divorce if either party is found seeking the life of the other, but the mental pressure of incompatibility can be a danger to a person's health and shorten his life; accordingly, divorce should also be permissible in the latter case[79].

Human society proceeds from the mind, otherwise it would not be more than a brutish society. The same must be the case with marriage, which is the basis for society[80]. As any other covenant, marriage is based on equity for the mutual good of both, but "extremity may dissolv it"[81]. After having entered the marriage covenant the situation could arise that a person may find himself unfit for the marriage estate, or that he was too quick in a choice which later is realized to be wrong. In such a case God is more "mild and good to man, then man to his brother, in all this liberty givn to divorcement, mentions not a word of our past errors and mistakes"[82]. The statement about liberty of divorce is a reference to Deuteronomy xxiv. 1 which is a law given to preserve the ideal of marriage. "And therfore doth in this Law, what best agrees with the goodnes, loosning a sacred thing to peace and charity, rather then binding it to hatred and contention; loosning only the outward and formal tie of that which is already inwardly, and really brokn, or els was really never joyn'd."[83]

It is within the framework of his understanding of the primary purpose of the marriage institution and the principle of Deuteronomy xxiv. 1 that Milton approaches his interpretation of the New Testament logia on divorce. The significance that Milton places upon Deu-

---

[77] Milton, *The Doctrine and Discipline of Divorce, Works*, III (II). 395, 400, 402, 404, 416.

[78] Milton, *Tetrachordon, Works*, IV. 128; *The Doctrine and Discipline of Divorce, Works*, III (II). 383.

[79] Milton, *The Doctrine and Discipline of Divorce, Works*, III (II). 420–21; See also pp. 390. 395, 400.

[80] Milton, *The Doctrine and Discipline of Divorce, Works*, III. (II). 422–23.

[81] Milton, *Tetrachordon, Works*. IV. 119.

[82] Milton, *Tetrachordon, Works*, IV. 125.

[83] Milton, *Tetrachordon, Works*, IV. 127.

teronomy XXIV. 1 he finds supported by Christ. He notices that in the Gospel of Luke, immediately before the statement against divorce, the sentence against abrogating the law is inserted, "as if it were call'd thither on purpose to defend the equity of this particular law against the foreseene rashnesse of common textuaries, who abolish lawes"[84]. Likewise in Matthew v. 18 Christ expresses Himself to the effect that He came not to abrogate the law "one jot or one tittle"[85]. In Mark x. 5 Christ refers to Deuteronomy as a law[86]. Milton realizes that on this point he is not in agreement with other English expositors and therefore makes the following remark: "All those expositors upon the fifth of Matthew confesse the Law of Moses to be the Law of the Lord, wherin no addition or diminution hath place; yet comming to the point of divorce, as if they fear'd not to be call'd least in the kingdom of heav'n, any slight evasion will content them to reconcile those contradictions which they make between Christ and Moses, between Christ and Christ."[87] Milton encourages the members of Parliament to follow the judgment of their predecessor Moses[88].

When evaluating Christ's statement on divorce, one should keep in mind the occasion which persuaded him to speak. Christ sought either to convince the Pharisees of their abuses of a good law or to give a rebuking reply to a tempting question. In such cases it would not be a right hermeneutical principle "to repose all upon the literall terms of so many words"[89].

Commenting on Christ's explanation that Moses allowed a letter of divorce for the hardness of the people's hearts, Milton expresses his disagreement with those who think that for this reason it ought to be abolished[90]. He further mentions "that these words of Christ, though a very appropriate answer to the Pharisees who tempted him, were never meant as a general explanation of the question of divorce. His intention was, as usual, to repress the arrogance of the Pharisees, and elude their snares; for his answer was only addressed to those who taught from Deut. XXIV. 1. that it was lawful to put away a wife for any cause whatever, provided a bill of divorcement were given"[91]. No

---

[84] Milton, *Tetrachordon, Works*, IV. 139.
[85] Milton, *Tetrachordon, Works*, IV. 138–39; *The Doctrine and Discipline of Divorce, Works*, III (II). 428–31, 466–68.
[86] Milton, *The Doctrine and Discipline of Divorce, Works*, III (II). 444.
[87] Milton, *The Doctrine and Discipline of Divorce, Works*, III (II). 462.
[88] Milton, *The Doctrine and Discipline of Divorce, Works*, III (II). 369, 375. 376.
[89] Milton, *The Doctrine and Discipline of Divorce, Works*, III (II). 429, 430, 466.
[90] Milton, *Tetrachordon, Works*, IV. 164.
[91] Milton, *Doctrina, Works*, XV. 159.

law would have been given which could permit sin, therefore the letter of divorce is good in itself[92].

Milton defines the hardness of heart, for which the letter of divorce was allowed, as the "imperfection and decay of man from original righteousnesse, it was that God suffer'd not divorce onely, but all that which by Civilians is term'd the secondary law of nature and of nations ... In the same manner, and for the same cause hee suffer'd divorce as well as mariage, our imperfect and degenerat condition of necessity requiring this law among the rest, as a remedy against intolerable wrong and servitude above the patience of man to beare"[93]. In other words since God allowed divorce for a cause, "therefore in relation to that cause he allow'd it"[94].

The word *suffered* is considered a legal word "denoting what by law a man may doe or not doe"[95]. In Matthew xix. 7—8 and Mark x. 3—4 the two words "command" and "suffer" go together as "all the precepts of law are divided into obligatorie and permissive, containing either what we must doe, or what wee may do; and of this latter sort are as many precepts, as of the former, and all as lawfull"[96]. Out of this argument grows a question with the answer implied. "But if it be plaine that the whole juridical law and civil power is only suffer'd under the Gospel, for the hardnes of our hearts, then wherefore should not that which Moses suffer'd, be suffer'd still by the same reason?"[97] In this latter argument Milton has moved from the concept of moral law to that of judicial law. But even considered on that lower level the divorce law is "just and pure", for it was given by God[98]. It is Milton's conviction that the interpretation which makes Christ's words mean that the Mosaic divorce law had been abolished, has changed an unhappy marriage into a captivity without any hope of relief[99]. Christ's practice too is contrary to this misinterpretation. "If we examine over all his sayings, we shall find him not so much interpreting the Law with his words, as referring his owne words to be interpreted by the Law."[100] Thus when Milton had ascertained the meaning of

---

[92] Milton, *The Doctrine and Discipline of Divorce, Works*, III (II). 389, 432—34, 443—44.

[93] Milton, *Tetrachordon, Works*, IV. 165. See also *The Doctrine and Discipline of Divorce, Works*, III (II). 493.

[94] Milton, *Tetrachordon, Works*, IV. 164.

[95] Milton, *Tetrachordon, Works*, IV. 164.

[96] Milton, *Tetrachordon, Works*, IV. 163.

[97] Milton, *Tetrachordon, Works*, IV. 166.

[98] Milton, *Tetrachordon, Works*, IV. 154.

[99] Milton, *The Doctrine and Discipline of Divorce, Works*, III (II). 381—82.

[100] Milton, *The Doctrine and Discipline of Divorce, Works*, III (II). 449.

the original law of marriage and divorce in order to obtain a better understanding of Christ's words, then he had followed what he considered a hermeneutical principle implied in the teaching of the Master. He therefore very categorically states that "Christ neither did, nor could abrogat the Law of divorce, but only reprove the abuse therof"[101]. The same is confirmed by the Apostle Paul. The case of unbelief mentioned by him as a legitimate reason for divorce equally well justifies it "wherever Christian liberty and peace are without fault equally obstructed"[102]. Not only through the concept of law, but also through the avenue of grace, Milton comes to the same result.

Since the Mosaic principle of divorce, as any other law, expressed equity and justice and was given to preserve peace in marriage, then "the mercy of this Mosaick Law was graciously exhibited"[103]. It would be against the nature of grace and charity or the liberty of the gospel if it should place heavier burdens on afflicted souls than the law[104]. Milton therefore exclaims: "O perversnes! that the Law should be made more provident of peacemaking then the Gospel! that the Gospel should be put to beg a most necessary help of mercy from the Law, but must not have it."[105]

The comments Milton makes in connection with his interpretation of the various phrases found in the divorce passage of Matthew xix further illustrate his exegesis. According to the Greek the words "to put away" one's wife mean to loose, set free or dissolve, thus confirming that here it is not spoken about a separation from board and bed but a divorce which set the person free to remarry[106]. When it is asked if a wife can be divorced "for every cause", then the problem for discussion is not whether or not divorce is allowed, but whether or not it is permissible to divorce for trivial reasons. The preposition "for", when read in the Greek, implies an abrupt action, thus indicating divorce prompted by any sudden feeling. In this connection Milton mentions the right of divorce by mutual consent. "In that our Saviour seemes here, as the case is most likely, not to condemne all divorce but all injury and violence in divorce. But no injury can be done to them who seeke it." Furthermore, "there can be nothing in

---

[101] Milton, *The Doctrines and Discipline of Divorce, Works*, III (II). 428. See also pp. 388, 474; *Tetrachordon, Works*, IV. 167; *Doctrina, Works*, XV. 169.

[102] Milton, *The Doctrine and Discipline of Divorce, Works*, III (II). 491–92. See also pp. 406–15, 490–92; *Doctrina, Works*, XV. 173.

[103] Milton, *The Doctrine and Discipline of Divorce, Works*, III (II). 392.

[104] Milton, *Tetrachordon, Works*, IV. 165; *The Doctrine and Discipline of Divorce, Works*, III (II). 425, 447, 449–51.

[105] Milton, *The Doctrine and Discipline of Divorce, Works*, III (II). 403.

[106] Milton, *Tetrachordon, Works*, IV. 144–46.

the equity of law, why divorce by consent may not be lawfull: leaving secrecies to conscience, the thing which our Saviour here aimes to rectifie, not to revoke the statutes of Moses"[107]. It should be noticed that Milton expects the magistrate to "see that the condition of divorce be just and equall"[108], and that he considers marriage "a civil ordinance"[109].

The connotation of "fornication" should be seen in the light of the meaning given to "some uncleanness" in Deuteronomy xxiv. 1. Thus Milton finds himself justified in letting fornication signify "not so much adultery, as the constant enmity, faithlessness, and disobedience of the wife, arising from the manifest and palpable alienation of the mind, rather than the body", or "whatever is found to be irreconcilably at variance with love, or fidelity, or help, or society, that is, with the objects of the original institution"[110].

The words " ... and whoso marrieth her which is put away doth commit adultery" indicate that Christ did not have in mind to give a finished creed for divorce but only to prohibit "such divorces as the Jewes then made through malice or through plotted licence, not those which are necessary and just causes; where charity and wisedome disjoyns, that which not God, but Error and Disastre joyn'd"[111]. If Christ's words should be understood differently, then the Apostles and the Churches of the Reformation would be wrong in allowing remarriage[112]. In this connection two other points should be noticed. Christ never intended His words to become a judicial law[113]. "It is therefore a most flagrant error to convert a gospel precept into a civil statute, and enforce it by legal penalties."[114] His precepts should be expounded "not by the written letter, but by that unerring paraphrase of Christian love and Charity, which is the summe of all commands, and the perfection"[115].

Another key statement by Christ is found in the words: "Wherefore they are no more twain, but one flesh. What therefore God hath joined together, let not man put asunder." The prohibition expressed "is not an absolute and tyrannicall command without reason", but is founded "upon some rationall cause not difficult to be apprehend-

---

[107] Milton, *Tetrachordon, Works*, IV. 145, 146.
[108] Milton, *The Doctrine and Discipline of Divorce, Works*, III (II). 497 ff.
[109] Milton, *Colasterion, Works*, IV. 264.
[110] Milton, *Doctrina, Works*, XV. 171, 179; *The Doctrine and Discipline of Divorce, Works*, III (II). 488.
[111] Milton, *Tetrachordon, Works*, IV. 185.
[112] Milton, *Tetrachordon, Works*, IV. 182.
[113] Milton, *Doctrina, Works*, XV. 173.   [114] Milton, *Doctrina, Works*, XV. 175.
[115] Milton, *Tetrachordon, Works*, IV. 186.

ed"[116]. That cause is the primeval purpose of marriage, for Christ refers back to "the beginning". The expression "some rationall cause" should be noticed because it supplies Milton with Christ's endorsement when he himself, as has been considered, explains at great length what the ends of marriage are, and by rational reasons points out causes which destroy the object of marriage. The prohibition of divorce expressed by Christ depends therefore "upon the plainer & more eminent causes omitted heere and referr'd to the institution ... and finde both here and in Genesis, that the forbidding is not absolute, but according to the reasons there taught us, not here"[117]. Where the cause for making husband and wife "one flesh" is absent, there God's joining is absent; consequently the reason for not putting asunder is not present[118]. Thus Milton finds his exegetical circle closed by the very teaching of Christ.

That Milton's exegesis of the divorce texts should be challenged was only to be expected and has already been noticed. He himself tells that he was opposed and critized from the pulpit and by pen[119]. The anonymous booklet written against his first book on divorce no doubt reflects the general content of these attacks[120]. The author of *An Answer* makes a clear denial of Milton's main theme. "Whatsoever other causes of Divorce may be allowed of, yet that disagreement of minde or disposition between husband and wife, yea though it shewes it selfe in much sharpnesse each to other, is not by the law of God allowed of for a just cause of divorce, neither ought to be allowed of by the lawes of man."[121] Ten arguments are presented as a support for this assertion. For example, the Bible gives no degree of height to which disagreement should reach before divorce is permissible. Paul neither said that a husband should put away an unbelieving wife, "much lesse may he put his wife away for disagreement of disposition". Since it is a Christian's duty to bear the burdens and infirmities of a fellow Christian, and a husband should love the wife as Christ loved the Church, "then ought not a man to put away his Wife for

---

[116] Milton, *Tetrachordon, Works*, IV. 148.
[117] Milton, *Tetrachordon, Works*, IV. 149.
[118] Milton, *The Doctrine and Discipline of Divorce, Works*, III (II). 382, 391, 456, 458, 479–80; *Tetrachordon, Works*, IV. 148–52, 171–72; *Doctrina, Works*, XV. 177.
[119] Milton, *Colasterion, Works*, IV. 233.
[120] Anon., *An Answer to a Book, Intituled, The Doctrine and Discipline of Divorce, or, A Plea for Ladies and Gentlewomen, and all other Maried Women against Divorce*, London, 1644.
[121] *An Answer*, p. 4.

weaknesse of nature, contrariety, or indisposition of minde". The same is born out by Christ's words and canon law[122].

Four propositions or conclusions are mentioned in order to destroy the main pillar of Milton's book: divorce for incompatibility of mind. There is no so-called unchangeable disposition which the grace of the gospel cannot alter. Men should rather seek divorce "with their own corruption, which is the cause of all discord and disagreement". The second proposition is similar to the first. Next, "that solace and peace which is contrary to discord and variance is not the main end of mariage", but is chiefly made up of the difference between the sexes. Finally, the "contrarietie of disposition is not so great a cause of natural frigidity"[123].

Ten further arguments are brought against Milton's theses, and can best be evaluated by examining the writer's exegesis of the divorce texts. It is restated that the significance of the original marriage estate was not that "Eve was a fit conversing soule for Adam", but that they were created as male and female[124]. Milton's interpretation of Deuteronomy XXIV. 1 is referred to as "this great Scare-crow and maine Pillar which he trusts in to hold up his whole Book, or most part of it"[125]. The uncleanness Moses speaks about has no reference to a displeasing nature, but to some shamefull acts committed before marriage. Deuteronomy XXIV. 1 should be understood in the light of chapter XXII. 13—15, where reference is made to fornication[126]. It is also suggested that Moses granted no divorce at all, but the law was given to safeguard a woman who was put away unjustly. Even if the text would allow both interpretations, it is now "altered by Christ under the Gospell"[127]. It should not be considered as a contradiction that Moses should allow a divorce which Christ would deny, for there were not only ceremonial but also judicial laws given to the Israelites, which are far from the spirit of the gospel[128].

Contrary to the opinion of Milton the anonymous writer thinks that Christ does not speak about the Pharisees' abusive use of the Mosaic divorce law, since His purpose was to abolish the law[129]. According to Matthew V. 1 Christ gave his speech to the disciples. Thus His words are not "an expressive resolution to repress and crosse the pride and false glosses of the Pharisies", but the New Testament logia on divorce, which prohibits divorce for any other reason than adultery, is "a direction binding all Christians under the Gospell"[130]. Fur-

[122] *An Answer*, pp. 5, 6.
[123] *An Answer*, pp. 11, 12.
[124] *An Answer*, p. 14.
[125] *An Answer*, p. 19.
[126] *An Answer*, pp. 21—25.
[127] *An Answer*, p. 29.
[128] *An Answer*, p. 30.
[129] *An Answer*, pp. 26—27.
[130] *An Answer*, p. 29.

thermore, the philosophy of Christ's whole sermon, of which the statement of divorce is only a part, gave "as it were new inlargements of lawes under the Gospell, requiring more spiritualness in observation, then the Mosaical government"[131].

In his reply Milton does not add anything new. He refers the unknown author to the second edition of his work on divorce which answers some of the questions raised in more detail[132]. He blames his opponent that he interprets Matthew v. 32 "after the old fashion, and never takes notice of what I brought against that exposition; Let him therefore seek his answer there"[133]. A few points should be noticed from his reply. Milton agrees with the writer's observation that Deuteronomy XXIV. 1 is one of the two pillars of his exegesis, however not the main one, which is Genesis I and II. He expresses his conviction that no one will be able to shake them. He also consents to the suggestion that difference of disposition even "in much sharpnes, is not alwaies a just cause of divorce", and grants that the other's infirmities should patiently be born, "but not outrages, not perpetual defraudments of truest conjugal society, not injuries and vexations as importunat as fire". Thus it is made evident that it is not something ordinary that Milton has in mind when he speaks about "contrarieties of minds"[134].

In the question of the relationship between the Mosaic law of divorce and the ceremonial laws of circumcision, sacrifices, etc., Milton reaffirms that the question of divorce is different as it is "of a morall point in houshold dutie, equally belonging to Jew and Gentile; divorce was then right, now wrong; then permitted in the rigorous time of Law, now forbidd'n by Law eevn to the most extremely afflicted in the favourable time of grace and freedom"[135]. The statement implies that this cannot be true.

Milton has been called "the first protagonist in Christendom" in favour of divorce by mutual consent[136]. To his contemporaries at large his proposals and exegesis sounded not only radical but heretical. However, seen in the light of the history of the interpretation of the divorce texts from the time of Erasmus, it must be asserted that Milton did not advocate one single point which had not been stated previously. The difference is that Milton, with renewed emphasis, pre-

---

[131] *An Answer*, p. 27.   [132] Milton, *Colasterion, Works*, IV. 237.
[133] Milton, *Colasterion, Works*, IV. 244.
[134] Milton, *Colasterion, Works*, IV. 241, 243, 251.
[135] Milton, *Colasterion, Works*, IV. 261.
[136] Edward Alexander Westermarck, *Christianity and Morals*, London, 1939, p. 358.

sents them as a whole and makes them subservient to his main objectives. Thomas More and Martin Bucer had suggested divorce by mutual consent. All the interpreters were guided by their concept of the purpose of the original marriage institution. The Reformed theologians sought to harmonize the divorce laws of the Old Testament with the words of Christ, and Zwingli, Bullinger, and Bucer read Christ's words in the light of Deuteronomy XXIV. 1. The naturalism seen in the young Luther is also reflected in Milton, and the former had raised the question as to whether the laws of Moses should be more gracious than Christian liberty. Milton was not merely a Puritan partisan, and for him Reformation and Renaissance were not contradictory terms. He employed rational reasoning as did Erasmus. The latter had suggested that when the same causes appeared in the Christian era, as among the Israelites, then the same remedies should also be applied. While Erasmus was a Christian humanist, he was above all else a Christian theologian, and it should be noticed that Milton also sought to synthesize the Reformation with humanism. This "is Milton's peculiar contribution to the cause and philosophy of humanism, and there is a special significance in the fact that his is the final word of the whole era"[137]. In his theological thinking Milton is not confined within the narrowness of Puritan thought but may also here be considered as the last great Protestant protagonist[138]. Accordingly, in his exegesis of the New Testament logia on divorce Milton exhausted the interpretations and arguments of the Renaissance and the Reformation period.

In his divorce tracts Milton had addressed the Westminster Assembly. The chapter on marriage and divorce in the *Westminster Confession of Faith*, 1647, gave this reply:

Although the corruption of man be such as is apt to study arguments, unduly to put asunder those whom God hath joined together in marriage; yet nothing but adultery, or such willful desertion as can no way be remedied by the Church or civil magistrate, is cause sufficient of dissolving the bond of marriage [Reference is made to Matthew XIX. 6, 8, 9 and 1 Corinthians VII. 15]; wherein a public and orderly course of proceeding is to be observed; and the persons concerned in it, not left to their own wills and discretion in their own case [Reference is made to Deuteronomy XXIV. 1—4][139].

---

[137] James Holly Hanford, "Milton and the Return to Humanism", *Studies in Philology*, XVI. 146.

[138] This is substantiated in a recent work in which Milton's concept of the central doctrines of the Christian faith are compared with historical Christianity. See C. A. Patrides, *Milton and the Christian Tradition*, Oxford, 1966.

[139] "The Westminster Confession of Faith, 1647", XXIV. VI, *Creeds of Christendom*, ed. Philip Schaff, III. 656—57.

Milton's teaching on divorce, like Bucer's, did not find response among the theologians. The Westminster Assembly counteracted Milton's interpretation and confirmed the conservative Calvin-Beza exegesis.

Summary and Conclusion

In the history of the interpretation of the New Testament logia on divorce during the sixteenth and early seventeenth centuries, there is a direct line from Erasmus to Milton. Erasmus was not merely a humanistic theorist but a Christian theologian and pragmatist with his teaching anchored on Scripture and centered in Christ. Milton was not confined within the narrowness of Puritan thought or the stereotyped creeds of Protestant orthodoxy, but he made use of all the philological, historical, and exegetical tools made available by the Christian humanists more than a century earlier. Regarding the question of divorce both men sought a reform based on research which was accomplished by the means just referred to. Furthermore, by his concept of divorce Erasmus began to draw a circle which was closed by Milton. Within this circle the exegetical arguments of the Reformation period were exhausted.

The specifically theological concepts of the major branches of Christendom are mirrored in their exegesis of the logia on divorce. The theological and doctrinal structures became a prism in which the rays from the divorce texts were broken for better or for worse.

Marriage conceived as one of the seven sacraments is the pivot around which Roman Catholic exegesis of the divorce texts moves. The Ancient Fathers' reference to marriage as a sacrament conveyed the meaning of mystery, secret, symbol, and a most holy thing. The theologians of early scholasticism made the sacraments a cause of grace, but considered marriage only remedial, even though it was numbered as one of the sacraments. Thomas Aquinas established marriage as a *causa gratiae*, and the Council of Trent confirmed the sacramental concept of marriage in the Thomistic sense to be an absolute truth of faith.

When the marriage institution, in the hands of the scholastic theologians, had become one of the seven sacraments, Ephesians v. 32 became the textual foundation for the Roman Catholic sacramental idea of marriage, making the marriage tie indissoluble. Accordingly, the exception clause in the Gospel of Matthew v. 32 and xix. 9 could only mean separation from board and bed, and this separation could be administered only in the case of adultery. Furthermore, in the records of Mark and Luke the exception clause is not mentioned, and the statement of Matthew should be read in the light of the sayings by the two former Evangelists. The Apostle Paul's statement in 1 Corinthians VII. 15 that a "brother or sister, is not under bondage" if an unbelieving partner departs, grants no permission to remarry, for verses nine and ten of the same chapter deny this. The same is supported by Romans VII. 1–3 stating that only death dissolves the marriage tie. The sacramental concept of marriage would also make the marriage estate an absolute ecclesiastical institution to be regulated by canon law. While the medieval Church taught the indissolubility of the marriage tie, it was possible through canon law, which listed a great number of impediments, to obtain an absolute annulment of the marriage tie by asserting that the marriage *ab initio* had been unlawfully contracted, and thus it could not be considered a proper marriage.

In his exegesis of the divorce texts Erasmus is indebted to the Christian humanists for his philological, historical, and exegetical approach, but not in the main for the findings in connection with his interpretation of the divorce texts. The publication of his New Testament, 1516, thus became the beginning of a reevaluation of marriage and divorce. The Greek *mysterion* of Ephesians v. 32 and its context could not justify the sacramental concept of marriage, which the theologians had arrived at from the use of the Latin *sacramentum* as found in Ephesians v. 32 of the Vulgate, together with the sacramental concept of Thomas Aquinas. Erasmus' approach to the interpretation of the divorce texts indicates that he was convinced that enlightenment would bring a reform regarding divorce matters. He seems to be motivated by the basic proposition that charity should come before any institutionalism, having preference over any ecclesiastical injunctions. Erasmus felt that the Church's rigid interpretation of the logia on divorce was contrary to the interpretation given to the other sayings in the Sermon on the Mount. The words of Matthew v. 32 clearly state that Christ made one exception for divorce, namely adultery. However, the words were spoken to the disciples, who represent Christ's true members of the kingdom of God, but within the Church are also found the imperfect ones. When the same causes appear among them as among the people of the Old Testament, then in principle the same remedy, which God permitted in former times, should be advocated, lest the people should do greater evil. Erasmus asserts that in Romans VII 2–3 as in 1 Corinthians VII. 39 the Apostle is not dealing with the question of divorce. In 1 Corinthians VII he finds two types of *departing*. In verses ten and eleven Paul has in mind equal marriages of Christians and a *departing* in such a case may be styled a separation with no permission to remarry. In verse fifteen the Apostle deals with actual divorce allowing a new marriage. The divorce texts of Mark and Luke should be read in the light of Christ's statements in the Gospel of Matthew.

Erasmus had hoped, through a biblical and Christological theology, to better the moral condition of his time, which had decayed partly on account of canon law, but since his exegesis expressed doubt regarding the very foundation and structure of the Roman Catholic concept of marriage and divorce, he was greatly opposed by prominent theologians, who confirmed, as did also the Council of Trent, the late medieval exegesis of the divorce texts. The annotations in the various vernacular Bibles, which were printed by both Roman Catholics and Protestants, reflect respectively the official Roman Catholic concept of divorce and that of Erasmus. Erasmus had desired a reform within the Church and he greatly detested the revolt of the Protestant reformers. While he did not recant his interpretation, he expressed his loyalty to the Church, and in the attack made upon him he intimated a willingness to submit his opinions to Her final judgment. To such a submission the Protestant reformers could not agree. However, the reformers were indebted to Erasmus as the one who "had laid the eggs", which they were determined to hatch.

The exegesis of Luther and his associates concerning the divorce texts is generally found in a context in which the high dignity of the marriage estate is emphasized. While Luther opposed the Thomistic sacramental concept of marriage, he considered matrimony to be a most sacred thing and expressed that in terms similar to those of the Fathers and theologians who lived before Thomas Aquinas. Luther's opposition to the Roman Catholic impediments was rooted in his high concept of the marriage vow, and the conservative Lutheran view on divorce is reflected in the assertion that Christ allowed adultery as the only cause for divorce. In his exegesis of the divorce texts in Matthew Luther generally brings his interpretation into relationship with the Pauline exception in 1 Corinthians VII. 15, making desertion the second reason for divorce. Since the believer and the deserted party were innocent, they had the right to remarry. In the case of adultery the marriage tie was severed by the adulterer himself and not by the innocent party, who was then free. The guilty party deserved capital punishment and even if it was not exercised the guilty one should be considered as dead in the eyes of God and in his relationship to the former spouse. Thus was fulfilled the obligation or permission of Romans VII. 2—3, that death of the one partner made remarriage permissible. Furthermore, if the permission to remarry was not inherent in the act of divorce, the latter would be a divorce in name but not in reality.

The secular aspect of marriage is reflected in the fact that the only means of punishment given to the Church is that of excommunication, while to the magistrate is given authority and the power of the sword whereby to declare a divorce legal and punish the guilty partner.

The doctrine of the two kingdoms was of basic importance in the Lutheran consideration of matrimonial matters. In secular society other laws operated than those in the kingdom of God. As Moses among the Israelites, so also the magistrate had to do his best under the given circumstances. The laws of the Christian emperors illustrated this principle. The Lutheran teaching about the two kingdoms could be applicable only in a society where marriage was considered not only a *res sacra* but also a *secular* matter.

While naturalism was present in Luther's thinking during the early period of his life and influenced him in his discussion of marriage matters, the Christological and soteriological emphasis was, however, prevalent. Marriage is compared with Christ's relationship to the Church by the fact that the vitalizing energy in the marriage relationship is that "fides" which is one of the fruits of the Spirit. Likewise, in all matrimonial matters the judgement of grace and love should prevail over any legalistic concept, having as its object the salvation of the individual person involved. This emphasized that the practical result of one's interpretation should be in harmony with "the Spirit of Christ". The innocent party should be willing to forgive the guilty party, and a repenting David should be restored. Christian liberty, as understood in the light of Paul's teaching, should be preserved. In their exegesis of the divorce texts the associates of Luther follow the Lutheran line of thought.

The exegesis of the reformers in Zürich and Geneva reveals a common denominator. They seek to harmonize the divorce laws of the Old Testament with the New Testament logia on divorce. Their hermeneutical principle is that God is ever the same and does not contradict Himself. The theological motivation is their bibliocratic concept regarding the administration of secular society, which ought to be ruled by a "thus saith the Lord". Accordingly, the laws and regulations, including discipline and punishment, which should guide the magistrate in the case of divorce and other marriage problems, had to be in harmony with the teaching of Christ. In spite of the fact that the reformers of Zürich and Geneva had this common starting point, they moved in opposite directions in their exegesis.

Zwingli and Bullinger asserted that when adultery was mentioned by Christ as a legitimate reason for divorce, He did not exclude other reasons or prescribe this only. Making adultery only one among many reasons for divorce, they attempted to harmonize Christ's statement with the Mosaic laws, which in their opinion allowed the letter of divorce for various reasons. The reformers of Zürich did not make the sharp distinction between the two kingdoms. They hoped to make the administration of their city bibliocratic or Christocratic, thus the injunction regarding divorce should be based upon a "thus saith the Lord". Theologically and exegetically they sought to unify the words of Christ with those of the Old Testament. God was ever the same and could not contradict Himself. Interpreting Christ's words to mean that adultery is only one among several reasons for divorce supplied them with a liberal concept, making it easier to deal with a secular society as a bibliocracy, while Luther, because of his *only-one-exception* concept, relegated divorce matters to the secular society.

Calvin and Beza contended that Christ allowed only one exception, and that the letter of divorce had been given only to safeguard the woman and to avoid polygamy. The one who wrote such a letter of divorce labelled himself as an adulterer; accordingly, in the Old Testament also there was only one legitimate cause for divorce.

While all the Reformed theologians thought that adultery deserved capital punishment, Calvin and Beza emphasized that adultery had become an exception only because the secular authorities neglected to apply this punishment. For a liberal application of the divorce texts Zwingli and Bullinger referred to the laws of the Christian emperors, but Beza opposed the use of these. The general opinion was that matrimony was instituted for the purpose of procreation and in order to avoid fornication, but Bullinger also placed weight on mental compatibility. Bucer, influenced by Bullinger, developed this point further and suggested divorce for mental incompatibility and by mutual consent. He also appealed for an exemplifying of the divorce laws given by the Christian emperors. However, in the early part of his life Bucer was rather Lutheran in his interpretation and so was his close associate Peter Martyr, even after the publication of the works of Bullinger and Bucer.

Calvin was one with Luther in asserting that the first marriage institution was a perpetual law. He also distinguished between the spiritual and secular societies. However, when he sought to make the government of Geneva what is commonly called a theocracy, he was following Zwingli. Attempting this he sought to bring the laws and regulations which had a bearing upon the secular society into harmony with God's will. In some way Calvin bridges the Lutheran and the Zwingli-Bullinger hermeneutical principles. He preserved Luther's interpretation of Christ's words, but like Zwingli he brought them into harmony with Deuteronomy XXIV. 1 and Malachi II. 14, 16.

Bringing the Old Testament and Christ's words to harmonize, he was theologically motivated in the same way as Zwingli, but the textual interpretation is different because he read the Old Testament divorce texts in the light of Christ's words and not vice versa as did Zwingli and Bullinger. While Calvin maintained the conservative Lutheran concept of the New Testament divorce texts, Bucer, under the influence of the Zwingli-Bullinger concept liberalized his Lutheran exegesis of Christ's words to mean more than one exception and applied this interpretation within his concept of the kingdom of God. The Zürcher Ehegericht became the real ancestor of the Genevan Consistory, but while Zürich applied the Zwingli-Bullinger liberal exegesis, Calvin and Beza brought their *only-one-exception* interpretation into relationship with their bibliocratic concept of the civil administration in Geneva.

The influences, principles, and attitudes revealed in the general development of the English Reformation are reflected in the history of the interpretations of the divorce texts by the English divines. A preparatory groundwork for their re-evaluation of the divorce question was made through the writings of Erasmus, especially in his New Testament with annotations. Luther's ideas found inroad into England through his own writings and through those of Tyndale.

During the year 1540 Cranmer was found earnestly seeking to better the moral condition in England by influencing the King to forbid divorce after the "Pope's law", which meant an abolishment of the various impediments which might justify an annulment of a marriage. Matrimony was not defined as a sacrament in the Thomistic sense, but neither were the reformers' interpretations of Christ's words accepted. On the contrary, Crammer was as much worried about the development among the Protestant reformers as he was about the impediments of canon law.

With the beginning of Edward's reign the influence of the Reformed theologians was more strongly felt as illustrated in the return of Hooper and the presence of such men as Peter Martyr and Bucer. The changed attitude of Cranmer is illustrated in the case of William Parr, who was first denied divorce but, after a re-study of the divorce texts, was granted permission to remarry. In the reformatory attempts during the time of Edward, England became a sort of melting pot for the various viewpoints which were advocated on the Continent. A liberal interpretation is reflected in the composition of *Reformatio Legum Ecclesiasticarum*. Prevailing opposition in Edward's reign hindered its acceptance and the conservatism of the Elizabethan Settlement and the Queen's ecclesiastical policies did likewise. Marriage as a sacrament was denied, but the old canon law remained in force allowing only separation from board and bed. However, the religious latitude of Elizabeth's ecclesiastical policies, as long as the advocates did not become politically dangerous, made it possible for English divines with Puritan sympathies to advocate the *only-one-exception* exegesis as expressed by Calvin and Beza. During the Puritan Revolution the pendulum swung to the extreme left in an attempt at further reform. In the interpretation of the divorce texts this is illustrated in Milton's views which were a restatement of Bucer's concept but reinforced. However, in the Westminster Confession the Puritans reaffirmed that adultery and desertion were the only biblical grounds for divorce.

In view of the fact that matrimonial matters belonged to the ecclesiastical courts, the Reformed concept of divorce, formulated as it was within the conception of a bibliocracy, had greater possibilities to appeal to Elizabethan divines than Luther's, which included the idea of the two kingdoms. Since the old canon law was still maintained, it seems also logical that the *only-one-exception* interpretation of Calvin and Beza, rather than that of Zwingli-Bullinger, could be advocated alongside the official position of the Church of England. Anglicans and Puritans, each in their own way, remained conservative in their exegesis.

One common denominator is found among all the expositors, namely, the emphasis upon the sanctity of the marriage institution, and that Christ Himself restored it to its original purpose. Accordingly, they detested anything which might destroy this concept. In the different and even contradictory interpretations which follow, there is still another common denominator. In their exegesis the expositors have this God-given and Christ-restored concept in mind and each is convinced that the practical application of his interpretation is the best way whereby it may be safeguarded. Thus they are all Christologically motivated in their exegesis.

Bibliography

Abelard, Peter, *Epitome Christianae Theologiae*. Printed in Migne, *Patrologia Latina*, CLXXVIII. Paris, 1885.
Aquinas, Thomas, *Commentum in Lib. IV. Sententiarum*. Printed in *Opera*, XI. Paris, 1874.
Aquinas, Thomas, *Summa Contra Gentiles*. Printed in *Opera*, XII. Paris, 1874.
Andrewes, Lancelot, *Two Answers to Cardinal Perron and other Miscellaneous Works*. Oxford, 1854.
An Answer to a Book, Intituled, The Doctrine and Discipline of Divorce, or, A Plea for Ladies and Gentlewomen, and all other Maried Women against Divorce. London, 1644.
Augustine, *Contra Julianum*. Printed in Migne, *Patrologia Latina*, XLIV. Paris, 1865.
Augustine, *De Bono Conjugali*. Printed in Migne, *Patrologia Latina*, XL. Paris, 1887.
Augustine, *De Genesi Ad Litteram*. Printed in Migne. *Patrologia Latina*, XXXIV. Paris, 1887.
Augustine, *De Gratia Christi Et De Peccato Originali*. Printed in Migne, *Patrologia Latina*, XLIV. Paris, 1865.
Augustine, *De Nuptiis et Concupiscentia ad Valerium Comitem Libri Duo*. Printed in Migne, *Patrologia Latina*, XLIV. Paris, 1865.
Augustine, *A Treatise on the Grace of Christ, and on Original Sin*. Printed in *A Select Library of the Nicene and Post-Nicene Fathers of the Christian Church*, ed. Philip Schaff, V, Grand Rapids, Mich., 1956.
Augustine, *On Marriage and Concupiscence*. Printed in *A Select Library of the Nicene and Post-Nicene Fathers of the Christian Church*, ed. Philip Schaff, V, Grand Rapids, Mich., 1956.
Augustine, *On the Good of Marriage*. Printed in *A Select Library of the Christian Church*, ed. Philip Schaff, III, Grand Rapids, Mich., 1956.
Augustine, *Saint Augustine Against Julian*. Printed in *The Fathers of the Church*, ed. Roy Joseph Defarrari, 35, New York, 1957.
Augustine, *The Good of Marriage*. Printed in *The Fathers of the Church*, ed. Roy Joseph Defarrari, 27, New York, 1955.
Bainton, Roland H., *Here I Stand, A Life of Martin Luther*. New York, 1950.
Becon, Thomas, *The Early Works of Thomas Becon, S.T.P. Chaplain to Archbishop Cranmer, Prebendary of Canterbury, &c. Being the Treatises published by him in the Reign of King Henry VIII*. Ed. John Ayre. (Parker Society) Cambridge, 1843.

Bedda, Natalis, *Annotationum Natalis Bedae Doctoris Theologi Parisien in Iacobum Fabrum Stapulensem libri duo: Et in Desiderium Erasmum Roterodamum liber vnus, qui ordine tertius est . . . in Paraphrases Erasmi super eadem quatuor Euangelia & omnes Apostolicas Epistolas.* [Paris] 1526.

Beza, Theodore, *Iesv Christi D. N. Nouum Testamentum, siue Nouum foedus. Cuius Graeco contextui respondent interpretationes duae: vna, vetus: altera, noua, Theodori Bezae, diligenter ab eo recognita. Eivsdem Th. Bezae Annotationes, quas itidem hac tertia editione recognouit, & accessione non parua locupletauit.* n. p., 1582.

Beza, Theodore, *Tractatio De Repvdiis et Divortiis: in qva pleraeqve de causis matrimonialibus (quas vocant) incidentes controuersiae ex verbo Dei deciduntur. Additur Iuris Ciuilis Romanorum, & veterum his de rebus canonum examen, ad eiusdem verbi Dei, & aequitatis normam. Ex Th. Bezae Vezelii praelectionibus in priorem ad Corinthios Epistolam.* Geneva, 1573.

Brenz, John, *Opervm Reverendi et Clarissimi Theologi . . . In qvo Continentur Commentarii in tres Euangelistas. In Matthaeum. Marcum. Lucam,* V. Tübingen, 1582.

Brenz, John, *Wie inn Eesachen vnnd den fellen so sich derhalben zütragen nach gotlichem billichem rechten Christenlich zuo handeln sey.* n. p., 1531.

Bucer, Martin, *De Regno Christi Iesu seruatoris nostri, Libri II. Ad Edvardvm VI. Angliae Regem, annis abhinc sex scripti: non solum Theologis atque Iurisperitis profuturi, uerum etiam cunctis Rempub. bene & feliciter administraturis cognitu cumprimis necessarii.* Basel, 1557.

Bucer, Martin, *Deux Livres dv Royavme de Iesvs Christ Nostre Savvevr.* n. p., 1558.

Bucer, Martin, *Enarrationes perpetvae in sacra qvatvor evangelia, recognitae nuper & locis compluribus auctae. In quibus praeterea habes syncerioris Theologiae locos communes supra centum, ad scripturarum fidem simpliciter & nullius cum insectatione tractatos.* Strassburg, 1530.

Bucer, Martin, *Enarrationvm in Evangelia Matthaei, Marci, & Lucae, libri duo. Loci communes syneceriosis Theologiae supra centum, ad simplicem scripturarum fidem, citra ullius insectationen aut criminationem.* Strassburg, 1527.

Bucer, Martin, *The Ivdgement of Martin Bucer, concerning Divorce, Writt'n to Edward the Sixt, in his second Book of the Kingdom of Christ. And now Englisht. Wherin a late Book restoring the Doctrine and Discipline of Divorce, is heer confirm'd and justify'd by the authoritie of Martin Bucer. To the Parlament of England.* London, 1644. Printed in the *Works of John Milton,* IV. New York, 1931.

Bucer, Martin, *Sacrorvm Psalmorvm Libri Qvinqve, ad ebraicam ueritatem genuina versione in Latinum traducti: primum ap pensis bona fide sententiis, deinde pari diligentia adnume ratis uerbis, tum familiari explanatione elucidati.* Strassburg, 1532.

Bucer, Martin, *Scripta Anglicana fere omnia Iis etiam, quae hactenus vel nondum, vel sparsim, vel peregrino saltem idiomate edita fuere, adiunctis a Con. Hvberto ad explicandas sedandasque religionis cum alias, tum praesertim Eucharisticas controuersias, singulari fide collecta.* Basel, 1577.

Bucer, Martin, *Vom Reich Christi vnsers Herren vnd Heilands, Wie das selbige* von allen Christlichen Oberkeiten anzustellen, vnd ins werck zubringen seye. Strassburg, 1563.

Buckley, Theodore Alios, trans., *The Canons and Decrees of the Council of Trent.* London, 1851.

Buckley, Theodore Alios, trans., *The Catechism of the Council of Trent.* London, 1852.

Bugenhagen, John, *Ehesachen, vom Ehebruch vnd Heimlichen weglauffen.* Wittenberg, 1540.

Bullinger, Heinrich, *Der christliche Ehestand.* Zürich, 1854.

Bullinger, Heinrich, *The Decades of Henry Bullinger, Minister of the Church of Zurich.* Ed. Thomas Harding. 5. vols. (Parker Society) Cambridge. 1849—52.

Bullinger, Heinrich, *Diarium.* Printed in *Quellen zur Schweizerischen Reformationsgeschichte.* Ed. Emil Egli. Basel, 1904.

Bullinger, Heinrich, *In Lvcvlentvm et sacrosanctum Euangelium domini nostri Iesu Christi secundum Lucam Commentariorum lib.* IX. Zürich, 1546.

Bullinger, Heinrich, *In Omnes Apostolicas Epistolas, divi videlicet Pavli* XIIII. *et* VII. *canonicas, commentarii.* Zürich, 1537.

Bullinger, Heinrich, *In Sacrosanctvm Euangelium Domini nostri Iesu Christi secundum Marcum, Commentariorum lib.* VI. Zürich, 1545.

Bullinger, Heinrich, *In Sacrosanctvm Iesu Christi Domini nostri Euangelium secundum Matthaeum, Commentariorum libri* XII. Zürich, 1542.

Bunny, Edmund, *Of Diuorce for Adulterie, and Marrying againe: that there is no sufficient warrant so to do. With a note . . . that R. P. many yeeres since was answered.* Oxford, 1610.

Burnet, Gilbert, *The History of the Reformation of the Church of England.* 2 vols. London, 1681—83.

Bush, Douglas, "John Milton", *Encyclopaedia Britannica*, XV. 506—15. London, 1964.

Calvin, John, *Commentaries on the Epistles of Paul to the Galatians and Ephesians.* Trans. William Pringle. Grand Rapids, Michigan, 1948.

Calvin, John, *Commentaries on the First Book of Moses called Genesis.* Trans. John King. 2 vols. Grand Rapids, Michigan, 1948.

Calvin, John, *Commentaries on the Four Last Books of Moses Arranged in the Form of a Harmony.* Trans. Charles W. Bingham. 4 vols. Grand Rapids, Michigan, 1950.

Calvin, John, *Commentaries on the Twelve Minor Prophets.* Trans. John Owen. 5 vols. Grand Rapids, Michigan, 1950.

Calvin, John, *Commentary on the Epistles of Paul the Apostle to the Corinthians.* Trans. John Pringle. Grand Rapids, Michigan, 1948.

Calvin, John, *Commentary on a Harmony of the Evangelists, Matthew, Mark, and Luke.* Trans. William Pringle. 3 vols. Grand Rapids, Michigan, 1949.

Calvin, John, *Institutes of the Christian Religion.* Trans. Henry Beveridge. 2 vols. Grand Rapids, Michigan, 1957.

Calvin, John, *Ioannis Calvini Opera*, printed in *Corpus Reformatorum.* 59 volumes. Brunsvigal and Berolini, 1863—1900.

Calvin, John, *Tracts and Treatises in Defense of the Reformed Faith.* Trans. Henry Beveridge. 3 vols. Grand Rapids, Michigan, 1958.

153

Colet, John, *An Exposition of St. Paul's Epistle to the Romans*. Trans. J. H. Lupton. London, 1873.

Colet, John, *An Exposition of St. Paul's First Epistle to the Corinthians*. Trans. J. H. Lupton. London, 1874.

Courvoisier, Jaques, *Zwingli, A Reformed Theologian*. London, 1964.

Cranmer, Thomas, *Miscellaneous Writings and Letters of Thomas Cranmer*. Ed. John Edmund Cox. (Parker Society) Cambridge, 1846.

Dibdin, Lewis and Healey, Charles E. H. Chadwyck, *English Church Law and Divorce*. Oxford, 1912.

Dove, John, Of *Diuorcement. A Sermon preached at Pauls Crosse the 10. of May. 1601*. London, 1601.

Dugmore, C. W., *The Mass and the English Reformers*. London, 1958.

Dungersheym, H., *Erzeigung der falscheit des unchristlichen Lutherischen coments über das sibende Capital d'ersten Epistel zu den Chorinthern, so weyt es bedrifft die geistlichen*. n. p. [1525?].

Egli, Emil, ed., *Actensammlung zur Geschichte der Zürcher Reformation in den Jahren 1519–1533*. Zürich, 1879.

Erasmus, Desiderius, *The Censure and Iudgement of the Famous Clark Erasmus of Roterodam: Whyther dyoursement betwene man and wyfe stondeth with the lawe of God . . . in the Book of his Annotations, upon these wordes of Paule*. Trans. Nicholas Lesse. London [1550?].

Erasmus, Desiderius, *Declarationes ad Censvras Lvtetiae Vvlgates Svb Nomine Facultatis Theologiae Parisiensis*. Printed in *Opera*, IX.

Erasmus, Desiderius, *Des. Erasmi Roterodami Liber Qvo Respondet Annotationibus Eduardi Lei, quibus ille locos aliquot taxare conatus est in quatuor euangeliis*. Printed in *Opera*, IX.

Erasmus, Desiderius, *Divinationes Erasmi Rot. Adnotata Per Beddam*. Printed in *Opera*, IX.

Erasmus, Desiderius, *The Lives of Jehan Vitrier, warden of the Franciscan Convent at St. Omer, and John Colet, dean of St. Paul's, London*. Trans. J. H. Lupton. London, 1883.

Erasmus, Desiderius, *Novvm Instrumentum omne . . . cum Annotationibus*. Basel, 1516.

Erasmus, Desiderius, *Novvm Testamentvm omne . . . cum Annotationibus*. Basel, 1519.

Erasmus, Desiderius, *Omnia Opera Des. Erasmi Roterodami, Qvaecvnqve ipse avtor pro svis agnovit, Novem Tomis Distincta*. Basel, 1540–41.

Erasmus, Desiderius, *Opvs Epistolarvm Des. Erasmi Roterodami*. Ed. P. S. and H. M. Allen. 11 vols. Oxford, 1906–47.

Erasmus, Desiderius, *The Paraphrase of Erasmus vpon the Newe Testamente*. 2 vols. London, 1548–49.

Erasmus, Desiderius, *Paraphrases Des. Erasmi Roterodami in Epistolas Pauli apostoli ad Rhomanos Corinthios & Galatas, quae commentarii uice esse possunt*. Basel, 1520.

Erasmus, Desiderius, *Paraphrasin in Euangelium Matthaei nunc primum natam & aeditam per D. Erasmvm Roterodamum: Paraphrases in omneis epistolas apostolicas, hoc est Pauli, Iacobi, Ioannis, Petri, Iudae, per eundem*. Basel, 1522.

Finsler, Georg, *Zwingli-Bibliographie. Verzeichnis der gedruckten Schriften von und über Ulrich Zwingli.* Zürich, 1897.

Flinner, Johann, "Johann Flinner an Conrad Hubert, Heidelberg 25. 8. 1557." Archive St. Thomas, Strasburg 156, no. 111.

Foxe, John, ed., *Reformatio Legvm Ecclesiasticarvm, Ex Avthoritate primum Regis Henrici. 8. inchoata: Deinde per Regem Edouardum 6. prouecta, adauctaq; in hunc modum, atq; nunc ad pleniorem ipsarum reformationem in lucem aedita.* London, 1571. Reprinted Oxford, 1850. Ed. Edward Cardwell.

Friedberg, Emil, *Das Recht der Eheschliessung in seiner Geschichtlichen Entwicklung.* Leipzig, 1865.

Fulke, William, *The Text of the New Testament of Iesvs Christ, translated ovt of the vulgar Latine by the Papists of the traiterous Seminarie at Rhemes . . . Whereunto is added the Translation out of the Original Greeke, commonly vsed in the Church of England, with a Confvtation.* London, 1589.

Goodman, Godfrey, *The Fall of Man or the Corruption of Nature proved by the light of our naturall Reason. Which being the First Ground and Occasion of Our Christian Faith and Religion, may likewise serue for the first step and degree of the naturall mans conuersion. First Preached in a Sermon, since enlarged, reduced to the forme of a treatise and dedicated to the Queenes most excellent Maiestie.* London, 1616.

Greenslade, S. L., ed., *The Cambridge History of the Bible. The West from the Reformation to the Present Day.* Cambridge, 1963.

Hall, Joseph, *The Works of Joseph Hall, D. D. successively Bishop of Exeter and Norwich: with some account of his life and sufferings, written by himself.* 12 vols. Oxford, London, 1837—39.

Hammond, Henry, *A Paraphrase, and Annotations upon all the Books of the New Testament: Briefly explaining all the difficult places thereof.* London, 1653.

Hammond, Henry, *A Practical Catechism.* Twelfth edition. London, 1684.

Hanford, James Holly, *A Milton Handbook,* London, 1934.

Hanford, James Holly, "Milton and the Return to Humanism", *Studies in Philology,* XVI. 126—47 (April, 1919).

Heppe, Heinrich, *Theodor Beza. Leben und ausgewählte Schriften.* Printed in *Leben und ausgewählte Schriften der Väter und Begründer der reformirten Kirche,* VI. Elberfeld, 1861.

Hooker, Richard, *Of the Lawes of Ecclesiastical Politie.* London, 1617.

Hooper, John, *Early Writings of John Hooper.* Ed. Samuel Carr. (Parker Society) Cambridge, 1843.

Howard, George Elliott, *A History of Matrimonial Institutions, chiefly in England and the United States, with an introductory analysis of the literature and the theories of primitive marriage and the family.* 3 vols. London, 1904.

Hugo of St. Victor, *Dogmatica.* Printed in Migne, *Patrologia Latina,* CLXXVI. Paris, 1880.

Joyce, George Hayward, *Christian Marriage: An Historical and Doctrinal Study.* London and New York, 1933.

Kidd, B. J., *Documents Illustrative Of The Continental Reformation.* Oxford, 1911.

Klaiber, Dr., ed., *Evangelische Volksbibliothek.* Stuttgart, 1863.

Köhler, Walther, *Zürcher Ehegericht und Genfer Konsistorium.* 2 vols. Leipzig, 1932–42.
Koellin, C., *Eversio Lutherani Epithalamii.* n. p., 1527.
Kohls, Ernst-Wilhelm, *Die Theologie des Erasmus.* 2 vols. Basel, 1966.
Lee, Edward, *Annotationes Edovardi Leei in Annotationes Novi Testamenti Desiderii Erasmi.* [Basel, 1520.]
Lefèvre, Jacques, of Étaples, *Commentarii Initiatorii in Qvatvor Evangelia.* [Paris] 1526.
Lefèvre, Jacques, of Étaples, *Epistolae Divi Pauli Apostoli.* [Paris] 1515.
Lombard, Peter, *Sententiarum Libri Quatuor.* Printed in Migne, *Patrologia Latina,* CXCII. Paris, 1880.
Luther, Martin, *Briefwechsel.* Printed in *D. Martin Luthers Werke. Kritische Gesamtausgabe.* 11 vols. Weimar, 1930–48.
Luther, Martin, *Die Deutsche Bibel.* Printed in *D. Martin Luthers Werke. Kritische Gesamtausgabe.* 12 vols. Weimar, 1906–61.
Luther, Martin, *An exposition in to the seventh chaptre of the first pistle to the Corinthians.* [Trans. W. Roy?] n. p., 1529.
Luther, Martin, *Luther's Works.* Ed. Jaroslav Pelikan and Helmut T. Lehmann. 55 volumes. Philadelphia, 1958–67.
Luther, Martin, *A Prelude on the Babylonian Capivity of the Church.* Printed in *Three Treatises.* Philadelphia, 1943.
Luther, Martin, *Tischreden.* Printed in *D. Martin Luthers Werke. Kritische Gesamtausgabe.* 6 vols. Weimar, 1912–21.
Luther, Martin, *D. Martin Luthers Werke. Kritische Gesamtausgabe.* 58 vols. Weimar, 1883–1948.
Mangan, John Joseph, *Life, Character & Influence of Desiderius Erasmus of Rotterdam.* 2 vols. New York, 1927.
Martyr, Peter, *In selectissimam D. Pauli priorem ad Corinthios epistolam . . . P. M. Vermilii . . . commentarii.* n. p., 1567.
Martyr, Peter, *In Selectissimam D. Pavli Priorem ad Corinthios Epistolam, D. Petri Martyris Vermilii Florentini, ad Sereniss. Regem Angliae, &c. Edvardvm VI. Commentarii doctissimi.* Zürich, 1572.
Martyr, Peter, *Loci communes. Ex variis ipsius authoris libris in unum volumen collecti, & quatuor classes distributi.* London, 1576.
Martyr, Peter, *Locorum Communium Theologicorum ex ipsius scriptis sincere decerptorum.* Basel, 1580.
Martyr, Peter, *The Common Places of . . . Peter Martyr, diuided into foure principall parts: with a large addition of manie theologicall and necessarie discourses, some never extant before.* Trans. A. Marten. London, 1583.
McNeill, John T. *The History and Character of Calvinism.* New York, 1957.
Melanchthon, Philip, *Argumentum et Brevis Explicatio Prioris Epistolae Ad Corinthios.* Printed in *Corpus Reformatorum,* XV. Ed. C. G. Bretschneider. 1848.
Melanchthon, Philip, *Breves Commentarii in Matthaeum.* Printed in *Corpus Reformatorum,* XIV. Ed. C. G. Bretschneider. 1847.
Melanchthon, Philip, *De Coniugio.* Printed in *Corpus Reformatorum,* XXI. Ed. C. G. Bretschneider and H. E. Bindseil. Brunsvig, 1854.

Mentz, F., *Zur 400 jährigen Geburtsfeier Martin Butzer's. Bibliographische Zusammenstellung der gedruckten Schriften Butzer's.* Strassburg, 1891.

Milton, John, *A Common-Place Book of John Milton, and a Latin Essay and Latin Verses presumed to be by Milton.* Ed. Alfred J. Horwood. London, 1877.

Milton, John, *The Works of John Milton.* 18 vols. New York, 1931–38.

More, Thomas, *Utopia.* Printed in *Ideal Commonwealths.* Ed. by Henry Morley. London, 1901.

Nichols, Francis Morgan, *The Epistles of Erasmus from His Earliest Letters to His Fifty-First Year. Aranged in Order of Time. English Translations from the Early Correspondence, with a Commentary Confirming the Chronological Arrangement and Supplying Futher Biographical Matter.* 3 vols. London, 1901 ff.

Nörskov Olsen, Viggo, "The Concept of the Church in the Writings of John Foxe." Ph. D. London, 1966.

"Les Ordonnances Ecclesiastiques de 1561." Printed in *Corpus Reformatorum,* XXXVIII, pars prior, cols. 91–124. Ed. G. Baum, E. Cunitz, E. Reuss. Brunsvig, 1871.

Original Letters Relative to the English Reformation, written during the Reigns of King Henry VIII, King Edward VI, and Queen Mary: Chiefly from the Archives of Zurich. Ed. Hastings Robinson. 2 vols. (Parker Society) Cambridge, 1846–47.

Patrides, C. A., *Milton and the Christian Tradition.* Oxford, 1966.

Pauck, W., *Das Reich Gottes auf Erden.* Berlin, 1928.

Perkins, William, *Christian Oeconomie: or, a short survey of the right manner of erecting and ordering a familie, according to the Scriptures ... Written in Latin ... and now set forth in the vulgar tongue ... by T. Pickering.* London, 1609.

Powell, Chilton Latham, *English Domestic Relations 1487–1653.* New York, 1917.

Raynolds, John, *A Defence of the Iudgment of the Reformed churches. That a man may lawfullie not onelie put awaie his wife for her adulterie, but also marrie another. Wherin both Robert Bellarmin the Jesuits Latin treatise, and an English pamphlet of a nameless author mainteyning the contrarie are confuted.* London, 1610.

Richter, Aemilius Ludwig, ed., *Die evangelischen Kirchenordnungen des sechszehnten Jahrhunderts.* 2 vols. Weimar, 1846.

Rockwell, William Walker, *Die Doppelehe des Landgrafen Philipp von Hessen.* Marburg, 1904.

Sarcerius, Erasmus, *Corpvs Ivris Matrimonialis.* Frankfurt, 1569.

Schaff, Philip, ed., *The Creeds of Christendom, with a History and Critical Notes.* 3 vols. Sixth edition, New York, 1931.

Schmidt, C., *Peter Martyr Vermigli. Leben und ausgewählte Schriften.* Printed in *Leben und ausgewählte Schriften der Väter und Begründer der reformirten Kirche,* VII. Elberfeld, 1858.

Smith, Henry, *A preparative to mariage.* London, 1591.

Smith, Preserved, "German Opinion of the Divorce of Henry VIII", *The English Historical Review,* XXVII. 671–81 (Oct. 1912).

Staehelin, Ernst, *Das Theologische Lebenswerk Johannes Oekolampads.* Leipzig, 1939. (Quellen und Forschungen zur Reformationsgeschichte. Bd. 21.)

Strype, John, *Memorials of Thomas Cranmer.* London, 1694.

Tyndale, William, *Doctrinal Treatises and Introductions to Different Portions of The Holy Scriptures.* Ed. Henry Walter. (Parker Society) Cambridge, 1848.
Tyndale, William, *Expositions and Notes on Sundry Portions of the Holy Scriptures together with The Practice of Prelates.* Ed. Henry Walter. (Parker Society) Cambridge, 1849.
Valla, Lorenzo, *Lavrentii Vallae, viri tam Graecae quam Latinae linguae doctissimi, in Nouum Testamentum Annotationes, appri me utiles. Cum Erasmi Praefatione, & cuisdem in hasce Annotationes castigationibus ad calcem adpositis.* Basel, 1541.
Vio, Thomas De (Cardinal Cajetan), *Epistolae Pavli et Aliorvm Apostolorum,* n. p., 1532
Vio, Thomas De (Cardinal Cajetan), *Evangelia cvm Commen. Caietani.* n. p., 1530.
Weber, Alfred, *Heinrich Bullingers "Christlicher Ehestand", seine zeitgenössischen Quellen und die Anfänge des Familienbuches in England.* Leipzig, 1929.
Westermarck, Edward Alexander, *Christianity and Morals.* London, 1939.
White, Francis, *The Orthodox Faith and Way to the Chvrch explaned and ivstified: In Answer to a Popish Treatise.* London, 1617.
Wither, George, *A View of the Marginal Notes of the Popish Testament, translated into English by the English fugitiue Papists resiant at Rhemes in France.* London [1588].
Württembergisches Glaubensbekenntniss (Confessio Württembergica) unter dem Herzog Christoph im Jahre 1551 von Johannes Brenz entworfen, von einer nach Stuttgart berufenen Synode geprüft, angenommen, und der grossen zu Trient gehaltenen Kirchenversammlung durch eine herzogliche Gesandtschaft überreicht. Stuttgart, 1848.
The Zurich Letters, Comprising the Correspondence of Several English Bishops and Others with some of the Helvetian Reformers, during the Reign of Queen Elizabeth. Ed. Hastings Robinson. 2 vols. (Parker Society) Cambridge, 1842—45.
Zwingli, Huldreich, *Huldrici Zuinglii Opera (Huldreich Zwingli's Werke).* Ed. M. Schuler and J. Schulthess. 8 vols. Zürich, 1828—42.
The Holie Bible Faithfvlly Translated into English . . . by the English College of Doway. Douai, 1609.
The Nevv Testament of Iesvs Christ, Translated Faithfvlly into English . . . in the English College of Rhemes. Rheims, 1582.

Index of Names

Abelard, Peter, 5
Allen, William, 40
Ambrose, 22
Andrewes, Lancelot, bishop of Chichester, Ely and Winchester, 126—27
Aquinas, Thomas, 4, 5, 6, 50, 143, 144, 145
Augustine, 2—4, 5, 7, 21, 24

Bedda, Natalis, 30—32, 33
Bellarmine, Robert, 122
Bemoist, Rene, 10
Beza, Theodore, 88, 104—09, 121, 127, 129, 147, 148, 149
Bourcher, Anne, 113—14
Brenz, John, 55, 56, 61—64
Bucer, Martin, 15, 75, 76—88, 89, 92, 94, 97, 100, 108, 112, 116, 118, 128, 129, 141, 142, 147, 148, 149
Bugenhagen, John, 56—57
Bullinger, Heinrich, 17, 70—76, 83, 85, 86, 89, 94, 97, 100, 101, 104, 108, 115, 117, 118, 119, 125, 141, 146, 147, 148, 149
Bunny, Edmund, archbishop of York, 127—28
Burcher, John, 86
Burnet, Gilbert, 113—14

Calvin, John, 3, 6, 70, 94—103, 104, 105, 107, 108, 121, 129, 147, 148, 149
Cajetan, Cardinal (Thomas De Vio), 33—36, 40
Caraccioli, Galeazzo, 99
Cartwright, Thomas, 121, 122
Catherine of Aragon, queen, 17, 68, 69, 111
Charles V, emperor, 36
Christian III, king, 57
Christoffer, duke, 61
Chrysostom, 21, 115
Colet, John, 13—14, 77, 117

Constantine, emperor, 74
Cranmer, Thomas, archbishop of Canterbury, 16, 80, 110, 112—15, 117, 119, 148

Dietenberger, Johann, 9
Dove, John, 126, 127

Eck, John, 9
Edward VI, king, 15, 80, 81, 110, 113, 114, 117, 118, 119, 120, 129, 148
Elizabeth I, queen, 40, 119, 120, 148, 149
Emser, Hieronymous, 9
Erasmus, Desiderius, 7, 8, 11, 12, 13, 14, 15—27, 28, 29—30, 31, 32—33, 40, 45, 76, 88, 113, 115, 117, 140, 141, 143—44, 145, 148

Fabiola, 26, 41, 107
Farel, Guillaume, 12
Fisher, Christopher, 11
Flinner, Johann, 87—88
Foxe, John, 119, 120
Francis I, king, 33
Froben, John, 8
Fulke, William, 42, 122

Gardiner, Stephen, bishop of Winchester, 15, 118
Goodman, Godfrey, bishop of Gloucester, 127
Grindal, Edmund, archbishop of York and Canterbury, 127

Hall, Joseph, bishop of Exeter and Norwich, 124—25
Hammond, Henry, 124, 125—26
Henry VIII, king, 14, 55, 68—69, 73, 110, 111, 112, 114, 117, 118
Hooker, Richard, 120
Hooper, John, bishop of Gloucester and Worcester, 86, 110, 115—17, 148

Hubert, Conrad, 87
Hugo of St. Victor, 5

Jerome, 6, 7, 26, 115
Justinian, emperor, 74, 79, 80, 90, 91

Lee, Edward, archbishop of York, 27–29, 30, 33, 113
Lefèvre, Jacques (Faber Stapulensis), 8–9, 12, 14, 31
Lombard, Peter, 5, 6
Luther, Martin, 2, 3, 6, 8, 9, 18, 19, 20, 24, 33, 40, 43–57, 58, 61, 62, 63, 64, 67, 68, 69, 70, 73, 74, 76, 85, 89, 96, 100, 107, 108, 112, 115, 116, 117, 123, 141, 145–46, 147, 148, 149

Martyr, Peter (Pietro Martire Vermigli), 18, 88–94, 116, 118, 119, 129, 147, 148
Mary I, queen, 119
Masson, Robert, 89
Melanchthon, Philip, 56, 57–60, 61, 68, 112
Micronius, Martin, 119
Milton, John, 15, 72, 73, 80, 82, 85, 120, 123, 124, 128–42, 143, 149
More, Sir Thomas, 14–15, 141

Oecolampadius, John, 17, 69, 73
Olivetan, Pierre Robert, 9
Origen, 21, 22
Osiander, Andreas, 112

Parr, William, 113–15, 117, 148
Perkins, William, 123
Philip of Hesse, 47, 55, 113
Pollentius, 3
Pope Pius IV, 39
Powell, Mary, 129

Raynolds, John, 122–23

Sarcerius, Erasmus, 56
Smith, Henry, 124
Stapulensis, Faber, see: Lefèvre, Jacques
Strype, John, 15, 16, 112

Tertullian, 22, 115
Theodosius, emperor, 60, 74, 79, 80, 91
Tyndale, William, 110–12, 117

Valla, Lorenzo, 11–12
Vermigli, Pietro Martire, see: Martyr, Peter
Vio, Thomas De see: Cajetan, Cardinal

White, Francis, bishop of Carlisle, Norwich and Ely, 123
Whitgift, John, archbishop of Canterbury, 118, 121
Wither, George, 122
Worthington, Thomas, 123

Zwingli, Huldreich, 64–70, 71, 73, 76, 83, 85, 88, 92, 97, 101, 104, 112, 125, 141, 146, 147, 148, 149

Index of Bible References

Genesis
i.   131, 140
i. 28   73
ii.   82, 102, 131, 140
ii. 23—24   38, 73
xvi.   51

Leviticus
xviii.   18, 39, 65, 73, 111
xviii. 16   68, 111
xx.   73
xx. 21   68

Deuteronomy
xix.   65
xxii. 13—15   139
xxiv. 1   34, 41, 81, 83, 84, 90, 92, 98, 101, 103, 105, 116, 125, 132, 133, 134, 137, 139, 140, 141, 147
xxiv. 1—4   141
xxv. 5   111

Malachi
ii. 14   34, 83, 90, 98, 101, 102, 147
ii. 16   98, 147

Matthew
v.   33, 52, 53, 62, 116, 134
v. 1   139
v. 18   134
v. 32   1, 25, 31, 33, 41, 47, 48, 52, 54, 64, 77, 85, 90, 104, 116, 124, 126, 140, 143, 144
xix. 3   20
xix. 6   31, 82, 141
xix. 7—8   135
xix. 8   67, 102, 105, 141
xix.   27, 29, 32, 33, 34, 38, 52, 55, 62, 105, 113, 116, 136
xix. 9   1, 29, 31, 33, 35, 41, 48, 51, 52, 60, 65, 67, 68, 70, 77, 83, 85, 90, 103, 116, 126, 127, 141, 143, 145
xix. 11   98, 105
xxii. 21   55

Mark
   x. 3—4   135
   x. 5   134
   x.   62, 104, 113
   x. 11—12   1, 31, 34, 35, 41, 66, 90, 116, 122, 126, 145

Luke
   xvi. 16—18 72, 113
   xvi. 18   1, 35, 41, 90, 104, 122, 126, 145

Romans
   vii. 1—3   12, 14, 25, 26, 31, 41, 84, 106, 113, 122, 126, 144, 145
   xiii. 21   55

1 Corinthians
   iv. 1   44
   v. 12   78
   vii.   13, 17, 18, 21, 26, 32, 34, 35, 48, 52, 58, 66, 69, 71, 72, 73, 96, 117, 141
   vii. 3—4   53
   vii. 4   3
   vii. 10—11 12, 26, 31, 35, 37, 40, 41, 51, 89, 104, 105, 106, 122, 126, 144
   vii. 15   1, 12, 26, 27, 31, 35, 41, 53, 83, 84, 85, 99, 105, 106, 107, 108, 111, 144, 145
   vii. 39   3, 26, 49, 144

Galatians
   v. 22   46

Ephesians
   iii. 9   95
   v. 25—26 38, 50
   v. 28—32 40
   v. 31—32 4, 44, 49
   v. 32   6—10, 12, 27, 28, 29, 36, 38, 39, 50, 67, 73, 95, 122, 143, 144

1 Timothy
   iii. 9   95
   iii. 16   44, 95
   v. 8   111

1 Peter
   ii. 13—15 55

1 John
   iii. 15   84

www.ingramcontent.com/pod-product-compliance
Lightning Source LLC
Chambersburg PA
CBHW060820190426
43197CB00038B/2172